GOD ON EARTH: EMPEROR DOMITIAN

 **sidestone**press

GOD ON EARTH: EMPEROR DOMITIAN

The re-invention of Rome at the end of the 1st century AD

edited by

Aurora Raimondi Cominesi, Nathalie de Haan,
Eric M. Moormann & Claire Stocks

PALMA 24

PAPERS ON ARCHAEOLOGY OF THE
LEIDEN MUSEUM OF ANTIQUITIES

PALMA: Papers on Archaeology of the Leiden Museum of Antiquities (volume 24)

Published by Sidestone Press, Leiden
www.sidestone.com

Layout & cover design: Sidestone Press
Photographs cover: Portrait of Domitian, c. 88. Rome, Musei Capitolini, Museo del Palazzo dei Conservatori, inv. MC 1156 (photo Musei in Comune – Roma).

ISBN 978-90-8890-954-2 (softcover)
ISBN 978-90-8890-955-9 (hardcover)
ISBN 978-90-8890-956-6 (PDF e-book)

ISSN 2034-550X

Contents

Preface: Anchoring a New Emperor

André Lardinois & Ineke Sluiter

The book in front of you is the product of two academic impulses. The first is the development in our historical perspective on the Emperor Domitian, traditionally known as one of the 'bad emperors'. Current scholarship, however, has moved beyond this by additionally investigating the ways in which this Emperor and his family before him managed to get and maintain power, his development of public space, and his relationship to the population of Rome. The second academic impulse provides one central conceptual instrument to study Domitian's position: the notion of 'anchoring innovation', used to understand the ways in which new phenomena become accepted to relevant social groups by their connection to what is already familiar.

'Anchoring innovation' is the title of a research programme carried out by a consortium of Dutch classicists, and funded by the Dutch Ministry of Education, Culture and Science (2017-2027) through a so-called 'Gravitation Grant'. It investigates the 'human factor' in innovation, the ways in which new ideas, inventions, and other phenomena become embedded ('anchored') among relevant social groups. For anything new to become an accepted innovation, people need to understand whatever is offered to them as new, they need to find it important, compatible with their beliefs, and morally right. This presupposes that they will be able to establish a cognitive link between what was presented as new and what they consider familiar. Successful innovation will be connected somehow – both in the ways it is communicated and perceived, and in terms of content – to what people know, believe, want, value, and can understand. This is true of new technologies or ideas, but also of new political regimes.[1]

The 'Anchoring Innovation' programme also emphasizes the importance of realizing that what is presented as 'new' is not always really new – and the same goes for 'old'. Certain groups may experience or construe a phenomenon as familiar or new. Secondly, 'old' and 'new' are not neutral terms. They frequently carry a value judgement, which may vary among members of a society. Thirdly, anchoring does not necessarily imply the slowing down of innovation – it can also safeguard its steady development.

Anchoring is a dynamic process. Anchors are being construed and adapted, their meaning and significance is open to negotiation and processes of anchoring should themselves be part of the historical understanding of a period. Finally, and importantly:

---

1   For a programmatic paper, see Ineke Sluiter, "Anchoring Innovation: a Classical Research Agenda", *European Review* 25 (2017), 20-38: DOI: https://doi.org/10.1017/S1062798716000442 (= Sluiter 2017). For an example of the way in which political regimes use cultural anchors to legitimate their rule, see André Lardinois, 'Creation or Confirmation of the Canon? The Measures of Lycurgus and the Canonisation of Athenian Tragedy in Antiquity', in: D. Agut-Labordère / M.J. Versluys (eds.), *Firm anchors. Textual canonization and cultural formation in the first millennium BC* (Euhormos. Greco-Roman Studies in Anchoring Innovation), Leiden/Boston: forthcoming.

innovation in no way implies moral progress. Dictators are frequently successful anchorers.[2] And in fact, so was Domitian.

Domitian shared this characteristic with the other Flavians. They could use Nero as a negative anchor, a foil from whom to distinguish themselves, while reaching back across this undesirable part of their past to the positive anchor Augustus. Domitian started 'new traditions' and found legitimation in them. One area in which this is apparent is religion. Some of his innovations in this area were more successful than others. In presenting his role as that of god on earth, he extended the familiar post mortem deification (bestowed, *e.g.*, on Caesar and Augustus) beyond the acceptable and relatable.

More successful was Domitian's use of Egypt, with its great appeal to the public imagination, and his self-representation as a Roman pharaoh. Part of the story of Domitian is also the *damnatio memoriae*, the official order to erase him from the record of Roman history. *Damnatio memoriae* is a paradoxical procedure in that the literal erasure of a name (*e.g.* from an inscription) automatically draws attention to the gap itself. The very visibility of the measure replaces the commemorative function of the inscription with the memory of condemnation and contempt. The inscription now becomes the anchor for wilful forgetting. In this way, it provides a negative example of what Roman rulers should strive for.

The anchoring innovation consortium is proud to have been able to sponsor the international exhibition on Domitian, first to be featured in the Dutch National Antiquities Museum in Leiden (RMO). But we are even happier to have been able to contribute to the intellectual foundation of this book.

---

2   The five points in these two paragraphs are derived from Ineke Sluiter, 'Oud is het nieuwe nieuw', *Lampas* 51.4 (2018), 289-295, here at 292: available in Open Access through the programme website: https://www.ru.nl/oikos/anchoring-innovation/.

Introduction: Domitian, the Neglected Emperor Who Wished to Be God

Aurora Raimondi Cominesi, Nathalie de Haan,

Eric M. Moormann & Claire Stocks

Why Domitian?

Sightseers in Rome today are confronted with the city's Roman past at every step. Each corner, each surviving monument, speaks of the deeds of Rome's most famous men and (less frequently) women, its emperors and empresses. The Mausoleum of Augustus; Agrippa's Pantheon; Nero's *Domus Aurea*; Trajan's column; the Baths of Caracalla. Domitian's name is not among them – in fact, few people today have even heard of him. And yet some of the crucial contributions to the appearance and the history of Rome owe their origin to that man.

The remembrance of Roman emperors, good or bad, and their survival into our own collective memories depends on a series of complex mechanisms. Between the famous names of the past – Augustus with his spotless reputation and the supposedly despotic Nero – are those of individuals who lie forgotten or overlooked, some of whom failed to leave a permanent mark on the Roman Empire, or were forcefully carved out of it. Among the latter is *Titus Flavius Domitianus.* A complex historical figure, Domitian contributed enormously to the shaping of Rome and the Roman Empire as we know it today, yet he was an unpopular figure in antiquity and since then his name has drifted into oblivion.

Now, as we head toward 2000 years since that emperor's birth (in AD 51), the time seems right to shine the spotlight back on Domitian, and to explore the complexities of one of Rome's most productive, loathed, and forgotten emperors. This book is the outcome of a collaborative effort of over thirty international scholars who wished to offer a portrait of the Emperor Domitian in all his facets. The research was carried out in tandem with an exhibition entitled *God on Earth. Emperor Domitian* planned for the fall of 2020, but postponed to fall 2021 due to the Covid-19 crisis. This exhibition aims to build on previous exhibitions that have taken a single Roman emperor or dynasty for their focus. Over the last two decades, various exhibitions in Rome and around the world have been organized to celebrate the lives and deeds of single Roman emperors or their families. On occasion, these events have been connected directly to a jubilee year, for example the 2014 exhibition on Augustus (*AVGVSTO*, Rome) and the 2009 show on Vespasian (*Divus Vespasianus. Il bimillenario dei Flavi*, Rome), which marked the bimillennia of their respective death and

Fig. 1. Cuirass statue of Domitian from Veleia. Parma, Museo Archeologico Nazionale Complesso Monumentale della Pilotta, inv. 1952.827 (courtesy Ministero per i Beni e le Attività Culturali e per il Turismo – Complesso Monumentale della Pilotta).

birth, or prompted by the location of the venue and its specific ties to an emperor (*e.g. Konstantin der Große*, Trier 2007; *Claude : Lyon, 10 avant J.-C.-Rome, 54 après J.-C. : un empereur au destin singulier*, Lyon 2018). Other exhibitions (*Giulio Cesare: l'uomo, le imprese, il mito*, Rome 2008-2009; *Rome, de droom van keizer Constantijn: kunstschatten uit de Eeuwige Stad*, Amsterdam 2015-2016; *Traiano: l'ottimo principe*, Rome 2017-2018) were conceptualized from different perspectives, such as the rise of Christianity under Constantine, or Trajan's empire as a proto-European union, offering the public a perspective of the ancient world through the lens of the modern.

By looking at the names of the emperors celebrated in these exhibitions, one can discern the fate of their respective reputations over the centuries. The high number of exhibitions dedicated to Augustus and Constantine reiterate the myth of their everlasting, positive marks on the Roman Empire at its two opposite ends (its beginning and its end). A fascination for Hadrian highlights our own interest in the sophistications of the Graeco-Hellenistic world (*Adriano e la Grecia. Villa Adriana tra classicità ed ellenismo* Tivoli, 2014; *Adriano e Atene. Dialogo con un mondo ideale*, Athens, 2017). The number of exhibitions centred around Nero (three only in the last decade)[1] reflects a die-hard interest in the emperor who more than any other incarnated all sorts of misbehaviours as he was presented as the opponent of Christianity and the embodiment of the iconic 'bad emperor'.

This volume, as stated above, accompanies the exhibition God on Earth. Emperor Domitian (Leiden, Rijksmuseum van Oudheden, 16 December 2021-22 May 2022 and Rome, Summer 2022) and both focus on Domitian as a man, emperor, and (almost) god. Additionally, they aim at more than shedding light on the complexities of memory and the controversial legacy of this emperor. As we will see, the initiative to compose the book and launch the exhibition is the result of a research topic within the Dutch research programme 'Anchoring Innovation', which highlights the connections between, and within, antiquity and beyond. The place of our volume and exhibition within this programme demonstrates that whilst Domitian is an emperor deserving of his spotlight, he should not be viewed in isolation. Rather his rule and its achievements are both anchored to the past and would serve as anchor points for emperors thereafter.

Changing the face of Rome

Born on 24 October 51 in the very heart of Rome on the Quirinal Hill, near a pomegranate tree (*ad malum punicum*),[2] the future Emperor descended from a well-fixed, yet relatively obscure family, the *Flavii*. His family's first, and then his own rise to power must have come as a shock to his contemporaries. However, the Flavians were able to impose themselves on the scene of Rome, and on 14 September 81, following the rule of his father, Vespasian, and then his brother, Titus, Domitian found himself unexpectedly seated on the imperial throne, at thirty years old.

Domitian must have been a complicated and fascinating personality. His fifteen-year long rule brought about many necessary changes that transformed the face of Rome. Religious currencies became much more polyvalent by the introduction or expansion of devotions directed to divinities up to then seen as alien or strange, such as Isis, Mithras, and Jupiter Dolichenus. Some of the traditional gods were venerated in a specific way and received special attention in Domitian's building politics; we may think of Jupiter in his various guises, as well as Minerva, and Hercules. A close bond with Egypt showed Domitian's interest in an extremely important province of his empire, being the producer of large amounts of grain for the many mouths to be fed in the consumer town that was Rome. As we will see in various contributions, this *Egyptianization* consisted of the expansion of old and new Isis sanctuaries, both in Rome and in the provinces, as in Benevento, and the depiction of himself as a pharaoh outside the province of Egypt.

Yet many of the innovations Domitian fostered did not form absolute novelties. In various of the papers collected in this volume, we can observe a specific attention for political, military, urbanistic, artistic, and literary achievements of the first and "greatest" Roman emperor, Augustus, and, what might surprise us, of the last of the Julio-Claudian dynasty, Nero. Part of these innovations can be connected with research being carried out by the Dutch National Research School in Classical Studies (OIKOS) and in particular the research programme "Anchoring Innovation", for which we may also refer to the Preface by André Lardinois and Ineke Sluiter.[3] The research question of this programme addresses processes of change and innovation in Antiquity in various fields of ancient studies, such as literature, linguistics, history, and material culture. According to this concept, innovation cannot be seen as a purely new step forward in a cultural, historical, or technical process of developments, but always takes up extant and sometimes traditional notions

---

1 *Nero: Sulle tracce dell'imperatore Nerone – culture, rilievi, affreschi, dipinti e reperti: una mostra itinerante tra i Fori, il Palatino e il Colosseo*, Rome, 2011, *Nero -Kaiser, Künstler und Tyrann*, Trier, 2016, *Nero.* upcoming exhibition at the British Museum, London, 2021.

2 Suet. *Domit.* 1.

3 See Sluiter 2017 for a good introduction to this programme and its assets.

and experiences. Old forms can be used for the design of new technical devices and language formulae may change significance or meaning, but remain in use for ages etc. Domitian is renowned for renewing rulership, Roman architecture and art, and additionally was a source of inspiration for literary authors, standing in a venerable tradition. In various contributions the connection with the past, especially with the Emperors Augustus and Nero,[4] is at stake. Eric Moormann sees strong bonds between the imperial building programmes of Augustus and Nero and that of the Flavians, all adding splendour to Rome as well as its emperors. Jane Fejfer illustrates the relation between Domitian's portraits and those of specific predecessors to strengthen the suggestion of a special relation. Claire Stocks demonstrates the strong traditional themes and poetic forms in epic poetry, especially the relationship of the Flavian poets with Virgil. Onno van Nijf, Robin van Vliet and Caroline Torenaar place the games organized in the stadium of Domitian in a long history of games, beginning with the oldest, the Olympic Games. Frederick G. Naerebout and Miguel John Versluys explain the preference for particular gods, partly from Egypt, as a display of connection with the past.

The many qualities of Domitian's rule and the everlasting impact of his interventions on the organizational structure of the Empire, as well as on the landscape of the city of Rome as we know it today (*e.g.* the Colosseum or Piazza Navona), proved ultimately successful. Domitian's re-invention of Rome survived the test of time. The memory of him, however, did not.

Reassessing Domitian's Legacy

In nearly every historical and contemporary society, regime changes cause fierce, even violent reactions against previous governments and their protagonists. In other words, the memory of Roman emperors, good or bad, depends on a series of complex mechanisms that took place both during and after a ruler's reign. Crucial for their reputation was the relationship between ruler and the senatorial elite, and the respect an emperor paid to its members in particular. Every emperor who failed to do so, and who succeeded in alienating the elite from himself and his entourage, would sooner or later blacken his name, arousing the Senate's secret disapproval during his lifetime, and receiving loud and open condemnation after his death, no matter what his merits in other domains might have been.

When Domitian was assassinated on 18 September 96, he left no children and no legitimate heirs. As Nero before him, he was the last of his dynasty, and as such he offered the opportunity to his successors to try and legitimize their own rule by denigrating a predecessor. All that is recorded about Domitian and kept in the stores of our collective memory seems to be utterly negative. 'Unknown, unloved' could serve as a brief summary of the man and his deeds. The memory sanctions bestowed upon him by the Senate, and the blackest-possible portrait immortalised in writing by his contemporaries are proof of this mechanism of power. Tacitus, Pliny the Younger, or Suetonius, were all eager to wash away any memory of their own entanglements with his rule. Certainly, these ancient authors had a decided influence in shaping our perception of many of Rome's emperors and how later generations would remember them.

The example of Nero, however, shows that a bad reputation, even a *damnatio memoriae*, was not necessarily followed by obscurity. It remains our task to explain, therefore, the reason why Domitian appears to have faded into obscurity, remembered as a 'bald Nero' (a *calvus Nero*, the ultimate insult to a man who had even published a book complaining about his loss of hair), and surpassed by his great successor, Trajan. It is striking, for example, that the more positive voices on Domitian and his rule such as those of the contemporary poets Statius or Martial, have been systematically forgotten, shouted down, or misunderstood, even if these authors themselves have not.

Overly positive approaches to specific rulers, combined with the denigration of others should be taken *cum grano salis* and we should not accept without question the judgements of the ancient authors, especially given their propensity for criticizing their leaders – after their deaths... As Olivier Hekster recently put it: "Antiquity knows only bad rulers."[5] Periods of complete peace were rare in antiquity, and all inhabitants could at any moment be subjected to some measurement countering their expectations of life.

An explicit aim of this volume, therefore, as well as being one of the main objectives of the accompanying exhibition, is to reflect on those contradictions that form an equally important part of Domitianic and post-Domitianic culture, and to give more of a voice to those individuals from the antiquity who have often been left on the side-lines. This follows a trend in historiographic, literary, and archaeological studies of the last decades to refrain from

---

4   For Flavian responses to Nero, see Frederick 2003 and Heerink/ Meijer in press.

5   O. Hekster, "Foute Heersers? Antieke en moderne beelden", *Hermeneus* 91 (2019) 183: "De oudheid kent alleen maar foute heersers." In this special edition of the periodical aimed at the general public ("foute heersers" or bad rulers), Domitian receives his own article: Tim Noens, "De wreedste heerser van de oudheid? Plinius, Tacitus en Martialis over Domitianus" (The cruelest ruler of the world? Pliny, Tacitus, and Martial on Domitian), *Hermeneus* 91 (2019) 244-247.

unilateral judgements, aiming instead at a more balanced reconstruction of the life and deeds of this emperor.[6]

Scholars nowadays acknowledge the fact, for example, that Domitian's military skills were good, and his grip on the empire's administration was no worse than many of the emperors before or after him. Rome benefitted from his building policy, and arts and literature flourished. Economy performed well under his governance, which one sees reflected in the prospering towns and countryside of the Mediterranean in these years. The tide, therefore, has begun to turn, as evidenced by one recent reassessment of Domitian, a collection of essays by the title 'Undamning Domitian', the results of which have partly converged with this volume.[7]

Ultimately, we hope that this volume and the exhibition will offer a more balanced view of Domitian, his rule, and his world, returning him to a prominent place in the history of Rome's emperors.

Volume Overview

Our reappraisal of Domitian begins with the advent of the Flavians. In Section One of this volume ('Ruling the Empire'), Olivier Hekster's and Domenico Palombi's papers focus on Rome prior to the arrival of Vespasian in 69, exploring what it meant to be an emperor (Hekster) and how the city evolved under the Julio-Claudian rule (Palombi). In the paper that follows, Barbara Levick discusses the emergence of the Flavians as a ready-made dynasty, which offered some stability for Rome following a debilitating year of civil war and constantly changing leadership. Francesca Morandini, Lilia Palmieri, and Marina Volonté consider some of the archaeological remains of this time, which shed light on the impact that this civil war had on Italy and its landscape.

In Section Two ('Building the Empire'), Eric Moormann explores the changing city-scape of Rome under the Flavians. The three articles that follow consider the idea of empire both within the city and at the empire's borders, with Claudio Parisi Presicce exploring the latest research on the Arch of Titus in the Circus Maximus and Barbara Birley and Frances McIntosh focusing on the evidence of Domitian's campaigns in Roman Britain. Jasper de Bruin's paper concludes this section with an overview of Rome's borders with Germany under Domitian, an area of particular importance to an emperor who had assumed the name Germanicus.

Section Three ('The Image of the Emperor') shifts the focus to the perception of Domitian as an emperor as well as his imperial household. Papers by Jane Fejfer, Paolo Liverani, and Claire Stocks, all explore the image of Domitian in portraits, historical reliefs and architecture, and literature respectively. The article by Lien Foubert discusses notions of 'soft power', exploring the role of the imperial women as style icons for their day.

In Section Four ('The World of Domitian'), we focus on the daily life of Domitian and his subjects, juxtaposing the opulent lifestyle of the emperor with that of his citizens. Aurora Raimondi Cominesi and Claire Stocks focus on Domitian's imperial palaces, which serve as a symbol for his public and private personae. Nathalie de Haan shifts attention back to the people by focusing on the living conditions in Rome and the public facilities that were available. We then move onto two papers that focus on specific aspects of life in Domitian's Rome: Daniëlle Slootjes considers the spectacles and entertainment that a Roman citizen could expect to enjoy, whilst Onno van Nijf, Robin van Vliet, and Caroline van Toor deal with the Capitolia, a new series of Greek-style athletic and artistic competitions and horse races introduced by Domitian in 86 which took into account previous events of this kind in a process of "Anchoring Innovation". The contribution by Natascha Sojc centres on the seat of imperial power in Rome: the Palatine. This was the place where the emperor lived, slept, and conducted imperial business. As such it served as a counter-point to the traditional seat of Roman power: the Senate. Claudia Valeri introduces the reader in Domitian's luxurious villa at Albano.

Section Five ('Man and God') considers how we should respond to an emperor who actively marketed himself as a god on earth. We consider this from three approaches: Frederick G. Naerebout focuses on religion under the Flavians, whilst Diane A. Conlin investigates how the divine and imperial intersect in the art and architecture of Domitian's reign. Finally, Antony Augoustakis and Emma Buckley consider the literary sources on Domitian both during and after his reign, and the effect that this has had upon how the emperor has been received. Miguel John Versluys' paper considers the importance of the Egyptian goddess Isis to the Flavians, and especially Domitian, noting how the prominence of this goddess suggests a special affinity between the Flavians and Egypt.

In the final section of this volume ('Fall and Afterlife'), we tackle the subject of Domitian and his memory. Carrie Vout's paper on portraiture and memory sanctions opens this section, exploring the effect of the memory sanctions (often referred to as damnatio memoriae) that were imposed by the Senate immediately following Domitian's assassination. Olaf Kaper explores the fascinating effect (or lack thereof) of the memory sanctions in the Domitianic remains in Egypt. From the immediate response to Domitian's fall in antiquity, we shift focus in Maria Paola

---

6   See, for example, the biographies of Domitian by Brian Jones (1992) and Pat Southern (1997) whose modern appraisal of the emperor contrasts strongly with that of Stéphane Gsell (1894).

7   Augustakis/Buckley/Stocks 2019. For post-Flavian literature, see i.a. Whitton 2018.

Del Moro's and Nine Miedema's papers to the reception of Domitian in late antiquity and the Middle Ages.

The structure of this volume, with its collection of individual yet connected papers, is designed to offer the reader the opportunity to 'dip into' specific topics at will, as well as to read the volume as a whole. Whichever method one chooses, we hope that the reader will enjoy this material and that – by engaging with this emperor for the first time, or by renewing that engagement – they will re-assess the last of the Flavians, his legacy and the reasons why his post-mortem reputation became so bad.

Acknowledgements

The editors are greatly indebted to all the authors of this volume for their willingness to share their knowledge on such a crucial historical figure and fascinating period of Roman history. This volume benefitted enormously from the most recent investigations, allowing us to present new data from archaeological excavations and academic research. In particular, we are grateful to the co-coordinators of the Flavian Literary Network (Antony Augoustakis, Emma Buckley, and Claire Stocks) for their collaborative efforts in setting up a series of conferences and publications centered around the Emperor Domitian and his time, from which this volume and exhibition have also profited.

In each case where we have used images, we have received permission to do so or have done our best to contact the person or organization that we thought is the copyright holder to gain permission.

Thanks are due to our colleagues at RMO, Lucas Petit and Tanja van der Zon, who carefully read all texts and provided us with both critical and stimulating questions and feedback. This study was supported by the Dutch ministry of Education, Culture and Science (OCW) through the Dutch Research Council (NWO), as part of the Anchoring Innovation Gravitation Grant research agenda of OIKOS, the National Research School in Classical Studies, the Netherlands (project number 024.003.012). For more information see www.ru.nl/oikos/anchoring-innovation. Further support was provided by the Rijksmuseum van Oudheden in Leiden.

We thank the various institutions and museums for giving us the permission to publish images. In the captions these sources are duly indicated. For images of monuments pertaining to the Parco Archeologico del Colosseo, we thank the relevant institution for the release of a publication permit (Su concessione del Ministero per i beni e le attività culturali e per il turismo - Parco archeologico del Colosseo).

Practical Information

The articles are original contributions, each conform to the wish of the author or authors, so that differences in the use of references may occur. Ancient authors are referred to with abbreviations that conform to *Oxford Classical Dictionary*, fourth edition (Oxford 1996; also available online: https://classics.oxfordre.com/staticfiles/images/ORECLA/OCD.ABBREVIATIONS.pdf). There is a general bibliography as well as a general index.

PART I

Ruling the Empire

Emperorship and Emperors before the Flavians Came to Power

Olivier Hekster

For a long time, Roman emperorship did not, officially, exist. There is no doubt that from Julius Caesar onwards, the Empire was led by sole rulers, but these rulers pretended, at least to some of their subjects, not to be in sole control. The assassination of Caesar (44 BC) had made clear that open dictatorship created much antagonism among the ruling senatorial elite, and his successors – from Augustus onwards – formulated their new powers in traditional magisterial terms. Moreover, in Roman legal terms political offices could not be inherited. That did not stop Roman emperorship, from the beginning of the period of sole rule, from being effectively dynastic. Taken together, this led to a situation in which from the late-first century BC onwards, the Empire had in practice become a dynastic monarchy, but officially remained a *Res Publica* in which there was a *princeps* or 'first citizen'. There was no formalized position for the man who ruled the Empire, and hence no formalized mode of succession.[1]

This was not so much of a problem for Julius Caesar's adoptive son, young Caesar (as he was known in antiquity), who from 28-27 BC went by the name Augustus ('consecrated one'). He derived his undoubted supreme position from on the one hand a real sense of gratitude for restoring order after decades of Civil War, and on the other hand massive military support. Several letters of Augustus to senators start with the phrase "I and the army are in good health". The combination of ruler and troops is noticeable.[2] Apparently Augustus felt no need to hide the military underpinning of his reign. Much has been written about the ways in which Augustus' power was formulated through combining already existing magistracies, including membership of the major priestly colleges, and from 13 BC onwards, the position of *pontifex maximus*, in many ways the chief priest of Rome. His formal role in Rome was given shape by combining standard Republican offices and powers, such as that of the power of the tribune (*tribunicia potestas*). In Augustus' own often-cited words: "I excelled all in influence (*auctoritas),* though I possessed no more official power (*potestas*) than others who were my colleagues in the several magistracies."[3] This made it easier for the traditional elite to accept Augustus' position: he paid them proper respect. This amalgamation of traditional powers and magistracies formed the basis of imperial power for the duration of the Empire.

---

1   See Levick 2010, 63-114, Hurlet/Mineo 2011, Cowan 2019.
2   For the phrase as traditional opening line see: Dio Cass. 69.14.3, Reynolds 1982, document 6, 12. Cf. Campbell 1984, 148-156.
3   *Res Gestae* 34.3.

Fig. 1. Portrait of Augustus with idealized 'ageless' face. New York, Metropolitan Museum of Art, Rogers Fund 190, inv. 08.258.47.

Yet few, if any, Roman subjects will have been in doubt about the power that he could wield. The many surviving epigraphic requests to Augustus to intervene personally throughout the Roman Empire make clear that people expected him to exert his position to their benefit.[4] Augustus may have formulated his formal position in republican terms, yet that does not mean he hid his power behind a republican façade. The Augustan portrait, for instance, was disseminated through statuary and on coins issued at the centre and in the provinces. The image of the Empire's ruler was highlighted on a scale that was unparalleled in Roman history. Moreover, the style of his portrait was markedly different from that of earlier figures in Roman history. The likes of Marius (157-86) and Sulla (138-78) were portrayed as experienced military leaders, with lines in their faces and a severe expression. Augustus, on the other hand, was displayed as an eternal youth. His image still employed the traditional Roman way of portraying a recognisable individual, but it heavily borrowed from the much more heroic idealising style of Hellenistic art.[5] This new scheme for portraiture simultaneously triggered associations with Hellenistic kings and Roman values. In this way, it anchored Augustus' innovative political position in two very different traditions. It did not, however, hide his supreme position. Augustus' elevated status was also clearly visible in the city of Rome. His house on the Palatine, for instance, was, like the palaces of Hellenistic kings, intrinsically linked to a major temple – that of Apollo Palatinus, which was highly visible through its conspicuous use of white and gilded marble.[6] It was also a richly decorated residential compound, including many Hellenistic elements and motives, especially inside. At the same time, Augustus defended the building of the temple by referring to traditional Roman reasons for temple dedication.[7] Once again, this shows Augustus anchoring himself within two different traditions.

Augustus ruled for forty-one years, outliving both his opponents and almost anyone who remembered a functioning Roman Republic. He also had enough time to prepare for his succession. Augustus' grandsons Gaius and Lucius, who had been preferred heirs, died young, but his adoptive son Tiberius, who was the son of Augustus' wife Livia from an earlier marriage, had been given sufficient powers and honours to guarantee a smooth transition of power. When Augustus died in 14, Tiberius, who was an accomplished military leader, commanded the soldiers and inherited an enormous estate. Consequently, there was little discussion that Tiberius was in practice in control of the state. But there was no formal emperorship which he could inherit, nor did Tiberius inherit the gratitude which Augustus had been given for restoring order after years of Civil War. Instead, the new ruler positioned himself as the rightful heir. Augustus was deified, allowing Tiberius to be described as 'son of a god' (*Divi Filius*) on many coins. He also took 'Augustus' as an honorific denoting his position; an example taken up by subsequent rulers to the point that it became the title for emperorship. Like Augustus, too, Tiberius held *tribunicia potestas* and was elected as *pontifex maximus*. Though, officially, there was still no position of emperor, Tiberius' actions made clear Augustus was the cornerstone against whom successors would be measured.

Tiberius reigned for twenty-three years. By the time of his death in 37, only Romans older than sixty-four had been alive in an age without Augustus or his adopted son. Single rule had become the new normal and Augustus and his family were the only known incumbents in what was effectively a monarchy. Small surprise that Tiberius was succeeded by close family, in this case Gaius Caesar, better known as Caligula, who was the son of Tiberius' nephew Germanicus. Unlike Tiberius, Caligula, who was only twenty-five when he came to power, had little military and administrative experience and received all the honours and powers that effectively constituted

---

4   See still Millar 1984.
5   Burnett 2011.

6   Zink/Pienig 2009, 114-115.
7   Raimondi Cominesi 2018, with Hekster/Rich 2006.

emperorship *en bloc* at Tiberius' death. Apparently, there was now a recognisable basis to single rule, transferable to a male heir. In a way, then, 'official' emperorship started with Caligula.[8] Certainly, Caligula emphasised his elevated position more than his predecessors. Where Augustus had used both Roman and Hellenistic traditions to anchor his position to recognisable precedents, which were acceptable to different groups in the Roman Empire, Caligula seems to have presented himself more like a Hellenistic monarch. In doing so, he disregarded Rome's traditional senatorial elite and was murdered within four years. Ancient literary sources, all written by the elite, portray him as insane.[9]

Caligula's ultimate unpopularity with senators did not dent the popularity of the Augustan household, of which some of the women were prominent in Roman public life, notably Augustus' wife Livia, his sister Octavia the Younger, and the latter's great-granddaughter Agrippina the Younger, who was Caligula's youngest sister. Agrippina was to marry Caligula's successor Claudius (41-54). Claudius was Livia's grandson and Caligula's uncle. After Caligula's assassination, he was put forward by the Emperors' guard, the Praetorians, who had been concentrated in barracks on the outskirts of Rome since 22. This had increased their importance to the extent that they could decide that Claudius was head of the Augustan household, giving him the financial and military support to become sole ruler.

Where Caligula seems to have used Hellenistic precedents as an anchor to make his position understood, Claudius was an antiquarian, and many of his actions can be interpreted as trying to formulate a 'proper' Roman emperorship. Claudius also paid much attention to the military. Most importantly, it was during his reign that the Romans conquered Britain (43), and thus extended their Empire 'across the Ocean'. The logistics of the invasion had been prepared under Caligula, but the conquest took place under the auspices of Claudius, though of course the actual fighting was done by his generals – one of whom was Domitian's father Vespasian.[10] But it was Claudius who held the triumph. After this massive military success, the Emperor's dependence on the Praetorians seems to have diminished, and references to them disappear from his coinage. This shows how important demonstrable military qualities were for Roman rulers. They were expected to guarantee peace, and in Rome that meant outfighting the enemy.

In 49, Claudius married his niece Agrippina and in doing so tightened the dynastic nodes of what is known as the Julio-Claudian household in modern literature, but was referred to as the *Domus Augusta* in ancient sources. Three years later, Claudius adopted Agrippina's son Nero,

effectively making him heir to the throne over his own son Britannicus, who was thirteen years younger. Nero was also engaged to Claudius' daughter Octavia, further strengthening Nero's claims. Claudius died in 54, with Britannicus still underage. Nero was the undisputed successor, and started his reign by strongly emphasizing his Augustan descent. In the first two years of his reign, all Neronian coins include ancestral references. But after 55, a year that also saw Nero's assassination of Britannicus, these references disappear. Instead, Nero's coins emphasise the city of Rome, and peace, as guaranteed by military success.[11]

This emphasis on Rome in Neronian coins is unsurprising, taking into account the emperor's prolific building activities.[12] Most discussed of his constructions is the so-called *Domus Aurea* (Golden House) in the centre of Rome, extensively described by Suetonius:

> He made a palace extending all the way from the Palatine to the Esquiline ... Its vestibule was large enough to contain a colossal statue of the emperor a hundred and twenty feet high... There was a pond too, like a sea, surrounded with buildings to represent cities ... In the rest of the house all parts were overlaid with gold and adorned with gems and mother-of-pearl. There were dining-rooms with fretted ceils of ivory, whose panels could turn and shower down flowers and were fitted with pipes for sprinkling the guests with perfumes. The main banquet hall was circular and constantly revolved day and night, like the heavens.... [13]

Much of the area covered by this new palace complex was already in imperial hands before Nero' Golden House was built, but the scale of the complex, and its clearly monarchical overtones alienated the senatorial elite. Suetonius' emphasis on dining rooms is noticeable: public dinners mirrored the Roman social order, and imperial behaviour at such events indicated styles of rule.[14] Nero, like Caligula before him and Domitian afterwards, showed that he was in absolute control.

Still, Nero's palace complex was built in an area that had previously mainly consisted of senatorial urban villae, and the opulent decorations of the complex made use of traditional motives. Nero's more openly monarchical status was formulated in a language that was understandable to Rome's population, and located in a part of Rome that had

---

8   Wiedemann 1996, 261-262.
9   Winterling 2003.
10   See in this volume Barbara Levick.

11   Hekster/Manders/Slootjes 2014, 35.
12   *RIC* I², 150-187. For Nero's building activities, see Elsner 1994, Perassi 2002, Moormann 2003. See Domenico Palombi in this volume.
13   Suet. *Nero* 31.1-2. Cf. Tac. *Ann.* 15.42.
14   Acton 2011, 103-104.

always been inaccessible to most of the city's population. Even the oft-discussed colossal statue of the sun god (possibly resembling the emperor) that was part of the complex was not entirely innovative. Roman emperors were responsible for a proper relationship with the divine and could be supported by gods. Augustus had highlighted his special relationship with Apollo. Nero did the same, though on a larger and perhaps more personalised scale.

The type of personalised leadership which Nero put forward ultimately led to his fall, and with it to the end of the Augustan Household. There was no obvious successor. Civil War arose, leading to the so-called year of the Four Emperors (69). At the end of it, Titus Flavius Vespasianus ended up in power. Like Augustus, he could claim to have brought stability and peace to the Empire. His dynasty, however, also like that of Augustus, would be faced with the tension between widely varying expectations of what a ruler should be and do, and the lack of constitutional basis for the position which the emperors held.

Rome AD 69: The City at the Crossroads

Domenico Palombi

"What an artist dies in me!"[1] The note of theatricality that Suetonius conveyed to his audience when narrating Nero's last moments, highlights the amazing vision of imperial power conceived by the last heir of Augustus: "lover of the impossible",[2] and eager, beyond all measure, "to perpetuate his memory and fame in eternity".[3] We can thus understand the magnitude of the monumental, urban and infrastructural programme conceived by Nero for Rome after the fire of 64 which had devastated the city: only four out of the fourteen regions were spared (I, V, VI, XIV), three were totally destroyed (XI, X, III) while the remaining seven were seriously damaged. The fire gave him the opportunity to "acquire glory by building a new city and calling it by its name."[4]

The irreparable loss of "everything that had remained worthy of being seen or remembered from antiquity"[5] would have been balanced by a *nova Urbs* (new city) that was founded upon a rational and efficient urban design: orthogonal, wide and straight streets; buildings of reduced height, built with fireproof materials; urban blocks with front porches and inside courtyards; efficient water network. These features were "things well accepted for their usefulness and which also gave beauty to the new city."[6] In the centre of Rome, the emperor planned an immense palace, called the *Domus Aurea*: it extended from the Palatine to the Esquiline, was accessible from the Forum Romanum through a gigantic *atrium* dominated by the Colossus of the Sun. The *domus* was scattered with pavilions of unusual richness, very long porticoes, vast gardens, and a pond that looked like a sea. All this happened because "there was nothing in which he was more prodigal than in building."[7]

---

1   Suet. *Nero* 49.
2   Tac. *Ann.* 15.42.2.
3   Suet. *Nero* 55.
4   Tac. *Ann.* 15.40.2.
5   Suet. *Nero* 28, cf. Tac. *Ann.* 41.
6   Tac. *Ann.* 43.
7   Suet. *Nero* 31, Tac. *Ann.* 43. On Nero and Rome, see, among others, Cizek 1984, 276-281, Griffin 1984, Sordi 1999, 105-112, Champlin 2005, 230-269, for the image of Neron as a builder, see Elsner 1994. For Neronian urbanistics: Croisille/Perrin 2002 (essays C. Perassi, V.M. Strocka, E.M. Moormann/P.G.P. Meyboom, P. Gros, J.-P. Morel/F. Villedieu, S. Ensoli, K. Welch, M. Sordi, J.-M. Croisille, G. Mazzoli, J.-M. André, A. Malissard, R. Carré), Tomei/Rea 2011 (essays C. Panella, A. Viscogliosi, H. von Hesberg, M.A. Tomei, A. Carandini/D. Bruno/F. Fraioli, H.-J. Beste), de Souza/Devillers 2019 (essays F. Villedieu, M. Ippoliti, E. Brienza, M. Mimmo).

In fact, Nero's project should be considered the first coherent plan for the urban reorganization of imperial Rome, after the general renewal carried out by Augustus according to the new political-administrative organization and ideological-cultural needs of the city that had now become the *caput imperii* and the seat of the *Domus Augusta*. Had Fate not abandoned Nero – marking the end both of an era and of a dynasty[8] – in the centuries to come Rome would certainly have preserved the layout and the forms of his *nova Urbs*, the completion of which, on the other hand, seemed inevitable to those who wished to succeed him.[9] However, when the struggle for succession ended in 69, Vespasian found Rome still struck by the consequences of that terrible disaster, so that "being the *Urbs* disfigured by ruins and old fires, it allowed anyone to build in the empty areas if the owners had not done so."[10]

In fact, as archaeological investigations reveal, the city's rebuilding after the fire of 64 was focused on the area of the imperial palace, while a vast urban planning had been drawn up – but only partly carried out – in the districts between the Palatine Hill and the Imperial Fora, around the Via Sacra and its extension towards the valley of the future Amphitheatre and along the Argiletum, in front of the Fora of Caesar and Augustus.[11]

Elsewhere, it is very difficult to find archaeological evidence of rebuilding: the functional contents and ideological orientations of Nero's urban project emerge from what has been handed down from written sources.[12]

The particular attention paid to rebuilding the *Circus Maximus* (before 66-68), ties in with a more ambitious programme dedicated to the buildings for the spectacle which, even before 64, focused on the completion of the *Circus* of Caligula in the Vatican (with its bridge over the Tiber, the so-called *Pons Neronianus*) and the construction of an Amphitheatre in the *Campus Martius* (57) built as an entirely wooden structure but of extraordinary richness.[13] In the same topographical context falls the construction, in 60 or 62, of the Neronian Baths and of the sumptuous *Gymnasium Neronis* (burnt-down soon after and not rebuilt), linked to the celebrations of the *Neronia*, the five-yearly games in honour of the emperor abolished after his death.[14]

In addition to the *Macellum Magnum* on the *Caelius* (59) which replaced the traditional food market north of the *Forum*, other noteworthy public services and urban infrastructures include the completion of the Harbour of Claudius and the project of a navigable canal between Ostia and Pozzuoli, forming a direct connection of the two main food supply ports of Rome.[15] *Annona* (grain), *balnea* (baths), and *spectacula* (spectacles) qualify Nero's *nova Urbs* as an expression of the emperor's *munificentia* (generosity) and *liberalitas* (kindness), whose *maiestas* (greatness) was expressed in an urban and monumental vision unprecedented in grandeur and coherence.

Thus, at the end of the Julio-Claudian dynasty, the substantial and symbolic requirements connected with the exercise of imperial power had resulted in a spectacular metamorphosis of the city, transforming it into an imperial megalopolis[16] that extended well beyond the confines of its ancient walls (even if the gates retained a symbolic value):[17] it was divided into fourteen regions and two hundred and sixty-five districts (this number had already been reached in the Flavian age),[18] settled around the representative centres of power (the palace and the imperial *fora*),[19] with an improved network of services and infrastructures (aqueducts, markets, thermal baths, entertainment buildings, etc.).[20] This new imperial megalopolis was also supplied by an efficient annonary organization (the

---

8   Suet. *Galba* 1.1. See Olivier Hekster in this volume.

9   Suet. *Otho* 7, *Vitell.* 11. Cf. Cosme 2012, 212-217.

10   Suet. *Vesp.* 8.

11   Medri 1996, Brienza 2016, Palombi 2016, esp. 94-95. On the material and ideological 'destiny' of the *Domus Aurea*: Flower 2006, 228-232, Daguet-Gagey 2007, esp. 119-120, Rosso 2008, Leithoff 2014, 134-140.

12   For the edifices mentioned in the following, see the entries in *LTUR* I-IV (1993-2000).

13   On the circus in the Vatican: Coarelli 2008-2009 and Gee 2011-2012. For the *theatrum Neronis* in the same *horti* of Agrippina in the Vatican: Liverani 2000-2001.

14   On the recent discoveries pertaining these structures, see Filippi 2010.

15   On the *Macellum Magnum* of the *Caelius* and its representations on coins: Bocciarelli/Bizet 2013. On the *fossa Neronis*: Johannowski 1994 and Giardina 2004. On the evolution of the "Pozzuoli-Ostia-Roma system": Zevi 2001 and 2000.

16   On the quantitative and qualitative characteristics of the Imperial megalopolis: Nicolet 2000. On its formation: Palombi 2012a.

17   On the extention of the town – based on Plin. *HN* 3.5.66-67 – and on the censure of Vespasian and Titus in 73-74, closed with the extention of the *pomerium* by Vespasian in 75, see Guilhembet 2006.

18   A. Fraschetti/D. Palombi, s.v. *Regiones quattuordecim*, *LTUR* IV (1999) 197-204, 518.

19   On the Imperial Fora within the new institutional and bureaucratic topography of the *Urbs*: Bonnefond 1987, Carnabuci 1996, Corbier 2006, 147-162, Bablitz 2007, De Angelis 2010 (essays F. De Angelis, M. Maiuro, E. Kondratieff, E. Metzger, R. Neudecker).

20   Indicative is the multiplication of aqueducts between Augustus (*aquae Iulia*, 33 BC, *Virgo* 19 BC, *Alsietina* 2 BC) and Claudius (*Anio Novus* and *aqua Claudia*): Bruun 1997, 121-155 and De Kleijn 2001. On the first public baths of Rome: Migliorati 2015. On the buildings for spectacles: Sear 2006, Moretti 2009, Ciancio Rossetto/Pisani Sartorio 2017. On the problem of the *macellum Liviae* on the Esquiline: Bertrand/Chillet 2016.

harbour of Ostia, Tiber harbours, and warehouses),[21] was controlled by an extensive military and paramilitary system (with army and police barracks and garrisons),[22] and was administered by a complex bureaucracy of officials (with their relevant administrative offices).[23] The physical and symbolic presence of the *princeps* and the *domus Augusta* was pervasive (with an extensive array of gardens and celebratory and funerary monuments in addition to the imperial palace)[24] and there were an increasing number of ceremonies and buildings dedicated to the imperial cult.[25]

The radical transformation of the republican city had started with Augustus who, in forty years of ruling, had created that "city of marble" (more than one hundred documented monumental, building and infrastructural works) which, in symbolic and substantial terms, constituted the foundation of the new imperial capital.[26] After Augustus, the Julio-Claudian emperors had acted in the vein of continuity and dynastic legitimation. Tiberius faced the reconstruction of the quarters destroyed by the fire of 27, while he was himself responsible for the creation of several great functional and infrastructural works (the *Castra Praetoria* and the improvement of the Tiber banks). He also carried out vast restorations in the *Forum Holitorium* and in the *Campus Martius*. Caligula built a *Circus* in the Vatican and an Amphitheatre in the *Campus Martius*. Claudius took particular care of the water supply system (two new aqueducts and a general restoration of the existing ones), and of the *annona* with the possible construction of the new *Porticus Minucia Frumentaria* in *Campus Martius* and the creation of the Harbour of Ostia (from 42 onwards).[27]

However, only Nero had the ambition – and the opportunity – to conceive a consistent urban project for the centre of Rome. His unfinished legacy influenced the monumental building activity of the Flavians who, at the crossroads between Augustan classicism and the Hellenizing utopia of Nero, interpreted it according to their specific perspectives, and passed it on to the Antonines and the Severans.[28]

---

21   On the *annona* in Rome: *Mémoire* 1998 (essays E. Lo Cascio, S. Panciera, G.E. Rickman, B. Sirks, M. Tarpin, C. Virlouvet), Virlouvet 2000, Tchernia 2000, Hesnard 2001, Andreau 2001.

22   On the 'militarisation' of Rome: Sablayrolles 2001, Busch 2011.

23   On the imperial bureaucratic and administrative system, its offices and its ideological implications: Daguet-Gagey 2000, Coarelli 2019. For the development of the imperial system, see Olivier Hekster in this volume.

24   On the 'symbiotic' rapport between *princeps* and *Urbs*: Benoist 2005.

25   On times, protagonists, practices and manifestations of the imperial cult in Rome: Palombi 2013.

26   To be quoted from the vast bibliography: *Augustus* 1988, F. Castagnoli, s.v. Roma, in *Enciclopedia Virgiliana* I (1988) 544-553, Zanker 1987, Fraschetti 1990, Wallace-Hadrill 1993, Favro 1996, D. Palombi, s.v. Roma, in *Enciclopedia Oraziana* I (1996) 533-553, Haselberger 2007, La Rocca 2014 (esp. essays E. La Rocca and A. Viscogliosi).

27   On the monumental and infrastructural policy of the Julio-Claudians: Thornton/Thornton 1989, Ghini 2015 (essays M. Barbera, F. Coarelli, H. Hurst), La Rocca 2018.

28   On Flavian Rome see, with bibliography: Darwall-Smith 1996, Boyle/Dominik 2003, Edmondson/Mason/ Rives 2005, Cavalieri 2005, Coarelli 2009b, Gering 2012, Ruff 2012, Leithoff 2014, Tatarkiewicz 2014, Moormann 2018. On the urbanistic programmes of the Antonines: Palombi 2012b, Palombi 2017. On that of the Severi: Palombi 2018.

The Rise of the Flavians

Barbara Levick

Flavian Antecedents and Vespasian's Early Career[1]

"Oh! I do think I'm turning into a god!", cried the Emperor Vespasian on his death-bed in June 79, so it is alleged. Justifiably too, after a reign that had been a signal success. When he was born, on 17 November 9, it would never have entered anyone's head that this member of an undistinguished Sabine family, born at Falacrina, near Reate (modern Rieti), would take over the office currently held by Caesar Augustus and destined for his heirs. Ancient sources, notably Suetonius (writing after the Flavian dynasty had ended with the assassination of Domitian and relying on hostile stories of his early career), naturally make much of the disreputable occupations of his father (tax-collecting in Asia and money-lending in the Alps) and the squalor of the house in which his younger son Domitian was born. Yet even Suetonius has to let a few telling facts through. Vespasian and his elder brother Sabinus had an uncle on the mother's side (her father held military tribunates) who was already in the Senate and had reached the praetorship, the second highest magistracy in the senatorial career. Sabinus passed into the Senate without trouble, evidently, and the only obstacle in Vespasian's way was his own reluctance: his mother had to persuade him to apply for permission to wear the *latus clavus*, the tunic with the broad purple stripe that denoted senatorial rank.

Vespasian's early career was inglorious – and that too was remembered. After a military tribunate in Thrace, he was allotted a first civil post as quaestor (financial officer) in the backwater province of Crete and Cyrene; he failed in his first attempt to become aedile (supervisor of markets at Rome), came in last at his second attempt, and was disgraced when he failed to keep Rome's streets clean: Emperor Gaius had mud stuffed down his toga. All the same he reached the praetorship and his sycophantic speeches, including one accepting an invitation to dinner, curried favour. Real progress came under Gaius' successor Claudius, allegedly from the patronage of Claudius' freedman Narcissus. Clientship of Claudius' friends the Vitellii could be mentioned, too, when he threw off allegiance to the Emperor Vitellius in 69. Help is also said to have come from his mistress Antonia Caenis, a freedwoman of Antonia, the mother of the Emperor Claudius, who was known to be influential at court.

Other men might have profited by distinguished marriage connections, but Vespasian's wife was not even of securely free birth, though she may have brought a fine dowry. And when he married, in the thirties or beginning of the forties (for Titus was

---

1   Suet. *Vesp.* 1-2.

born 30 December 39), it was to a woman of low status, Flavia Domitilla. She had, according to Suetonius, formerly been the mistress of a Roman knight, Statilius Capella of Sabratha (Sabratah) in Africa. Her father was Flavius Liberalis, quaestor's secretary of Ferentium (near Viterbo), and his daughter had only Junian Latin status, that is, she was a slave freed informally, who had to be declared fully freed and of Roman status by a special board. Besides Titus and Domitian, Domitilla also gave Vespasian a daughter, but both mother and daughter died before Vespasian came to power. After his wife's death he took back Caenis and kept her until she died, having made a good business of her intimacy with the Emperor. Without regard for Domitilla's origins she was deified, to the advantage of her sons.

Military Distinction – and Humiliation[2]

The reign of Claudius saw the beginning of Vespasian's military distinction (Thrace may have given him the chance to shine). He was sent first as a legionary legate to Germany, then to Britain, where his conquest of two tribes, twenty *oppida* (settled communities, such as those of formidable Maiden Castle in Dorset and Isca Dumnoniorum, Exeter, in Devon), and the Isle of Wight brought him the triumphal regalia, two priesthoods, and a consulship at the tail end of 51. Vespasian's elder brother also served in Britain, not as his subordinate, as the text of Cassius Dio seems to suggest, but also as a legionary legate, subordinate of the supreme commander A. Plautius, and achieving his consulship four years before Vespasian.[3]

After their consulships the brothers passed to diverse offices. Sabinus was entrusted with the governorship of Moesia, an increasingly onerous post on the Danube, while Vespasian was allocated, literally by the lot and well after the prescribed five-year interval, to the governorship of the public province of Africa (*c.* 63), which contained no legions. This apparent snub may have resulted from the deaths of Claudius and his freedman Narcissus in 54, for neither young Nero's masterful mother Agrippina the Younger nor his constitutionally minded advisers Sex. Afranius Burrus, Prefect of the Praetorian Guard and the philosopher the younger Seneca were known to have favoured him.

Here again a hostile source makes the most of an uncomfortable episode: Vespasian was pelted with turnips in the market place of Hadrumetum (Sousse).[4] But the Emperor Claudius himself had been pelted in the Roman Forum with stale crusts in a time of grain shortage at Rome.[5] Perhaps Vespasian had loyally sent Africa's grain to Rome during another shortage and so earned the hatred of his subjects. And the poverty for which he was derided on his return to Italy, putting all his property into his brother's hands, may have been due to expenses incurred during his governorship. He earned the nickname of 'muleteer' (either for dealing in mules or for carrying on long distance trade with them); he is also said to have been convicted of taking a substantial bribe.

So far, Vespasian and his brother in the early sixties were loyal middle-ranking servants of the Emperor Nero. In 62 Nero dismissed his adviser the philosopher Seneca – the Prefect Burrus opportunely died – in favour of men more to his own taste, such as Ofonius Tigellinus. He had already freed himself in 59 from the encumbrance of his domineering mother and not everyone believed his story of a conspiracy of hers hatched against him. Without Agrippina's threatening presence Seneca and Burrus had few cards to play.

Nero's problems continued to deepen. His divorce and subsequent execution of Octavia, Claudius' daughter, in the year 62, added to the unpopularity aroused by his murder of Claudius' wife (Agrippina), the hero Germanicus' daughter. Worse, there was a long drawn out war against the Parthians, with a staged success in 66, a destructive revolt in Britain in 60-61, and in 64 the great fires at Lugdunum and Rome to be made up for. Such costs, and Nero's lavish expenditure could not be met by normal revenues. Nero turned rapacious, and the proportion of precious metal in the nominally silver coinage was reduced. Men of rank and wealth were afraid. In 65 came a real conspiracy which aimed to replace Nero with the senator C. Calpurnius Piso. That led to the deaths of Seneca and a succession of other senators and *equites*, guilty and innocent, in the following years. A second plot, focused on Beneventum was exposed in 66.

The Flavians in Moesia and Greece[6]

The Flavians did not move in dangerous circles. On the contrary, they were trusties. Sabinus' remaining offices are controverted because of difficulties in the sources, including a possible error in Tacitus,[7] but they culminated in the Prefecture of the City of Rome, which Sabinus held under Galba until Galba was murdered in 69. After his consulship he held the governorship of Moesia for the unusually prolonged period of seven years, 53-60. Sabinus still outstripped Vespasian in wealth and seniority when Vespasian came back from his proconsulship of Africa (*c.* 64). The story of

---

2   Suet. *Vesp.* 4, Dio Cass. 60.20.
3   Dio Cass. 60.20.
4   Suet. *Vesp.* 4.5.
5   Suet. *Claud.* 18.2.

6   Suet. *Vesp.* 4.3-4.
7   On Sabinus' prefecture: Suet. *Vesp.* 1, Tac. *Hist.* 1. 46 and 3. 75. See Griffin 1976, 256-257.

Vespasian's having to mortgage all his property to his brother, putting them on bad terms because of it, may be no more than inference.[8]

Vespasian accordingly followed Nero to Greece where in 66 the Emperor resolved to restore his popularity with a tour, appearing (and winning) at all the Hellenic festivals and as a culminating gesture freeing Greece from Roman rule. The Liberation of Greece was an old ploy, going back to 196 BC, but the exemption from tax that went with it would mean solid benefits. Here if anywhere, the philhellene Nero would win the adulation he craved. And this is where we next find Vespasian, a member of the entourage, with no province and no prospects. It was a precarious position. Worse, Vespasian nodded off at one of the performances and was banished from the Presence, so it was said.[9]

Vespasian and the Jewish War[10]

Fortunately for Vespasian, Nero was fighting to recover control of Judaea, which had broken out into open rebellion in 66, and forced an incompetent general, the governor of Syria, L. Cestius, to retreat; Cestius died in disgrace. Nero had had another general in the East: Cn. Domitius Corbulo, bold and boastful, and, worst of all, half-brother of the Emperor Gaius' last wife Milonia. He had won a resounding diplomatic victory against the Parthians in 62 and would have been the obvious choice for commander-in-chief against the Jewish rebels. But he would have been a dangerous choice. Corbulo, summoned to Greece, was promptly ordered to commit suicide on the grounds that he was implicated in the conspiracies of 65 and 66 – a warning to other generals of birth in

8   Suet. *Vesp.* 4.3.
9   Suet. *Vesp.* 4.4.
10   Jos. *BJ* 3-4, Suet. *Vesp.* 4.5.

Fig. 2. Arch of Titus in the Forum Romanum, northern relief: Titus enters Rome. Rome (photo Wikimedia Commons).

Fig. 3. Arch of Titus in the Forum Romanum, southern relief: spoils captured in Jerusalem are carried through the *Porta Triumphalis*. Rome (photo Wikimedia Commons, Beeldresearch: CKD, RU).

charge of armies (two brothers Scribonius had also been forced to die). Vespasian, with his humble ancestry and blemished career, was a thoroughly safe choice. Nero was reminded of Vespasian's achievements in Britain against wild tribes and over rough terrain: there had been the successful assaults on hill forts, with skilful use of siege engines on the formidable Maiden Castle. The thoroughly safe nobody was despatched to Judaea with three legions.

Vespasian had another enormous boon: his brave, attractive, and ambitious son Titus (born 39) as one of his legates. Titus was assigned to XV Apollinaris in Egypt, Vespasian took over Corbulo's X Fretensis and V Macedonica at Antioch. Collaboration between the legions was important in dealing with the rebellion. It soon became essential for another reason. It was while Nero was still in Greece that news reached him in 68 of the rebellion of Julius Vindex, governor of a Gallic province, probably Lugdunensis. This was an unarmed province but wealthy and tired of Nero's taxes; besides that it was close to the armies of the Rhine and to the single legion that the elderly and aristocratic Ser. Sulpicius Galba commanded in his province of Tarraconensian (Nearer) Spain. Vindex appealed to all his fellow governors; only Galba responded. L. Verginius Rufus, commander of the Upper Rhine army, marched into Gaul and crushed Vindex's revolt at the battle of Vesontio (Besançon). The leader killed himself. But Nero, back at Rome, did not hear the news quickly enough: in despair he too committed suicide as Galba accepted the Principate and marched from his province towards Rome.

There was much for the legionary commanders in the East to discuss: aside from Vespasian, these were C. Licinius Mucianus, the governor of Syria, and so inevitably a rival of Vespasian, who needed to be reconciled by the diplomacy and charm of Titus, along with Tiberius Julius Alexander, the equestrian governor of Egypt. They could assume that the new Princeps would expect them to repress the Jewish revolt; whether they would be replaced was another matter. Collaboration was indicated. Vespasian continued the conquest of Judaea from north to south, graphically described by the Jewish historian Flavius Josephus, who began as a commander on the rebel side but went on as a faithful follower of the Romans, a chronicler of their success, and a Roman citizen. Against the Jewish rebels the new commander was uniformly successful. He soon took Gabara, besieged and took Jotapata, where he was wounded in the leg, taking Josephus captive. He was at Ptolemais in July 67 and captured Gadara in March of the following year. In 69 he invaded Judaea from Caesarea, and in 70 Jerusalem was under siege from Titus.

The Year of the Four Emperors[11]

At the opening of 69 Ser. Sulpicius Galba was in Rome, apparently secure in his Principate. He had fine patrician lineage, military distinction and the *gravitas* of age that Nero had palpably lacked. He was also short of money, a result of Nero's expenditures, and needed to pay off his political debts, especially to the military. This was where he went wrong, as well as in a harshness that he could also ill afford. Nor did he have an heir to guard his back. Meanwhile, as treachery boiled up within the court, Vespasian's son Titus was making his way to Rome, sent by his father to discover what the new emperor's intentions were for Judaea, or rather towards Vespasian himself. Titus was soon to find his mission superseded.

Among Galba's supporters had been M. Salvius Otho, governor of Lusitania. Once in Rome, Otho, whose nobility went back only to the Triumviral period just before Augustus had taken over the state, noted Galba's failings and in particular his unpopularity with the people, who had been devoted to Nero and his lavish spectacles, and with the Praetorian Guard, and took advantage of it. Galba was torn from his carriage and lynched, along with his closest agents (15 January 69). Otho was proclaimed Emperor in his stead. Not surprisingly, Titus at Corinth gave up his mission and returned to his father, visiting the oracle of Paphian Aphrodite on the way – and Romans in post.

This was not the only opposition that Galba had had to face. Otho's regime was as ephemeral as Galba's. He had the support of the Praetorian Guard but they could not withstand the invading legions of Vitellius. Four legions from the lower Rhine army followed the example of the three from the upper, once under the command of Verginius Rufus, in refusing Galba the oath of loyalty on 1 January and declared for their commander A. Vitellius. They were preparing to march on Italy. The Vitellii had been intimates of the imperial family since the end of Augustus' principate, with Aulus' father a close ally of the people's favourite Germanicus Caesar and his son, sharing consulship and censorship with the Emperor Claudius.

Yet another massive group of legions had to be taken account of: those in the Danubian provinces, one in Dalmatia, two in Pannonia, three in Moesia, and it is not clear whether they were not first in the field. At any rate they were not in time to come to the aid of Otho, who had moved up into northern Italy. In a decisive battle (the first battle of Bedriacum) his forces were overwhelmed by the Vitellians. Otho committed suicide (16 April) and the third emperor to rule in 69 was recognized by Senate and People. So the movement in favour of Vespasian was helped by the discontent of troops in Moesia who were left without a leader and little to look forward to.

---

11   Tac. *Hist.* 1-5, Suet. *Vesp.* 6-7.

The Flavian Move on Italy[12]

When in the East consultation turned into planning is uncertain. What Vitellius' attitude to commanders in position would be was uncertain. Nothing was made clear until the beginning of July, first of all in Egypt, then in Syria, leaving Vespasian in the clear, as Vitellius had been. The figurehead might have been Mucianus rather than Vespasian but for several factors: Mucianus, a notorious homosexual, was childless, while Vespasian had a son of proven military talent to back him up and to succeed him if he became emperor; Vespasian's record in Britain and now in Judaea showed him to be a first-rate general; and Mucianus may have lacked ambition. Alexander, Greek-speaking *eques*, was not in contention, though his role as ruler of Egypt and so controller of a high proportion of Rome's grain supplies was vital.

There was no open declaration of power until 1 July, Alexander proclaimed Vespasian in Egypt; the troops in Judaea saluted him in person on 3 July, allegedly spurred on by an appeal from the defeated emperor Otho. C. Licinius Mucianus, governor of Syria, a former possible rival, came out as a powerful force behind him at Antioch (Josephus gives Alexander a secondary place).[13] A host of favourable omens supported his ambitions. Vespasian was made to seem like an emperor who had been reluctantly recruited, and 1 July was taken for the day of his accession to power (when his annual renewal of *tribunicia potestas* – tribunician power - was celebrated). The greeting of the soldiers passed for a vote of the people in Rome.

Vespasian himself stayed in the East, moving into Egypt and asserting his authority there through a series of apparent miracles, though there was the possibility of his marching on his old province of Africa, another breadbasket and where there had already been an abortive rising. Mucianus was put in charge of the Flavian expeditionary force, two legions which were to make their way into Italy by way of the Balkans and in collaboration with the superior Danubian forces. But these troops were under the strenuous leadership of M. Antonius Primus, legate of VII Galbiana, who at a conference held at Poetovio (Ptuj) in August argued for an immediate invasion of Italy, without waiting for Mucianus. He won the day and he carried out his gamble largely with auxiliary forces: Vitellius' backup had no time to arrive, and Vespasian had an apparent ally in the Batavian leader Julius Civilis. It was the Flavians who won the decisive second battle of Bedriacum and who perpetrated the atrocious sack of Cremona. Vitellius summoned further reinforcements and within Italy had a newly recruited Praetorian guard, fourteen cohorts, and a legion of marines, II Adiutrix, all men with everything to lose, and cavalry support. But Primus continued the march and the defection of the fleet at Misenum meant the opening up of a second front south of Rome. Vitellius, dividing his forces, weakened those available for the final battle.

Primus, Mucianus, and Flavius Sabinus in the City offered Vitellius the option of abdication, and Vitellius was ready to accept (17 December). The people would not hear of it and Sabinus had to retreat to the Capitol, joined by Domitian. The Flavian advance guard of a thousand cavalry failed in an attack and followers of Vitellius stormed the Capitol. The temple of Jupiter Optimus Maximus was burnt to the ground. Flavius Sabinus, still Prefect of the City, and negotiating on the Flavian side, was taken prisoner and killed by the Vitellians, while Vespasian's son Domitian, in disguise, had a lucky escape. Antonius Primus entered Rome on 20 December and the Senate met on the following day to confer on Vespasian all the necessary powers. His rival Mucianus was not far behind. By the time Vespasian arrived in Rome the Flavians were in complete control of the city: he and his son Titus had only to celebrate their triumphs. The new dynasty was established.

---

12 Tac. *Hist.* 3-4, Suet. *Vesp.* 6-7.
13 References to omens of Vespasian's success: Jos. *BJ.* 4.622-629, Suet. *Vesp.* 5, Tac. *Hist.* 2.78.

Impact of Empire: Cremona, Bedriacum and Brescia

Francesca Morandini, Lilia Palmieri & Marina Volonté

In the framework of the civil war following Nero's death, three cities in Northern Italy, all located within a short radius, stand out with clarity as testimonies of the troubled political environment of the time and the consequences derived from supporting different contenders to the *imperium*. Bedriacum, where the two decisive battles for the throne took place,[1] carries the traces of a significant reconstruction after the year 69. Cremona, rich and flourishing, never fully recovered from the devastation perpetrated by Vespasian's troops as retaliation for the city's support for Vitellius. Brixia (modern Brescia), faithful to Vespasian throughout the ordeal of the civil war, was encouraged by the emperor himself to acquire new monuments and public spaces, and after 69 experienced a long period of prosperity.

Bedriacum (L.P.)

The small town of Bedriacum went down in Roman history thanks to the mentions in literary sources of the two battles fought near the site in the year 69 that determined the rise to power of Vespasian and the beginning of the Flavian dynasty. It is the historian Tacitus who repeatedly cites the *infaustus vicus*, additionally and conveniently providing its topographical position.[2]

The identification of the site (38 km away from Cremona) dates back to the first half of the 1800's. In 1836, a fragmentary bronze statue of a Victory dedicated to the emperors Marcus Aurelius and Lucius Verus (161-169) was found.[3] A first excavation campaign in the 1900's (1957-1961) brought to light some wealthy private houses, but it is thanks to the excavations carried out by the University of Milan in the last thirty years (1988-2018) that it is now possible to reconstruct the development of the town.[4]

Located in the *ager Cremonensis* at the meeting point between the Via Postumia and the Oglio river, Bedriacum was founded in the second half of the second century BC to be a service centre for the mid-Po Valley. This strategic position was decisive for the economic success of the town between the first century BC and the first century.

---

1 See also Levick in this volume.

2 Tac. *Hist.* 2.23.5.

3 The "Calvatone Victory", sold in 1841 to the Antikenmuseum of Berlin and disappeared during the Second World War, today is in the Hermitage Museum in St. Petersburg. See *Die Victoria von Calvatone* 2020.

4 Grassi 2016.

Fig. 1. Fragments of wall paintings. Calvatone, Bedriacum (courtesy UniMI Archive).

Fig. 2. Mosaic of the Labyrinth from Bedriacum. Piadena, Archaeological Museum (courtesy UniMI Archive).

The House of the Labyrinth, the most famous house of Bedriacum, dates back to the Tiberian-Claudian period.[5] Unusually equipped with two dining rooms for seasonal use, with an elegant decorative apparatus characterized by concrete floors with marbles and wall paintings, it shows in one of the floors of the dining rooms a mosaic *emblema* depicting a labyrinth with the dying Minotaur in the middle (figs. 1 and 2).

During the excavations no evident traces of destruction due to the battles of 69 were found at the site. However, fragments of high-quality wall paintings dating back to the second half of the first century, presumably to the Flavian age, attest a renovation of the houses, which could perhaps be connected to a partial post-war reconstruction.[6] A large room decorated by a polychrome mosaic floor dated between the end of the second and the beginning of the third century attest the persistence of an articulated urban planning, characterized by the combination of residential and productive quarters.

The discovery of a hoard in the roof collapse of a room consisting of 144 *antoniniani* dating back to the age of Gallienus (253-268) suggests a period of strong crisis for the town, which was already abandoned and had fallen into ruin (or at least a part of it) by the mid-third century, reflecting the general crisis scenario of the Empire.[7] Bedriacum was, however, inhabited until the fifth century, as proved by the existence of coin circulation and economic activities in town, with wide-range trades with the East and Africa.[8]

Cremona (M.V.)

The Latin colony of Cremona,[9] together with its "twin" Placentia, was founded in 218 BC near a bend in the Po river in a border area occupied by the Celtic tribes of Insubres and Cenomani. In 190 BC Rome sent out new settlers because of the losses suffered during the Gallic War. The Via Postumia, the main road built by the consul Spurius Postumius Albinus in 148 BC to connect Genoa to Aquileia, crossed the city and its territory. In the second century BC, the city reached a significant economic and cultural level and after the Lex Iulia, it became a *municipium* in 89 BC. In the civil war following the assassination of Julius Caesar in 44 BC, having supported Mark Antony instead of Octavian caused land confiscations and redistributions to the future Emperor's veterans.

Nevertheless, at the end of the first century BC the city had achieved great economic prosperity, as reflected in the

---

5   Grassi 2013.
6   Nava, *forthcoming*.
7   Crisà/Palmieri, *forthcoming*.
8   Palmieri, *forthcoming*.
9   Tozzi 2003.

Fig. 3. Fragment of polychrome mosaic from Piazza Marconi, domus of the Nymphaeum. Cremona, Museo Archeologico (courtesy Ministero per i Beni e le Attività Culturali e per il Turismo).

Fig. 4. The Nymphaeum from Piazza Marconi. Cremona, Museo Archeologico (courtesy Ministero per i Beni e le Attività Culturali e per il Turismo).

increase of building renovations and the construction of numerous wealthy *domus*. During the Augustan period, new houses were built or the older ones were enlarged. In this phase, the floor, wall paintings and furniture, albeit very fragmentary, show contacts with Rome and the arrival in the heart of the Po Valley of valuable objects from various regions of the Empire.

To this phase, for example, belong the *domus* found in Via Cadolini, best known for the mosaic with the labyrinth in which we see in the middle Theseus killing the Minotaur,[10] and the *domus* of the Nymphaeum discovered in Piazza Marconi, whose important excavation has recently been the object of an extensive publication.[11]

This latest *domus* is particularly significant not only as it attests the luxury of the houses belonging to the local elites' houses but most importantly because it testifies of the destruction caused by the civil war of the year 69. As we know from the sources,[12] in October 69 Vespasian's troops burnt and plundered the *municipium* of Cremona, guilty of supporting Vitellius. Signs of this destruction

are very well evident in the material retrieved from the *domus* (figs. 3 and 4).

The appearance of new elegant houses attests of a post-war reconstruction, which, according to the sources, began on the order of Vespasian himself.[13] A large mosaic with the busts of the Seasons,[14] discovered in Via Cadolini not far from the *domus* of the labyrinth, is an evidence of this new phase. If we are to believe the archaeological data, the city, however, never returned to its ancient prosperity, perhaps also as a consequence of its distance from the new strategic routes of the Empire set up in the Flavian period. In Late Antiquity, the mention in several written sources of the harbour on the Po river up to the fifth century, the presence of an imperial shield workshop (*fabrica scutaria*) and the allocation of a Sarmatian warrior unit are evidence of a renewed, albeit temporary, strategic importance of the city. The city was ultimately destructed by Agilulf and the Lombards in August 603.

---

10   Volonté 2003, 177-178.
11   *Amoenissimis ... aedificiis* I, 2017, II, 2018.
12   Santangelo 2017, 83-84.

13   Santangelo 2017, 86.
14   Volonté 2003, 178.

Brescia – Brixia (F.M.)

The modern city of Brescia, at the foot of the Cidneo hill, returned traces of occupation from the Bronze age and dynamic commercial exchanges with Padanian Etruria thanks to the richness and variety of its natural resources and connections. From the Iron age, it became a reference point in the region for the Celtic tribe of the Cenomani, which, according to Livy, elected it as their chief town (*Brixia caput Cenomanorum*). Thanks to its steady economic and diplomatic relationships with Rome, it soon became a full-fledged Roman centre, as evidenced by inscriptions and public buildings at the beginning of the first century BC.[15]

In 89 BC, Brixia obtained the *ius latinum*, and between 49 BC and 42 BC, the full *ius romanum*. To the beginning of the first century BC dates a sanctuary in an excellent state of preservation with four *aulae*: its architecture and its mural decorations denounce a strong and precocious adherence of *Brixia* to the culture of Rome. During the Augustan age, the city wall was erected and the city defined urbanistically, with the main public area confirmed on the southern slopes of the Cidneo hill; the public aqueduct also dates back to this period.

As a result of the military confrontations of 69 and the proclamation of Vespasian, supported by the people of Brixia, as emperor, the city was the object of a monumental urban and architectural redevelopment, made it easier by the close presence of white limestone

Fig. 5. View of the *Capitolium*. Brescia (courtesy Archivio Fotografico Civici Musei di Brescia, Fotostudio Rapuzzi).

---

15 Morandini, Rossi 2015. Malnati/Manzelli 2015, 86-88, 179.

Fig. 6. Victory from Brescia after recent restoration (courtesy Archivio Fotografico Civici Musei di Brescia, Fotostudio Rapuzzi)

quarries, which led to the expansion of the area of the *forum*, the erection of a basilica and the construction of the *Capitolium*, all part of a single project of monumentalisation.

The temple, with three large halls decorated by polychrome *sectilia* and the pronaos projecting from two wings of the portico, was dedicated in 73: on its pediment, it mentions the emperor himself. It has been suggested that the renown bronze statue of the Winged Victory, found in the 1800's in the vicinity of the *Capitolium*, may have been a gift by Vespasian for the military success achieved thanks to the city's support (fig. 6).[16]

During this flourishing period for *Brixia*, numerous existing houses were enlarged, showing a predilection for new representative architectural solutions, with the addition of large floors decorated with mosaics and polychrome marbles, or the frequent introduction of floor and wall heating in private thermal baths – a reflection of wealthy clients who sought to express their social status through elevated architectural standards.[17]

If not for a few architectural interventions during the Severan age (*frons scenae* of the theater), the Flavian layout will continue to characterise the city into Late Antiquity when the centre of the city, after the adoption of the Christian cult, will move to the west. After an occupation by the Goths, in 568 the Lombards took possession of the city. The city graced them with important rulers, among whom Rothari and Desiderius, the last king of the Lombards, defeated by Charlemagne in 774.

---

16   Dell'Acqua 2020 65-118, about the Winged Victory see Morandini 2020 and Morandini, Patera forthcoming.
17   Morandini 2012.

PART II

Building the Empire

Domitian's Reshaping of Rome

Eric M. Moormann

When Vespasian became emperor, he was far from Rome and needed to gain support in the capital of his Empire. Rome had become the unavoidable holy see of power from the time of Augustus onwards, when it was stylized as a metropolis and main centre of the world. Thanks to his huge building projects, the town had changed into a conglomerate of shining public buildings amidst the traditionally shabby and poor living quarters of the increased masses. Repeated fires devastated these slum areas, whereas the constructions of marble and brick were relatively well protected, although they remained susceptible to fire. After the great fire in 64, Nero dictated rules to improve the building standard of house blocks and built public baths for the people in order to contribute notably to the public interest of the town. At the same time, he appropriated large properties on and around the Palatine to create the Golden House, a private landscape garden with pavilions and works of art. With this intervention he transgressed in terms of what people saw as appropriate behaviour, for he displayed – at least in the eyes of the elite – an extreme penchant for *luxuria* (luxury).[1]

Vespasian and Titus saw the relevance of creating monuments to enhance their modest family prestige and profited from the bad name Nero had acquired.[2] In the centre of the Golden House's area, they erected a huge amphitheatre, a commodity hitherto known from temporary wooden installations only, and usually constructed at a city's edges, in order to avoid large crowds in the urban centre. The two Emperors also rebuilt (or continued the construction of) the large temple devoted to *divus* Claudius on the southern limit of Nero's former properties, the Caelius. The Templum Pacis was a kind of forum similar to the Forum Augustum, with a shrine dedicated to the goddess of Peace (Pax) at the eastern side. Pax recorded Vespasian's victories over the Germans in the Low Countries and – more lavishly – the Jews in Judea. Works of art from both Nero's Golden House and the conquered areas made the garden resemble a showcase of imperial power. For Pliny, the complex was one of "the most beautiful works ever seen in the world."[3]

A new great fire in 80 rudely interrupted their projects, especially in the down town area of the Campus Martius. As in previous instances, works included large-scale restorations of damaged buildings as well as entirely new structures. Due to Titus'

---

1   Moormann 2003, Edelmann-Singer 2014, Welch 2018. See Domenico Palombi in this volume.
2   Fundamental Darwall-Smith 1996 and Pierre Gros in Coarelli 2009a, 98-109.
3   Plin. *HN* 36.101. See Meneghini/Rea 2014, 242-341, Tucci 2017, Varner 2017, 252-255, Moormann in press.

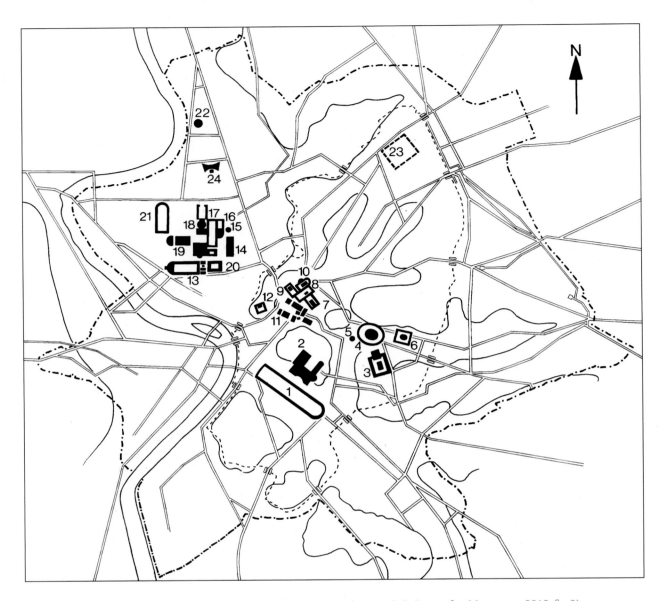

Fig. 1. Map of Rome with interventions undertaken under Domitian (drawing R. Reijnen; after Moormann 2018, fig. 3).

premature death in September 81, Domitian could shape the town into a real Domitianopolis without trespassing the ambitions of his father and brother (fig. 1).[4]

First, he amplified the Colosseum, and added the four training facilities, the *ludi*. He reconstructed at its western side an Augustan fountain, the Meta Sudans. With this intervention he anchored his work[5] in that of the first Emperor, and annulled the last traces of Nero's Golden House which had covered a couple of venerated Augustan

monuments like the Meta and the Curiae Veteres in this area, both reconstructed under the Flavians.[6] The area was further filled with various triumphal and memorial arches, seen as a specific form of self-representation Domitian displayed.[7] The recently excavated and thoroughly studied remains of an arch in the Circus Maximus date to 81 and might still belong to Titus' reign, whereas the well-known arch on the Sacra Via was built by Domitian. The Circus Maximus Arch stood in the vicinity of Titus' birth place

---

4   On Domitian's rebuilding of Rome, see, among others, Frederick 2003 and, most recently, Moormann 2018.

5   For the concept of 'anchoring innovation' as a leading issue of our work, see the Introduction. Frederick 2003 connects Domitian with Augustus.

6   On the first Meta and the various phases of the Curiae Veteres, see Panella 1996, 70-91, Panella et al. 2019, Coarelli 2020, 234-236. See also Moormann 2018, 165-166, fig. 3.

7   Suet. *Dom.* 13.2 and Dio Cass. 68.1.

Fig. 2. Relief from the Tomb of the Haterii depicting monuments built under Domitian. Vatican Museums, Museo Gregoriano Profano ex Lateranense, inv. 9997 (courtesy Governorato SCV – Direzione dei Musei, all rights reserved).

Fig. 3. View of the eastern side, including the podium of the shrine dedicated to Pax. Rome, Templum Pacis (photo Lidy Peters).

prope Septizodium.[8] The crude relief from Quintus Haterius Tychicus' tomb shows some of these arches as well as the Colosseum (fig. 2). Haterius belonged to the *redemptores*, the contractors of complexes erected under Domitian and eternized some of them in a neutral way, not specifically alluding at Domitian.[9]

Domitian turned the Templum Pacis (fig. 3) into a public facility by adding a public library and an administration building in which a predecessor of the marble city plan of the Severi, the Forma Urbis Romae, may have had a place of pride.[10]

Domitian created one more forum, the Forum Transitorium, dominated by a temple dedicated to his patroness Minerva. By means of this 'transition market', Forum Romanum and Subura were connected in a monumental way. Again, this was a clear proof of paying attention to public works, since the transit disclosed a densely inhabited area towards the commercial, administrative, and religious centres in and around the forums. There might have come a third, much more monumental forum at the west side of the Forum

---

8 Suet. *Titus* 1. Cf. *Arco* 2017, 171.

9 See most recently Steinby 2018 and Paolo Liverani in this volume. On the Arch of Titus in the Circus Maximus, see *Arco* 2017 and Claudio Parisi Presicce in this volume.

10 Tucci 2017, 126-173.

Augustum, some elements of which are recognizable in the Forum of Trajan.[11] The Emperor may have envisaged to connect the forums through this piazza with the hill where he was born, the Quirinal.

Concerning Domitian's interventions on the Forum Romanum I only mention the three-partite aula at the foot of the Palatine which was connected with the palace by a monumental ramp. Its function would have been that of an entrance with reception hall for the citizens who could greet the Emperor here.[12] Part of this complex was probably, again, dedicated to Minerva.[13]

The Palatine, the emblem of Neronian luxury, was neglected by Vespasian and Titus. In contrast, Domitian was keen to revive the tradition of imperial residences: in great splendour, he constructed a new version of the houses of Augustus, Tiberius, Claudius, and Nero by covering the remains of their dwellings with a multiple complex known as the Domus Flavia and Domus Augustana, allegedly the private and public sections respectively that met the wishes of the emperor in all senses.[14] It displayed Domitian's desire for luxury by applying peculiar architectural techniques and shapes and embellishment that incorporated works of art, marble ornaments and precious floor and wall coverings in *opus sectile*. By designating a large part as a public residence, with the aforementioned public entrance on the Forum Romanum, audience halls and rooms for festivities, receptions, and banquets, Domitian avoided association with Nero's selfish building projects, and implied that his building projects were for the people of Rome, although, in practice, the majority of citizens would never have contact with these new areas.

On the Quirinal, Domitian erected an ambitious complex in memory of his father and brother, the *Templum Gentis Flaviae*, allegedly at the spot of his birth, *ad malum punicum*.[15] This *altum Flaviae decus gentis* ('high grace of the Flavian family'), as Martial (9.1.8) called the complex in 93-94, however, has left no visible traces. Due to the dearth of concrete remains, the exact location and reconstruction of this mausoleum cum temple have been problematic, but investigations under the Planetario, an octagonal hall within the Baths of Diocletian, and in its surroundings have yielded proof of its position. Filippo Coarelli has proposed a square podium topped by a round Pantheon-like temple; within the podium it would contain the tomb of the *divi* Vespasian and Titus and Julia Titi, venerated here maybe in combination with other members of the family.[16] The shape of the mausoleum's nucleus would have copied that of Augustus and the Pantheon-like part reflected the Augustan Pantheon restored by Domitian. However, most scholars argue for a rectangular complex surrounded by a portico measuring up to 123 x 83 m.[17] If, one more time, we may believe Coarelli, next to the monument stood the obelisk which now graces Bernini's Four Rivers Fountain in Piazza Navona and which was brought there from the Circus of Maxentius.[18] Whilst the monument surely enhanced Domitian's prestige, the emperor seems to have been keen to have shifted direct focus away from himself, onto the memory of his predecessors, again avoiding the worst of Nero's self-promotion works. This anchoring to the past was also achieved by establishing an ideological link with Augustus' Pantheon and Mausoleum where, before the construction of the Templum, Vespasian had been buried by Titus.

Simultaneously, Domitian linked the Templum both topographically and functionally with the Temple of Quirinus. This shrine was dedicated to the mythical founder of Rome, Romulus, who as Quirinus had become the name-giver of the hill. It had Republican origins, but the monumental distyle temple was erected by Caesar and reconstructed by Augustus.[19] Coarelli observed a connection with the Flavii in the etymology of the name Quirinus, which, according to ancient sources, derived from the Sabine word for a lance, *cures*. This origin could have been connected with the region of Vespasian's

---

11 Pierre Gros in Coarelli 2009a, 107-108, Moormann 2018, 167. See Claudio Parisi Presicce in this volume.

12 Sommaini 2019, 230-240, esp. 239: "cerniera tra Foro Romano e Palatino unificante gli spazi della *civitas* e quelli del *princeps*." For further interventions on the Forum Romanum, see Moormann 2018, 168-169, Coarelli 2020, 151-160 (Equus Domitiani, see also J. Fejfer in this volume; Temple of Vespasian).

13 Sommaini 2019, 239: the area was known as *ad Mineruam*. Cf. J. Aronen, *LTUR* III (1996) 249-250.

14 See the contributions in this volume by Aurora Raimondi Cominesi & Claire Stocks and Natascha Sojc.

15 Suet. *Dom.* 1.1. cf. Martial, *Ep.* 9.20.2: "the ground knew about the infant-master." See Coarelli 2009b, 93-94, Eugenio La Rocca in Coarelli 2009a, 224-233, Coarelli 2014, 194-207, Moormann 2018, 169-170, Kaderka 2018, 186, 196-208. On the houses of the Flavii, see Coarelli 2014, 271-274.

16 And Domitian himself, despite his *damnatio memoriae* (Suet. *Dom.* 17.3). See Coarelli 2014, 200-204, fig. 52.

17 Most recently Borg 2019, 244-251. Häuber 2021. I follow this view, which is supported by Borg's well-founded critique (Borg 2019, 249).

18 Jean-Claude Grenier in Coarelli 2009a, 234-238, Coarelli 2014, 205-207. I have doubts concerning this pedigree and prefer the traditional attribution to the *Iseum Campense* (Moormann 2018, 171-172, note 65). See Häuber 2017, 158-164, Versluys/Bülow-Clausen/Capriotti Vittozzi 2018, 32-33 (Katja Lembke: Iseum), 188 (Stefan Pfeiffer: Iseum), Nagel 2019, 1073-1077.

19 Coarelli 2014, 83-112, esp. 96-97, figs. 21-25. A description of its outlay is implicitly given by Vitruvius in his section on types of temples, i.c. dipteral temples (3.2.7). For the Hartwig reliefs, see Rita Paris in Coarelli 2009a, 460-468, Coarelli 2014, 98-106, Kaderka 2018, 186-196.

Fig. 4. Archaeological area of Largo Argentina with four Republican temples and the Porticus Minucia Frumentaria, all restored under Domitian. Rome, Largo Argentina (photo Lidy Peters).

provenance.[20] If this etymology really played such an important role, it would constitute one more case of anchoring through this 'visualisation' of the Flavians' roots in both the Sabine area and on the Quirinal. The presence of the Romulus-Quirinus myth in the temple's pediment as visible on the Flavian Hartwig relief might substantiate the importance of this connection.[21]

The Capitol Hill saw various paramount interventions during Domitian's reign. The most important shrine of Rome, the Temple of Jupiter Optimus Maximus, had been rebuilt by his father after a devastating fire in December 69 during the fights between the Vitellian and Vespasian factions, but the 80 fire made a new reconstruction necessary. Domitian rendered the building very luxurious, with gilded bronze rooftiles, Pentelic marble columns, and a chryselephantine cult statue by Apollonios. Plutarch tells that the Greek poet Epicharmus compared Domitian to the gold-greedy Midas.[22]

Despite a lightning strike in 96, this temple would remain more or less intact for the next two centuries.[23]

The Capitol got two more Domitianic shrines, first, a small temple dedicated to Jupiter Custos, then a larger one for Jupiter Conservator.[24] They were connected with the personal biography: the young prince escaped, if we may believe Suetonius and Tacitus, from here in the guise of an Isis follower during the turmoil of the December 69 conflict.[25] Like Minerva, Jupiter became Domitian's personal patron rather than the Isis whose followers gave him undercover.[26] The emperor had himself depicted on a relief adorning the altar as well as a statuette in the hand of the cult statue. It is unclear whether there was an old shrine dedicated to Isis relevant in this respect. I tend to follow Coarelli rather than Miguel John Versluys in virtue of the strong evidence adduced by the Roman scholar for

20 Coarelli 2014, 83, 97. Among the sources quoted is Ovid. *Fasti* 2.477-478, a text well-known in the Flavian era (sources in Coarelli 2014, 83 note 4).

21 See for a lengthy discussion of the connection between the Templum, Quirinus and the Flavian origins Leithoff 2014, 179-197. Kaderka 2018, 206-208 also stresses the Flavian veneration of Romulus and Remus. For one fragment, see Conlin, fig. 7.

22 PLut. *Publ.* 15.5. Translation from Frederick 2003, 200. For a full quotation, see Nathalie de Haan in this volume.

23 See S. De Angeli, *LTUR* III (1996) 151-152, Frederick 2003, 199-200.

24 Tac. *Hist.* 3.74.2. On these temples, C. Reusser, *LTUR* III (1996) 131-132, Arata 1997, 146-154 (he also suggests the presence of a mithraeum).

25 Suet. *Dom.* 1.2, Tac. *Hist.* 3.74.1. On the conflict Arata 1997, 149-151, Coarelli 2018, 69. The story has also been seen as fictitious and as a trope known from other persons as well: Gasparini/Veymiers 2018, 12, 89-90 note 82 [Giulia Sfameni Gasparro], 291-292 [Ludovine Beaudrin], 557-558 [Emmanuelle Rosso], Nagel 2019, 1048-1049, 1054-1055.

26 Emmanuelle Rosso in Gasparini/Veymiers 2018, 558. See now Coarelli 2018, 61-70.

Fig. 5. Façade which corresponds with the outline of the Odeum of Domitian. Rome, Palazzo Massimo alle Colonne (photo Lidy Peters).

its existence.[27] It should be searched for under the church of S. Maria in Aracoeli and possessed at least one obelisk, the 'Obelisk Mattei', erected by Domitian.[28] A first-century wall with semi-circular protrusions has been connected with this shrine.[29]

In the densely crowded Campus Martius,[30] massive restorations dating back to Domitian are visible on Largo Argentina, where the four temples of the republican era and the surrounding piazza and porticoes were repaired after the fire and a new travertine pavement was installed. The complex was of enormous importance, for it included the Porticus Minucia frumentaria, the accommodation for the *frumenta* and oil distribution of the greater part of the lower classes. The Emperor could demonstrate his concern to maintain these accommodations despite the recent disaster and the death of his brother, who had been much-loved by the people. At the same time he copied works of Augustus who had 'travertinized' the temples and the piazza's pavement and perhaps incremented the distribution accommodations.

The Campus offered further possibilities to execute building projects, despite the presence of venerable complexes like the Augustan Pantheon and the Baths of Agrippa and Nero. A large space of 220 by 70 m was destined for the *Iseum Campense*, the temple for Isis and Sarapis, located at the east side of the Saepta.[31] The complex emanated the Flavian connection with the Land of the Nile and had a sensible relation with the grain distribution in the nearby Porticus Minucia frumentaria. It must have been a fairy-tale-like setting, with palms, obelisks, and Egyptian and egyptianizing statuary along the Euripus, which, at its turn, reflected one of the Nile arms in the Delta. Water constituted a paramount component as expressed by the Euripus and other fountains. The Iseum clearly mirrors the Campus Martius with its perennial Tiber flooding and sacral spaces dedicated to water gods like those on Largo Argentina. Domitian fostered a special relationship with the land of the Nile, as did his father who grasped power in that country. Domitian was honoured as a pharaoh and stylised in that dignity in the shape of

27 See Coarelli 2018, 62-69. For the topography of this area Tucci 2006. The monograph announced by Tucci on this topic (p. 63, note 4) has not yet come out.

28 For this obelisk, nowadays in the Villa Mattei on the Caelius, see Coarelli 2018, 69, with bibliography.

29 Tucci 2006, 64-66, fig. 2. Cf. Arata 1997, Pier Luigi Tucci in Coarelli 2009, 218-221, Nagel 2019, 1049-1050.

30 See Moormann 2018, 170-173 for an overview, with bibliography.

31 Numbers given by Filippo Coarelli, *LTUR* III (1996), 108. See Versluys/Bülow Clausen/Capriotti Vittozzi 2018, Nagel 2019, 1056-1081, see in this book Miguel John Versluys.

portraits (Versluys, fig. 4).[32] Contemporary Isea are known as well from other towns in Italy and farther away.[33]

An impressive undertaking was the stadium constructed around 90, probably on top of Augustus' and Nero's stadiums, but much larger (275 x 106 m).[34] Its Greek architectural format tied in with its function to host Greek-style sport manifestations.[35] Next to it, the similarly Greek-styled Odeum, a roofed theatre, accommodated recitals, both of poetry and music. Its outlines can still be recognized in the façade of Palazzo Massimo alle Colonne (fig. 5).[36] With the propagation of Greek festivals, Domitian followed Nero, but also Augustus: both had embraced aspects from the classical Greek culture and visualized them in their versions of Rome (see note 35).

All these constructions show how Domitian meticulously anchored his projects in the building programmes of Augustus and Nero. Regardless of how he was perceived after his assassination, he assiduously sought to avoid being labelled a tyrant like Nero[37] by stressing the importance of public building as had been done by his father and brother in the previous decades.

32 See most recently Emmanuelle Rosso in Gasparini/Veymiers 2018, 560-561, figs. 18.14-15, Irene Bragantini in Versluys/Bülow Clausen/Capriotti Vittozzi 2018, 249-250, fig. 1 (portraits at Benevento, here Versluys, fig. 4, and in Palazzo Altemps), Nagel 2019, 1056 (as sign of "Herrscherlegitimation").

33 The rebuilt Iseum of Pompeii (Nagel 2019, 1125-1151) dates to the last years before the eruption of Vesuvius and that in Beneventum is from Domitian's era (see Irene Bragantini in Versluys/Bülow Clausen/Capriotti Vittozzi 2018, 243-259, Nagel 2019, 1163-1168).

34 Maria Letizia Caldelli in Bernard 2014, 44-45, Pierre Gros, ibidem 87-88, Jean-François Bernard/Paola Ciancio Rossetto, ibidem, 138-139. For measurements and further data see ibidem, 140-142.

35 For the stadium and its 'successive' stages of Piazza Navona, see Bernard 2014. On spectacles, see in this volume contributions by Daniëlle Slootjes and Onno van Nijf, Robin van Vliet & Caroline van Toor.

36 Djamilla Fellague in Bernard 2014, 117-134.

37 Eric Varner (2017, 237) typifies this relation with Nero as "a careful recalibration of the Neronian visual program." See on their relationship Heerink/Meijer in press.

The Arch of Titus in the Circus Maximus

Claudio Parisi Presicce

The arch erected at the centre of the semicircle in the Circus Maximus is the oldest commemorative monument of the Flavian dynasty, realized only a few months before the death of Titus in 81. By multiplying the dedications in favour of his father and brother, Domitian seems to have had the necessary consensus to display the images of a new *adventus* in a pervasive way and to finalize a political strategy of revision of the urban landscape, to be set against the monuments of the Augustan era, which neither Vespasian nor Titus had had the power to promote. The largest and most significant architectural projects from the perspective of the new dynastic ideology are shown together with the Amphitheatre on the funerary monument of the Haterii (Moormann, fig. 2): the arch *in summa sacra via*, (Levick, figs. 1-3), the entrance arch of the *Iseum Campense*, and an arch with one single passage not yet identified. In contrast, the dedication of the Arch in the Circus Maximus on behalf of the Senate and the Roman people to commemorate the victory over, and submission of the Jewish people, as well as the destruction of Jerusalem ten years earlier, that the Flavians celebrated with a triumphal procession reflects an attempt to put the emperor to the test: the emperor was the leader of the army, but it was the prerogative of the Senate, as the representative of the state, to commemorate its victories.

The inscription (fig. 1) which clearly indicates a belated proposal to celebrate the triumph, constitutes one of the novel elements of the Arch. The Arch represents a monumental transposition of a type of ceremony, with a clear theological allusion which had been absent during the entire reign of Vespasian for whom, it seems, no triumphal arch was ever erected. The reliefs added to the body of the monument would have amplified the prestige and the affirmation of personal power, derived from the achievement of an endeavour never before realized:[1]

---

1   CIL VI, 944. The commemorative inscription, now lost, was still *in situ* in the ninth century, when it was copied by the Anonymus of Einsiedeln: Valentini, Zucchetti 1942, 155-160. Some fragments of the blocks of the attic, with incisions made for the insertion of the bronze letters of the dedicatory inscription came to light in 2016 and have allowed us to reconstruct the attic: it most likely reached a height of 4,7 m and the text was articulated over seven lines: (Maria Grazia Granino Cecere in *Arco* 2017, 229-235).

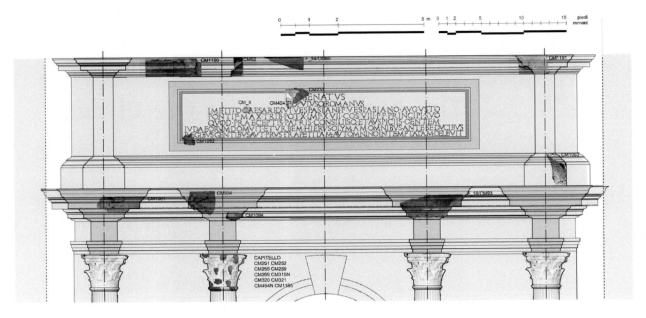

Fig. 1. Reconstruction of the inscription of the Arch of Titus (photo Sovrintendenza Capitolina ai Beni Culturali, Rome).

Senatus | populusq(ue) Romanus | Imp(eratori) Tito Caesari divi Vespasiani f(ilio) Vespasian[o] Augusto | pontif(ici) max(imo) trib(unicia) pot(estate) X imp(eratori) XVII [c]o(n)s(uli) VIII p(atri) p(atriae) principi suo | quod praeceptis patriae consiliisq(ue) et auspiciis gentem | Iudaeorum domuit et urbem Hierusolymam omnibus ante se ducibus | regibus gentibus aut frustra petitam aut omnino intemptatam delevit.

The Senate and the People of Rome erected this for Imperator Titus Caesar Vespasianus Augustus, son of the divine Vespasian, pontifex maximus, with tribunician power for the tenth time, imperator for the seventeenth time, in his eighth consulship, father of the fatherland, to their Emperor, because, by the orders and advice of his father and the auspices he subdued the Jewish people and destroyed the city of Jerusalem, a thing either attempted in vain by all generals, kings and peoples before him or untried entirely.

The *virtus* of the winner, central point in the phrasing of the propagandistic message, is relevant for the theme of continuity of the imperial family. The connection with the rebirth of the ideology of triumph was rendered explicit by means of the quadriga placed on top of the attic and was tied to the spot chosen for the erection of the Arch, at the entrance of the Circus Maximus and along the route of the triumphal procession.

The monument does not belong to the category of arches connected with the street grids of urban quarters, but was equivalent to the honorary arches used as main entrances to urban areas with various functions, either religious or civil. As to the first category, the function of a visual margin and prospective backdrop prevails, with the latter serving to accentuate and centralise the central passage. The Arch of Titus was the first to be constructed not as a passage through the urban walls or as an entrance in a fortress wall, but rather as a scenic backdrop positioned at the centre of a semi-circular series of arcades on the axe of the *spina* of the Circus Maximus. It constitutes an architectural realisation in line with the particular attention paid by the Flavian dynasty to spectacle buildings, a monumental typology chosen on purpose to serve as dynastic propaganda.[2]

---

2   See on spectacles in this volume contributions by Danielle Slootjes and Onno van Nijf, Robin van Vliet & Caroline van Toor.

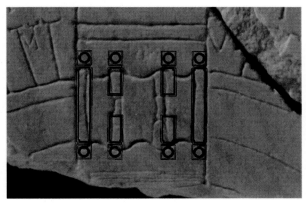

Fig. 2. The Arch of Titus as represented on the Forma Urbis Romae (courtesy Jon Arnold Images Ltd.).

Fig. 3. The arch of Titus on the mosaic with the circus games at Piazza Armerina, and, on a relief from Foligno (photo Sovrintendenza Capitolina ai Beni Culturali, Rome).

Until the end of the Julio-Claudian era, the honorary arches that did not stand isolated but were rather inserted within the *continuum* of a wall in an architectural structure by way of a more relevant passage, possessed a purely illusory architectonic system of framing of the fornix derived from Republican traditions. The applied order, of rectilinear nature, consists at most of lesenes, half-columns, or three-quarter corner columns. Under Domitian, in Rome the practice to frame the archway with a pair of columns set against the pillars, came into being, as is testified by the Arch of Titus at the foot of the Palatine (Levick, fig. 1) and the four-sided Arch of Domitian that features on the reliefs of Marcus Aurelius. The Arch of Titus in the Circus Maximus displayed, for the first time in Rome, the type with four entirely round columns on the front sides – two on the outside and two in the middle between the central major passage and the

two lateral ones – completely detached from the body of the structure. This scheme, which is also visible in the Arch of the Iseum Campense, probably Domitianic, and reproduced on the relief of the Tomb of the Haterii (Moormann, fig. 2), would become standard in the three-arched arches of the middle Empire. It obviously determined a different way of realising another rectilinear element of the architectural framework – now horizontal and not vertical – that is the cornice, articulated with elements protruding in respect to other elements on a recessing plan. This complex building syntax, which would become canonical, was still in its infancy when the Arch of Titus was constructed: the architectural order is limited to columns resting

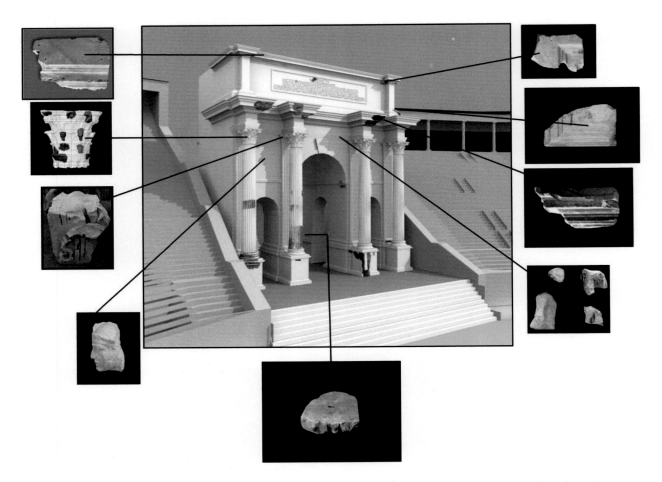

Fig. 4. Reconstruction of the Arch of Titus, with the surviving key fragments indicated (photo Sovrintendenza Capitolina ai Beni Culturali, Rome).

on pedestals and crowned by an entablature, which, although worked in the round and separately, rested against the body of the Arch, even touching the pedestals of the back wall sections.

The position of the Arch with three barrel vaults is documented on a fragmentary plaque of the Severan *Forma Urbis Romae*,[3] and on a number of depictions of circus scenes in relief and mosaic (figs. 2-3).[4] They demonstrate the fame of the monument, forming the main entrance to the most important and oldest circus complex of Rome,[5] which could accommodate up to 250,000 spectators during the Flavian era.[6] The excavations carried out in the area

of the Arch of Titus over an extremely long lapse of time,[7] have made clear that the monument's façades were c. 18 metres wide and were worked out extensively in the height. The aperture of the central passageway was much wider than those of the two lateral ones, probably in order to accommodate the passing of the train during the triumphal processions. The supporting structure in *opus quadratum* of peperino tuff and travertine was completely clad with Luni marble. Over the centuries, the architectural decorations have been almost completely stripped away; only a few fragments are still *in situ*. Some fragmentary

3   Carettoni et al. 1960, pl. XVII, fr. 7c.
4   Humphrey 1986, 123, 243-244, 223-225, 246-248.
5   Marcattili 2009, esp. 221-233.
6   Plin. *HN* 36.15.102.

7   See Parisi Presicce 2008, 348-354, first, on the exploration trench dug in 1928, which brought to light the basis of the triumphal arch (recorded as early as in a passage of the *Mirabilia Urbis Romae* and mentioned by Poggio Bracciolini in the mid-fifteenth century). Secondly, on the almost complete clearing of the area of the Circus Maximus from the constructions of the old gas plant as well as the barracks flanking it, realized in 1934. Thirdly, on the large exhibitions organised in the Circus Maximus, when the zone in 1936 was temporarily ceded by the Governatorato to the Partito Nazionale Fascista.

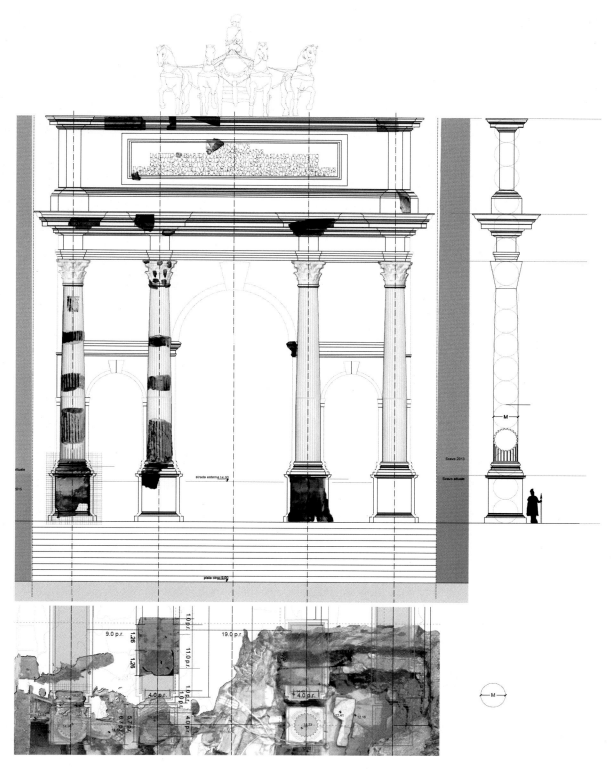

Fig. 5. Reconstruction of the Arch of Titus (photo Sovrintendenza Capitolina ai Beni Culturali, Rome).

Fig. 6. Reconstruction of the Arch of Titus in its setting in the Circus Maximus (photo Sovrintendenza Capitolina ai Beni Culturali, Rome).

plaques of historical reliefs found in the area have been attributed to the figural decoration of the Arch.[8] The frieze decorating the Arch of Titus in the Circus Maximus, at the moment only documented by a few surviving elements, offers nonetheless an initial framework for the style and the political message underlying its figural scenes.

For now, the retraced fragments document the presence of persons who, although placed in a paratactic fashion as on the Cancelleria Reliefs (Liverani, figs. 2-3), recall the coloristic style and the dynamic tension of the way of representation documented on the Arch of Titus at the foot of the Palatine (Levick, figs. 2-3).

The columns in Luni marble, 9-10 m high and with a diameter of 1,30 m, a base of 0,59 m high rising on a protruding plinth of 2,45 m, and the sustaining structure of the travertine pillars clad with marble plaques, attest to the Arch's exceptional dimensions: 17,35 m wide, 15 m deep, while it might have reached a height of some 20 metres.[9]

During the most recent archaeological explorations, it was possible to establish conclusively that, from the outset, the monument possessed three communicating passages (the central one measuring 5 m, the lateral ones 2,2 m), as documented on the fragment of the *Forma Urbis* and the mosaic from Luni. In contrast, it is depicted with one passage only – probably in abbreviated form – on sesterces of Trajan and Caracalla,[10] on several contorniate medallions of the fourth century, on the mosaic with the circus games at Piazza Armerina, and, finally, on a well-known relief from Foligno with a chariot race (fig. 3). One aspect still debated is the difference of level between the Arch and the arena, rising to some 2,5-3 m,[11] which was covered with a flight of steps descending towards the arena from a flat area extending from the Arch until the interior of the Circus for at least 5 m. This level difference maybe only occurred in correspondence with the central passage and was flanked by ramps inclined in correspondence with the lateral passages,[12] in order to facilitate an easier transit for the animals during the triumphal processions. At the opposite side, however, the level difference was remediated by two low steps, as wide as the complete Arch's façade, just as drawn on the marble plan.

---

8   La Rocca 1974, Parisi Presicce 2008, Caterina Coletti & Stefania Pergola in *Arco* 2017, 201-227.

9   Marialetizia Buonfiglio in *Arco* 2017.

10   RIC II, 284 n. 571, Banti 1983, 172-173, nos. 272-275, Banti 1986, 161-163., nos. 45-49.

11   Marialetizia Buonfiglio in *Arco* 2017, 171.

12   The level difference could be remediated along the 20 m forming the height between the 15 m of depth of the Arch and the at least 5 m width of the flat area in front of it.

Material Culture in Britannia under Domitian; a Northern Focus

Barbara Birley & Frances McIntosh

When Domitian came to power in 81, Britain had been part of the Roman Empire for around 40 years. Even before the invasion of AD 43, Roman material had made its way into Britannia but the floodgates opened once it became a province. This short article will look at the material culture of northern England in the last quarter of the first century focusing on four sites, Corbridge (Coria), Vindolanda, Carlisle and Carvoran with particular emphasis on the first two.

Introduction

First, the background of Roman occupation in this area will be discussed. It was only in the early 70s AD that the army made its way into Northern England and Scotland (fig. 1). The Roman governor Agricola had taken the army as far as the River Tay in Scotland by AD 79. This advance halted presumably due to Vespasian's death in AD 79 and was not resumed until AD 82, now under Domitian's reign. The famous battle of Mons Graupius (location unknown) marked a stopping point in further advancement, and the building of forts. The withdrawal of the II Adiutrix legion to the Danube also played a role in the abandonment of continued advance into Scotland. By the turn of the first century, the army had withdrawn to the Tyne-Solway line.

All the sites were linked via what is now known as the Stanegate road. An east-west line of forts each approximately a day's march apart, this was not a set frontier like Hadrian's Wall, but more a strategic road system. Of the forts on this line, Carlisle (*Luguvalium*) has the earliest known foundation date of c. 71-74, with the first fort at Corbridge dated to possibly 72 and Vindolanda being founded in 85. For the other sites, there is no detailed dating evidence due to lack of excavation. Coin loss in the Flavian period at Carlisle shows a peak, indicating an enlarged military presence. Both Carlisle and Corbridge were part of the network of forts on the route north founded under Agricola, whilst Vindolanda was one of the bases linking the two, on the Tyne-Solway line; Carvoran (*Magna*), about 10 Roman miles west of Vindolanda, was at the junction between the Stanegate and the Maiden Way, a Roman road coming north from the Lake District.

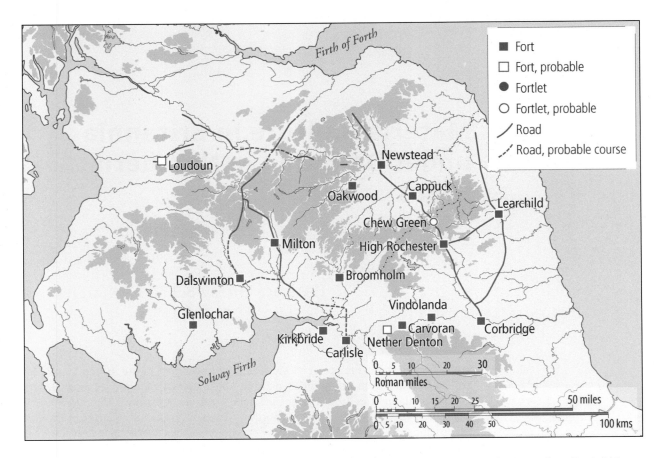

Fig. 1. The known forts in northern Britain in the late first century, including those in Scotland and along the Tyne-Solway line (which would later become the line of Hadrian's Wall). http://www.museen-mainlimes.de/content/6-media/pdfs.en.php (courtesy David Breeze).

Material Culture of the Late Flavian Period

It would be easy to fill an entire article simply on the militaria which the army brought into the region, but that represents only a small part of the new material which was introduced. Roman material culture differs from the preceding Iron Age not just in an increase in volume, but also in the number of categories of different items available. New forms of pottery, jewellery and military equipment arrived with the invading force. The Roman army brought literacy and currency which had a big impact on trade. Literacy also links to inscribed altars and tombstones, alongside the vast array of new deities introduced to the province, which were depicted in various forms and material.

Initially when the army moved into an area, they would bring everything they needed with them, and were as self-sufficient as possible. However, once they set up base, they would very quickly source supplies as locally as possible, as well as maintaining their long distance trade contracts. One such contract was with the terra sigillata producers of Gaul (fig. 2). The discovery of a hoard of such vessels in the bottom of the period I ditch at Vindolanda helped to provide clues to the dating of the fort. Within the cache, which was probably broken in transport to the site, there was a host of form Dragendorff 37s but no Dragendorff 29s – the 29 being a common vessel in Agricolan Scotland but one which ceased importation c. 85. On top of the pottery were hundreds of unopened oyster shells, presumably found to be unfit for eating upon arrival.

The military attire of both infantry and cavalry soldiers of the Roman army offer a myriad of objects to be lost, and then found by archaeologists. The painted replica of a late first century cavalry soldier, Flavinus, shows harness and a scabbard with copper alloy fittings, the shield with its metal binding around the outside and a detailed helmet. The amazing anaerobic or oxygen free conditions at Vindolanda have also helped to preserve military objects not usually seen at other sites. One such item is the delicate hair moss helmet crest. Found discarded in one of the outer defensive ditches dating to 85-90, it would have been a russet red when new. Soldiers enjoyed accentuating their armour and harness fittings demonstrating personal style, as seen on the Flavinus tombstone (fig. 3). There are numerous

Fig. 2. This fine collection of terra sigillata (samian ware) was imported from the famous La Graufesenque potteries in southern France. The pottery has been broken in transit and was thrown, unused, into the ditch at Vindolanda. Hexham, Chesterholm Museum (courtesy Vindolanda Trust).

Fig. 3. The first-century Flavinus cavalry tombstone was cast and painted to show the possible original colour scheme of the tombstone. The inscription reads "To the spirits of the departed, Flavinus, trooper of the *Ala Petriana*, standard-bearer, from the troop of Candidus, aged 25, of 7 years' service, lies buried here." Corbridge, Corbridge Roman Town, inv. CO23334 (courtesy English Heritage Trust). Helmet crest made of locally grown hair moss. Hexham, Roman Army Museum, SF 8454. Set of three melon beads found strung on a leather strap. Hexham, Roman Army Museum, SF 4460 (courtesy Vindolanda Trust). A large ornate penannular in silver with the knobs shaped as acorns, a type known as O2 that occurred in the first century and probably imported. Corbridge, Corbridge Roman Town, inv. CO6332 (courtesy English Heritage Trust).

objects throughout Britain, some very ostentatious and others quite understated, like the three large glass and faience melon beads from Vindolanda. What is unusual about these beads is that they were found complete with their thick leather strap, possibly used to decorate horse harness as seen on tombstones from the continent.

As well as fittings for belts, scabbards, and harness, soldiers also wore brooches to fasten their tunics. Over time, British produced types such as the trumpet, headstud and dolphin were incorporated into their dress. One soldier in Corbridge brought his Omega brooch with him from the Continent. This silver brooch is a rare find in Britain.

Literacy played a key role in the organisation of the army, and the Empire. The equipment of writing survives more often than the writing itself in Britannia, but again, the conditions at Vindolanda allow us a snapshot into the bureaucracy of the army. A strength report, written with ink on a thin piece of wood, of the First Cohort of Tungrians dating to c. 85-90 gives us great insight into the movements of the troops. At the time the cohort had

752 men, including 6 centurions but 337 men including 2 centurions are absent in *Coria*. The absentees were probably new recruits being trained (before they returned to the fort when it was enlarged to accommodate the increased garrison). Others are away doing various tasks leaving just 296 men including 1 centurion at Vindolanda (fig. 4). Of those left 15 are described as 'sick', six 'wounded' and 10 suffering from conjunctivitis. This leaves only 265 soldiers fit for duty at Vindolanda.

In 2017, around 24 almost complete and fragments of new ink writing tablets were discovered scattered on a road surface outside the Vindolanda period I commanding officer's residence. Four of the longest and most complete letters of Iulius Verecundus have now been interpreted and give new information into the personal life of the first commanding officer at the site. Verecundus is known from other tablets at the site but the most recent texts show that

Fig. 4. Vindolanda writing tablet , a draft version of a strength report found at Vindolanda and now on display at the British Museum. Tab Vindol. 154, 88.841 (courtesy Vindolanda Trust). Iron ink well lid with silver inlay. Corbridge, Corbridge Roman Town, inv. CO6335 (courtesy English Heritage Trust). Silver stylus pen used on the wax writing tablets. Hexham, Roman Army Museum, inv. SF4017 (courtesy Vindolanda Trust).

he was interested in his vegetables, including shoots of cabbage and turnip.[1] In addition to this, there are leave requests for soldiers as well as an appeal for the correct keys to be sent and the return of a cleaving knife.[2] There is also a request from Andangius to ask for lighter duties for Crispus the *mensor*.[3] *Mensor* means 'measurer'. Without more information in the tablet there are a couple of possible jobs for Crispus as a measurer. He could either be a surveyor or possibly the person responsible for the corn ration. If the second, then he would have used a modius like the one from Carvoran.

Vindolanda has produced two wooden pens with metal nibs plus several metal nibs for writing with ink. All four sites have produced many styli or pens for use on the well-known waxed tablets. These pens were made in a range of materials such as wood, bone, copper alloy, iron and silver. Indeed at Carlisle, the Flavian period produced the most styli, perhaps again indicating an increased military

1   WT 2017.15, 890. WT means Vindolanda Writing Tablet.
2   WT2017.24+26, 892, WT2017.15, 890, WT2017.24+26, 892.
3   WT2017.16, 891.

Fig. 5. Ceramic lamp with a boar motif, first century. Corbridge, Corbridge Roman Town, inv. CO4 (courtesy English Heritage Trust).

Fig. 6 (right). Copper-alloy *modius* (grain measure) found at Carvoran. Inscribed: IMP [/////////] CAESARE / AVG GERMANICO XV COS / EXACTVS AD S XVIIS / HABET P XXXIIX. 'In the fifteenth consulship of the Emperor Domitian Caesar Augustus Germanicus: tested to the capacity of 17 1/2 *sextarii*: weight 38 pounds.' Hexham, Clayton Museum, Chesters Roman Fort, inv. CH1823 (courtesy English Heritage Trust/Trustees of the Clayton Collection).

presence as with the coins. Less common are inkwells which could be made from pottery or metal. An ornate example from Corbridge survives only as the lid, whilst a complete Samian one from Chesters dates to the second century.

Ways to light homes, offices and barracks diversified with the Romans' arrival. Small, mould made ceramic lamps with decoration, candlesticks, both ceramic and metal, joined the simpler, open lamps for consumers to choose from. The decoration on the mould made lamps ranged widely, with two from Corbridge being decorated with a running boar, the symbol of the Twentieth Legion (fig. 5).

Vindolanda's leather collection reveals secrets regarding the early use of the material on the site. Archaeologist have discovered objects ranging from a complete 44 panel goat skin tent to small personal objects like draw string bags. Boots and shoes from Vindolanda show that there were many different styles available even at this early date. There are a variety of sizes from small children's shoe to large men's marching boots. Many of the shoes from this period are found in the first forts defensive ditches and include both openwork decorations usually used on less practical footwear and very utilitarian boots.

Whilst the fort of Carvoran has been little excavated, it has produced the most fascinating find specifically dating to the Domitianic period on the northern frontier (fig. 6). The copper alloy *modius*, or grain measure was commissioned in 90-91 and is an extremely rare find, not just in the province but across the Empire. It states that is has a capacity of 17 ½ *sextarii* of grain, which could be a soldier's weekly grain ration. Mysteriously however, the vessel holds more than the stated amount. After Domitian's assassination in 96, his name was erased from the vessel under the *damnatio memoriae*. This beautifully made piece has many layers to the stories it can tell.

Conclusion

The material culture in Britannia under Domitian differed greatly from that of the late Iron Age, particularly in the North of Britain. The occupying force had a lasting impact on the area and brought with it a possible sense of establishment. It changed the frontier for the next 300 plus years. Imported goods were bought in from afar, highly decorative, if not ostentatious, military life collided with the physical landscape, literacy and bureaucracy was initiated, fashions were changed and trade was standardized. The short 15 year period under Domitian established unique traits, forms and types of items that had much longer life spans within the Tyne-Solway area but it is also the period about which the least is known. Only small glimpses of remains and artefacts are available due to later Roman or post Roman building or lack of archaeological excavation. Hadrian's Wall is best known as the linear feature in the landscape, but it is actually the earlier forts and settlements which established the Roman influence in the area, forts like Corbridge, Vindolanda, Carlisle and Carvoran. Continuing research and excavations, especially on this earliest period of Roman occupation in Northern England will help expand our knowledge and understanding.

Domitian and the Lower German *Limes* (The Netherlands)

Jasper de Bruin

Introduction

Domitian's foreign policy focused particularly on Rome's Northern frontiers, like the Lower German *limes*, located on the Lower Rhine river in The Netherlands (fig. 1). At the start of his reign in 81, the area had already been in the spotlight of the Roman administration for over a century. Actions of the emperors of the Julio-Claudian dynasty and their generals and officials had added fortresses, a civic centre, hydraulic engineering works and a line of watchtowers and fortifications to the banks of the Lower Rhine. Archaeological research of these structures in the past decades has led, for example, to a re-evaluation of Caligula's skills as a general and military strategist, who seems to have been the mastermind behind the conquest of *Britannia* and responsible for the initial start of the Lower German *limes*.[1] Similarly, recent research has also led to a reappraisal of the previously negative assessments of the Emperor Domitian in this area.[2] Fairly recently, archaeological research in The Netherlands has provided more detailed information on the effects of Domitian's reign here. The question is what these archaeological data add to the knowledge of the actual, material deposit of Domitian's imperial policies along the Lower German *limes*.

Archaeology and Written Sources

An example of how archaeological data can contribute to a better image of known historical events is the research of the channel that was dug by Domitian's father-in-law Corbulo in 47, the *fossa Corbulonis* or Corbulo Canal. This canal, well-known from written sources,[3] was first excavated near Leiden in 1990 (fig. 2),[4] after which it was identified at more than a dozen other locations.[5] The wood for the revetments of the channel was, according to dendrochronological dating, cut in the spring to summer of 50,[6] suggesting that its construction took slightly longer than the historical sources suggested. Yet, the

---

1   De Bruin 2019, 223.
2   Galimberti 2016, 105.
3   Dio Cass. 60.30.6, Tac. *Ann.* 11.20.
4   Hessing 1990, 342-343.
5   De Bruin 2019, 78.
6   Vos et al. 2007, 9.

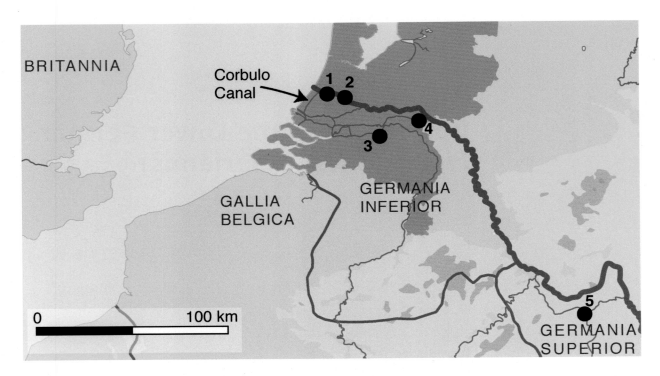

Fig. 1. The Lower German *limes* (thick red line) and the Roman provinces *Britannia, Germania Inferior, Gallia Belgica* and *Germania Superior*. Sites mentioned in the text: 1. Alphen aan den Rijn; 2. De Meern; 3. Empel; 4. Nijmegen; 5. Mainz. The territory of The Netherlands is in dark green. Image based on open source data from the Frontiers of the Roman Empire project.

most surprising discovery was that the canal was preceded by an older one that could have been dug under Caligula or even earlier.[7] Therefore, it seems that the initiator of the canal was deliberately omitted in the written sources or it was simply not known that Corbulo was not the first one who ordered the creation of a waterway between the Rhine and the Meuse. Thus, it remains a question who ordered the construction of the earlier canal. Besides Caligula, Tiberius is also a candidate.

Domitian and the Germanic *Limes*: Historical Information

As the example of the Corbulo Canal shows, some prudence should be shown when assessing the written sources which mention historical events. Yet, the written sources also provide historical overviews that can be very useful for understanding or contextualizing archaeological finds. A good example is the tombstone of Tiberius Claudius Zosimus,[8] that was found in Mainz (ancient *Mogontiacum*, in the Roman province of *Germania Superior*). Zosimus was head of Domitian's food tasters and therefore part of the imperial court. So, the tombstone proves the historical known presence of Domitian's court and the emperor

himself in Mainz. What is more, the tombstone can be dated accurately, because we know that Domitian was in Mainz in 83. Besides, the honorific title *Germanicus* for Domitian that is mentioned on the tombstone seems to suggest that this title was granted by the Senate while the Emperor was still in Mainz, so directly after or maybe even during the military campaign against the Germanic tribe of the *Chatti*.[9] Thus, the tombstone also shows that these honorific titles were granted even before the final outcome of the battle was known.

Probably, Domitian never visited the Lower German *limes* himself, but he was quite near, during the aforementioned war against the *Chatti* in 82-83,[10] which he coordinated from Mainz. From 83 onwards, the *limes* of *Germania Superior* was expanded. Around 85, Domitian transformed the military zone along the Rhine definitively into two new provinces: *Germania Inferior* and *Germania Superior* (Lower and Upper Germany). In 89, a second military campaign targeted the *Chatti* and in the same year, Lucius Antonius Saturninus proclaimed himself Emperor, again in Mainz. This rebellion was quickly oppressed by loyal troops of *Germania Inferior* that were granted afterwards the honorary titles *pia*

---

7   De Kort/Raczynski-Henk 2014, 59.
8   *Année Epigraphique* 1976, 504.

9   Lebek 1989, 80.
10 Most of the historical events mentioned in this section are derived from Galimberti 2016, 97-99, unless stated otherwise.

Fig. 2. Cross-section of the *Fossa Corbulonis* (Corbulo Canal) near Leiden (photo M. van Veen).

fidelis Domitiana ('faithful and loyal to Domitian'). So, historically, quite a lot is known of Domitian's activities in *Germania Superior*, but relatively little of the effects of Domitian's foreign policy on the Lower German *limes* in The Netherlands. Archaeological sources could potentially help to fill the gap.

Domitian and the Lower German *Limes*

Between 82 and 83, a remarkable amount of otherwise quite rare *quadrantes* ("the smallest denomination in the Roman monetary system"),[11] issued by Domitian, was distributed to legionary fortresses of the Rhine army, including Nijmegen, where the *legio X Gemina* (the Tenth Legion) was encamped. These coins compensated for the lack of small change and can be associated with the presence of the imperial court in Mainz during the Chattian campaigns, where the shortage of lower coin denominations was probably recognized and dealt with.[12] In turn, this had a profound effect on the type of available coins for the people of Nijmegen (and other legionary

settlements of the Rhine army) in the late-Flavian period. In 90-91, after the rebellion of Saturninus of 89 was crushed by the army of *Germania Inferior*, a new influx of Domitian coins in Nijmegen can be observed.[13] Almost half of these coins show on the reverse side a depiction of *Virtus* (bravery, courage, martiality), a remarkable number compared to other contemporary coin assemblages, suggesting that Domitian applied a sophisticated monetary policy to deliver an important message (and, possibly, a reward) to his loyal troops in Nijmegen.[14]

Around 10% of the brick stamps, found in the fortress of the Tenth Legion, show the abbreviation of the legion (LXG), supplemented with the letters PFD (*pia fidelis Domitiana*, fig. 3).[15] They suggest building activities in the fort and it is possible that the soldiers received new housing as some kind of reward for their support of the reigning emperor. Possibly, detachments of the legion were stationed in the area surrounding Nijmegen,[16] the homeland of the rural community of the *Batavi*. Also,

---

11 Kemmers 2005, 42.
12 Kemmers 2005, 42.

13 Kemmers 2005, 46.
14 Kemmers 2005, 46.
15 Brunsting/Steures 1995, 91.
16 Derks 2017, 272.

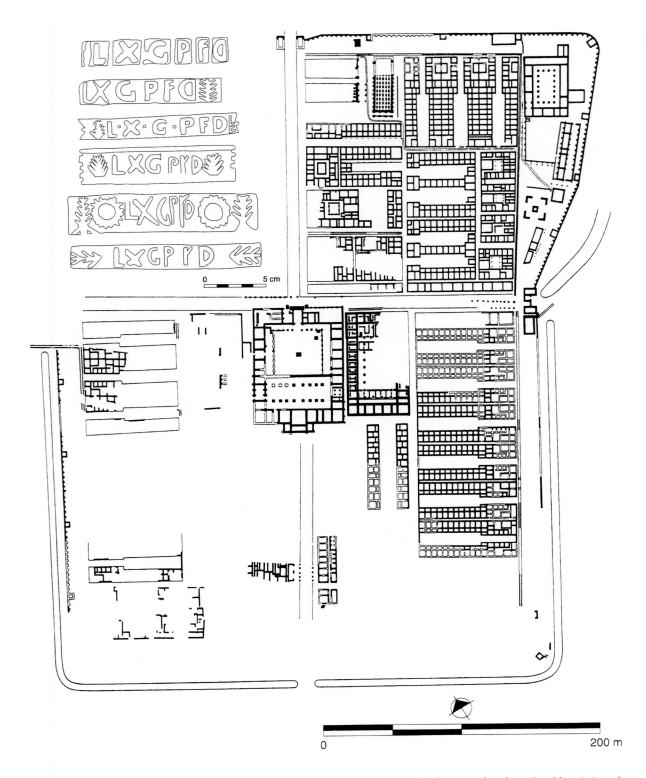

Fig. 3. The stone-built fortress of the *legio X Gemina* in Nijmegen. Top left: some of the brick stamps that show the abbreviation of the Tenth Legion (LXG), supplemented with the letters PFD (*pia fidelis Domitiana*), found in the fortress. Image based on Willems/Van Enckevort 2009, 49, fig. 16 (camp) and Brunsting/Steures 1995, 94, fig. 4 (stamps).

Fig. 4. Private Collection. Votive plaque, silver-plated bronze, found at the temple of Empel. The inscription mentions Julius Genialis, veteran of the Tenth Legion. Dimensions 6,5 x 7 cm (photo F. Gijbels).

Fig. 5. Fragment of a brick stamp of the *cohors I Classica pia fidelis Domitiana*, found in De Meern, plotted on a drawing of the complete stamp. Utrecht, Provinciaal Utrechts Genootschap van Kunsten en Wetenschappen (photo of the brick National Museum of Antiquities; drawing of the stamp based on Haalebos 2000, 49, fig. 10).

Fig. 6. Heavily constructed wooden quay works in Alphen aan den Rijn, dated to 93 (photo Radboud University, Nijmegen).

individual soldiers and veterans might have been present. The veteran who dedicated a votive inscription at the temple in Empel, some 25 kilometres away from Nijmegen, was probably not an exception (fig. 4).[17]

Moreover, there is ample evidence of the (indirect) involvement of the Tenth Legion with the construction of stone temples and *villae* in the Batavian countryside.[18] In the rural settlements of the *Batavi*, finds indicate that the locally manufactured handmade pottery was quickly replaced with wheel thrown vessels during the Flavian period, suggesting a rather rapid economic integration in the Roman Empire.[19] At the same time, remarkably rich burials appear in the countryside, showing a quickly developing and socially stratified society.[20] These phenomena can be seen as unintended spin-off effects of the activities of the Tenth Legion, which in turn were

---

17 Roymans/Derks 1994.
18 Van Enckevort 2005, 89, Van Enckevort 2012, 273, 275, 279, Willems/Van Enckevort 2009, 150.
19 Heeren 2014, 165.
20 Van der Feijst/Verniers 2017, 80-92.

financed by Domitian's government. It demonstrates how far imperial policies could intervene in the lives of many individuals, even in more remote rural areas.

Other building activities under Domitian took place in the auxiliary fort in De Meern near Utrecht, based on brick stamps of the *cohors I Classica* showing the honorary titles *pia fidelis Domitiana*, dated between 89 and 96 (fig. 5). These building activities suggest, again, that auxiliary units might have been 'rewarded' with new barracks. More evidence for a large scale refurbishment of the Lower German *limes* can be obtained from another rich source of information: constructions made from oak wood that are preserved under the high groundwater level in The Netherlands. There is a significant cluster of dendrochronological datings between 89 and 93 from heavily constructed quay works along the Lower Rhine (fig. 6) and even the first phase of the road that connected the forts (the *limes* road) can be dated to this period.[21] Erik Graafstal sees these activities in the light of the strategic completion of the *limes* along the Lower Rhine, as a conscious policy to strengthen this area before the Roman military could turn its attention to *Dacia*.[22] Graafstal's suggestion that Trajan executed these building programmes before he became emperor and that he was responsible for its completion after Domitian's death seems plausible.[23] It implies that it was Domitian who laid the foundation for the successful reign of Trajan.

Concluding Remarks

It is clear, that archaeological research can provide a better understanding of the impact of Domitian's imperial policies at the Lower German *limes*, down to the level of individual forts and even rural settlements. It shows how increasingly entangled Rome had become with its frontier regions during the Flavian period. Moreover, the evidence suggests that up until the end of Domitian's reign, his foreign policy remained intact. Although it is not clear if the emperor was personally involved in every decision, he also made no attempt to change this policy, indicated by the large-scale military building campaigns between 89 and 96. Therefore, the archaeological evidence is additional proof that the rehabilitation of Domitian as a competent emperor is indeed justified.

---

21   Aarts 2012, 259-260, Graafstal 2002, 9, Luksen-IJtsma 2010, 82.

22   Graafstal 2002, 8-9.

23   Graafstal 2002, 8.

PART III

The Image of the Emperor

The Image of the Emperor: Seeing Domitian

Jane Fejfer

Seeing Domitian: Reading Biography and Character – a Curse?

From antiquity to the present day, portraiture and biography have been closely intertwined. It is a near to intuitive practice to explore a portrait and the person portrayed from what we know about that person. Through biography people have engaged with and made sense of a portrait, today and in the past: does Domitian look like an emperor, or does he come across as a ruler who demanded that his subjects address him as *dominus et deus*? Similarly, reading a person's character from that person's outer appearance has been closely linked to portraiture: but what, if anything does Domitian's soft skin and high forehead reveal about his inner self? Is he strong and trustworthy or the opposite? Both ways of looking, to engage through life stories and to judge the inner qualities of a person by appearance, have been practiced since the Hellenistic period and character reading was specifically widespread among the elite during the second century.[1] Life stories lent themselves to being read into the face of emperors, when they were alive and even more so after their death, whether an emperor was deified or condemned as Domitian. For Tacitus, Domitian's face was red and filled with shame,[2] while Statius' approach was almost the opposite. He celebrated in a panegyric poem the inauguration of Domitian's colossal equestrian statue in the Forum Romanum from the viewer's perspective: he anticipated possible critics by vaunting its gargantuan size as stunning but appropriate and praising the emperor's shine and divine look "with its mingled traces of war and kind peace."[3]

In modern research on Roman portraiture biography is a troublesome entity. Biographical readings are seen as fallacy, coined 'biographical fallacy', a methodological obstacle for scholars, because a sitter's ideas of self-representation might have been manipulative.[4] In short, slander and strange behaviour reported in literary sources

---

1   I am grateful to Rolf Michael Schneider for his comments on the text. Any mistakes are of course my own. Overview of the pseudoscience of physiognomy in antiquity in Rohrbacher 2010.

2   Tac. *Agr.* 45.2. Domitian's face colour is discussed in Bradley 2009, 156-157. Suet. *Dom.* 18ff. For the changing attitude towards Domitian after his death by Pliny the Younger and Martial, see Cordes 2017, 50, 58 and *passim*.

3   *Silvae* 1,1 discussed in Cordes 2014 using *preferred reading* approach to Statius. See also Cordes 2017, 76-86 and 135-153. On the statue also Muth 2010.

4   For a discussion of the various aspects of the biographical fallacy in reading Roman portraits, see Smith 1998, 60.

should not be brought up when it comes to reading portraiture. Biography and psychological readings of individual emperors in hindsight, as has been reasoned, overshadow general historical questions on individual emperors and dynasties. As a result, ancient historians have tended to avoid research on the individual emperor and concentrated on the structures and systems around the imperial power in long term perspectives instead: the emperor himself has almost disappeared.[5] In archaeological research the problem of the biographic fallacy has been sidestepped by shifting the focus towards ideological messages and socio-historical context, and not least towards typology: for example, how individual portrait types of an emperor are interrelated to each other; how serial copies of them relate to their (lost) prototypes; and how chronological and geographical issues impacted the style and technique of single copies.[6]

Be that as it may, we all tend to read biographical or psychological aspects into a portrait. The psychologist Alexander Todorov has convincingly demonstrated that, when confronted with the face of another person, we make up our minds about that person in a snap of time: we cannot escape what he calls "the curse of knowledge". Even when confronting a person we are not familiar with, we take "the magic path" from outer appearance to inner character.[7]

Roman portraits were almost always accompanied by a text informing the viewer about the identity of the portrayed, whether emperors or private people, whether in form of statues erected on tall bases in public spaces or in the bust format for intimate viewing. After a first encounter, the viewer inevitably correlated the patron's biographical details in the inscription with the portrait image, perceiving its styling accordingly. A telling example is here the small index plate which separates the bust from its foot. When not inscribed with a name but left plain or ornamented, its sheer presence makes a conspicuous reference to the (unnamed) identity and biography of the sitter. Biography is an intrinsic part of engaging with a portrait, most obviously documented in Rome's imperial coinage. Later, from the Renaissance to the modern era, Domitian's biography has continued to spark renewed

interest in his portraits. My focus in this paper is on the Domitian portrait's possible communicative impact and meaning and its relationship to the different social agents within the contemporary society. What is the significance of the material evidence, the style, the iconography and the context of Domitian's portrait. How do his portraits inform us about his rule? What might they have meant to the viewer? And does his portrait image provide evidence which supports the traditional reading of Domitian as an Emperor who radically converted the imperial office from principate to monarchy, and of the Emperor from being *primus inter pares* to *dominus et deus*? To answer these questions I focus on three aspects of the Domitian portrait: first its design and making, then its media and contexts, and finally, what it means seeing the Emperor. Will these aspects take me beyond biography?

Reviewing Design, Making, Format, Context

a. The Portrait Types in Coinage and Sculpture

Due to the memory sanctions confined upon Domitian posthumously, most of his portraits must have been destroyed or alternatively re-carved into portraits of his follower Nerva (fig. 1).[8] However, a number of Domitian portraits have survived: some as originally carved, others as re-carved from portraits of Nero, others still as re-carved into portraits of Nerva, while new portraits of him continue to surface.[9]

Domitian was an eighteen year old adult, when his father, Vespasian became Emperor in 69. Over the next 22 years Domitian figured continuously in Rome's imperial coinage until he was assassinated on 18 September 96. Most scholars have agreed that the coinage shows him in three consecutive portrait types, supposedly identifiable also in his three-dimensional portraits. The earliest portrait type issued between 69 and 75, shows him with a squat head and a short

---

5 Winterling 2011, 2-11. See, however, the work on Commodus by Olivier Hekster in 2002 and by Egon Flaig on Nero, most notable the 2003 article.

6 Exemplified in the series *Das römische Herrscherbild*. Overview by Fittschen 2010 and Fittschen 2015. There are a number of exceptions, in particular on Augustus, see Zanker 1987. On Caligula, see von den Hoff 2009. On Nero and Vespasian, see Schneider 2003. On Hadrian, see Opper 2008. On imperial family members, on Livia, see Bartman 1999. On Julio-Claudian groups: see Rose 1997 and Boschung 2002. On imperial groups from Vespasian to Constantine, see Deppmeyer 2008.

7 Todorov 2017, 261 and *passim*.

8 Domitian portraits were also carved into portraits of, for example, Titus, Trajan and Constantine, see Varner 2004, 115-125.

9 On memory sanctions, see Caroline Vout in this volume. Also Caroline Vout 2008, Varner 2000, Varner 2004, Flower 2006. Although it is problematic to give exact figures it seems that well over 25 Domitian portraits in the round have survived. The exquisite bust in Toledo (fig. 7) appeared to the academic world in 1990. The head for insertion into a statue found in excavations in Munigua, Spain in 1982 probably also represents Domitian. A fragmented and eroded togate statue found 1966-1971 near a statue base commemorating Domitian originally from the *scaenae frons* of the theatre of Aphrodisias has been identified as Domitian, but according to Smith 2006, 105 this is not secure and the statue is more likely to represent a young local Aphrodisian of the mid first century. For the Toledo bust see Zanker 2018, for the Munigua head in Sevilla Archaeological Museum inv. 1996/8, see Prusac 2016, 137 cat. 110 and Varner 2004, 253 cat. 2.56.

Fig. 1 (above left). Head of Domitian reworked as Nerva. Berlin, Staatliche Museen zu Berlin, Antikensammlung, inv. 352 (courtesy Staatliche Museen zu Berlin, Antikensammlung, photo Universität zu Köln, Archäologisches Institut, CoDArchLab, 105830_FA-SPerg000357-01_Gisela Geng).

Fig. 2 (above right). Head of Domitian with *corona civica*. Naples, Museo Archeologico Nazionale, inv. 6058 (courtesy Museo Archeologico Nazionale).

fleshy neck. The thick front hair locks are combed deeply into the forehead forming a soft continuous curve over a low forehead which is sometimes marked by one or two furrows. The sculpted portraits associated with this coin type show a parallel arrangement of comma-shaped locks above the forehead including a small parting to the right above the right eye and a fork motif at each temple (fig. 1).

A second type, perhaps introduced in 75, represents the emperor with a higher forehead, less hair and a hairline forming a sharp angle above each temple. It is assumed that only five sculpted portraits are related to this type II (see figs. 2-3).[10]

A last, third coin type, believed to have been made to celebrate Domitian's accession to the throne in 81, shows him with a longer neck and head, a more open engaging face and a very high occasionally furrowed forehead, now crowned by a continuous slightly curved row of short comma-shaped locks. In short, there is a tendency towards slimmer portraits sporting a longer and slimmer neck and a head with less hair and an open more engaging face (fig. 4).

---

10   1. Naples, Museo Nazionale Archeologico 6058 with *corona civica* (according to Daltrop 1966, 103 not representing Domitian) in Gasparri 2009, 81, 2. Copenhagen, Ny Carlsberg Glyptotek IN 768 miniature bronze bust, in Johansen 1995, 38, cat. 8, 3. Naples, Museo Nazionale Archeologico 150-216 from Minturno does not have the characteristic arrangement of fronthair locks and may represent Titus, in Bergmann/Zanker 1981, 360-364 fig. 35,4. Athens, National Museum 345 an unfinished and/or reused head in Daltrop 1966 pl. 32,c-d; 5. Naples, Museo Nazionale Archeologico 5907 the only head of type II recut from a portrait of Nero (into Domitian?), in Bergmann/Zanker 1981, 366-367 fig. 37.

b. Carving and Re-carving

However, this division of the Domitian portrait into three separate consecutive types, is not at all clear-cut. It is not even clear if the third so-called Accession type can be identified in the coinage. One may ask if continuity of the Domitian portrait was not more important than flagging change? Anyway, as far as the three-dimensional portraits are concerned, we are left with a 'Typenchaos'.[11] This chaos is primarily related to the technical challenges in re-carving an existing portrait into a portrait of someone else. As noted by M. Bergmann and P. Zanker in their seminal article on the iconography of the Flavian Emperors and re-carved portraits of Nero and Domitian, a sculptor, challenged to recarve an existing emperor portrait into that of another emperor, had to compromise between existing and the new facial details. In the case of Domitian, the vast majority of the surviving portraits were re-carved from existing portraits of Nero and they therefore show smaller or larger variations making it difficult to sort out specific portrait types, and how individual copies within a type relate to each other.[12]

Fig. 3 (above left). Miniature bronze bust representing Domitian. Copenhagen, Ny Carlsberg Glyptotek, inv. IN 768 (photo Ny Carlsberg Glyptotek, Copenhagen).

Fig.4 (above right). Head of Domitian in type III. Naples, Museo Nazionale inv. 6061 (courtesy Museo Archeologico Nazionale).

---

11   On the so-called "Typenchaos" in Flavian imperial portraiture due to re-carving from already existing imperial portraits, see Bergmann/Zanker 1981, 318. On typology and Roman imperial portraiture, see most recently Fittschen 2015.

12   Bergmann/Zanker 1981, 318. Zanker 2018 revised the typology by associating the portraits previously assigned to type II as a later development of type I and dividing the former type III into type II and III. Significantly Daltrop 1966 dismissed two of the previous type II portraits as representations of Domitian arguing that one represented Titus while dismissing the other as Domitian, the portrait with *corona civica* in Naples, Museo Nazionale Archeologico 6058 and the head from Minturno likewise in Naples, Museo Nazionale Archeologico 150-216, see Daltrop 1966, 103.

Further, the Domitian portraits are so similar to those of his elder brother Titus, that it is hard to distinguish the two.[13] The fact that also portraits of Titus were re-carved from portraits of Nero blurs the typology and physiognomic features further. Perhaps the appearance of the two brothers were either alike or made to look alike in their portraits so as to propagate them as equal hereditary partners during the early part of the reign of their father, Vespasian.[14] There is also an extraordinary iconographic closeness between portraits of Domitian (and Titus) and those of contemporary private individuals,[15] the *princeps* and *privati*. In fact this closeness has made it very difficult to distinguish the decontextualised imperial portraits from those of private individuals. Not downplaying time-typical conventions and trends, the role of the so-called *Zeitgesicht*, this overlap touches upon the difficulty in recognizing a face in real life and in portraiture when a portrait does not sport either a very distinct physiognomy as the first portrait type of Vespasian or a recognizable typological feature such as a distinct arrangement of the front hair locks, repeated again and again in serial copies.[16] Without such markers we cannot easily see whether a decontextualised portrait shows Domitian, Titus or a private person. All this raises fundamental questions about what similarity means and how it is visually conceptualised. When we agree that new developments in portrait styling followed not a strict top-down model but reflected a mediating process between imperial and private faces, still the emperor portrait styling had a multiplying effect which went far beyond the elites in Rome. Which were the advantages for private people whose face was not familiar and whose social identity perhaps not interesting, to assimilate the imperial styling in their portraits so-called *Bildnisangleichung?* Blending in one's portrait and flattering the emperor's face by copying his styling no doubt played a role, but so did also biography. A familiar face, such as that of the emperor with its associated qualities and histories, seems to have influenced the verdict over how unfamiliar faces styled like the emperor were perceived by the viewer. The effect was that the qualities of the emperor were transferred to the unfamiliar *privati*.[17]

The evidence clearly suggests that leading portrait workshops in Rome worked for both the Emperor and the elite. These workshops were probably continuously engaged in flattering the Emperor by defining and updating his portrait image, mediating not only the emperor's ideological and aesthetic desire for his self-representation but also new trends within the political, economic and intellectual elite. The imperial portrait types once approved by the court, were distributed across the Empire and copied in numerous local workshops.[18] A good example here is an unfinished portrait, roughed-out for insertion into a statue of Domitian, as it shows an early phase of transferring a model into marble. Reported to have been found in Asia Minor the roughing-out may have taken place in or close to the quarry site, which would have saved up to fifty percent of the original marble block's weight before it was transported to and finished in a workshop close to the location where it was intended to be set up.[19]

c. Media, Body Formats, Context

The Domitian portrait has survived in a variety of materials and forms: in flat art such as large scale state reliefs in marble; in miniature in metal on coins, on military equipment, on luxury objects including a silver mirror (fig. 5) and in gems in precious stones.

In three dimensional art Domitian images survive in bronze such as a life-size full figure equestrian statue (fig. 6) and as a miniature bust (fig. 3): in marble, such

---

13 Jucker 1981, 304. Fittschen 1977, 64: that without the legend on coins it would be impossible on the basis of their portraits to distinguish them from each other. Varner 2004, 127 note 128. Also Daltrop 1966, 37 that neither of his first two groups associated with Domitian can with certainty be identified as Domitian. In Daltrop's group two is an over life-size portrait in the Vatican Museums, Braccio Nuovo 129 (126) which he dates to the reign of Titus. Also Bergmann/Zanker 1981, 354 no.15 identify it as Domitian but of the first type. The front-hair locks are however not arranged in the typical pattern and it may represent Titus and not Domitian. The portrait Naples 6038 with *corona civica* according to Daltrop 1966, 103 cannot represent Domitian while others including Bergmann/Zanker 1981, 362-364 identify it as Domitian type II. The identification of the colossal head of an acrolith statue from the temple of Domitian in Ephesos likewise oscillates between an identification as Domitian and Titus, Varner 2004, 128 note 138 as does a head from Almedinella in the National Archaeological Museum in Madrid, Daltrop 1966, 39 pl. 19).

14 Seelentag 2010. For the scarce evidence of imperial groups of the Flavians, see Deppmeyer 2008, 42-45.

15 Cain 1993, 111. Take just the discussion of whether a portrait in Ostia found in the tomb of Iulia Procula, represents Domitian or not, Varner 2004, 127.

16 Todorov 2017 shows, contrarily towards what is usually assumed, how difficult it is to recognize faces.

17 Todorov 2017, 246-263.

18 The workshop practice of early nineteenth century Danish sculptor Bertel Thorvaldsen and analogies with ancient Roman practices is now described by Fejfer/Schneider 2020. Some portraits in plaster survive from the Roman period and it has been suggested that the under life-size plaster portrait of Septimius Severus from North Africa was in fact a model from which marble copies could be made.

19 Pfanner 1989, 194 with fig. 16 illustrating the whole process. Varner 2000b, 158-161. Compare also the roughed-out head on a statue of an emperor from the Proconnesian quarries at Marmara in Asia Minor, in W. Wooton, B. Russell, Peter Rockwell, "Stoneworking Techniques and Processes at The Art of Making in Antiquity", in: *Stoneworking in the Roman World* at http://www.artofmaking.ac.uk/. Michael Pfanner's research is essential here. See latest Pfanner 2020.

Fig. 5. Silver mirror with portrait of Domitian, signed by Euporos. Karlsruhe, Badisches Landesmuseum, inv. 68/40 (courtesy Badisches Landesmuseum Karlsruhe, photo Thomas Goldschmidt).

Fig. 6. Equestrian portrait of Domitian with face replaced by that of Nerva. Castello di Bacoli, Museo dei Campi Flegrei, inv. 155743 (courtesy Ministero per i Beni e le Attività Culturali e per il Turismo – Museo dei Campi Flgrei).

as 'extremities' of a colossal acrolith statue, life-size statues and as busts. The choice of the portrait medium was usually linked to function and context, balancing the ambiguity between honorific permanence and momentary presence when the image of the emperor replaced him in person. The most famed portrait statue of Domitian was the *Equus Domitiani,* a colossal bronze set up for him by the Senate and the Roman People in the Forum Romanum in 90 or 91 so as to praise his victories over the Germans. The statue did not survive, possibly except for its foundations from which it was removed right after Domitian' assassination.[20] Depicted on coins and praised, as mentioned above by Statius, it showed the emperor as military commander holding in his left hand a figure of his patron goddess Minerva while raising his right arm in a *vetat pugnas* (banning battles) gesture. According again to Statius, Domitian's horse rested "its bronze hoof paws" not on "a vacuous clod of earth .... [but] at the flowing tresses of captive Rhine." The unique location of the colossus in the middle of the Forum Romanum close to the famous rostra and facing the temple of the deified Caesar, made a clear statement about the emperor's place among the most eminent people in Rome's history, as the new guardian of peace achieved through his military strength and *virtus*.[21]

Another Domitian statue of enormous proportions in Rome, the *Palatinus colossus,* is lost as well, apart from a possible related fragment of its cuirass.[22] Some five meters high was a colossal acrolith statue from the temple of Domitian in Ephesos, in Asia Minor, of which in marble the Emperor's head and parts of the arms and legs survive. Originally, this statue would have shown Domitian standing, dressed in a cuirass and with a lance in his raised right hand. In context of the temple in which it probably served as a cult statue, it testifies to the divine honours given to the living Emperor in the Roman East.[23] Another statue of Domitian in military guise, made in life-size bronze and found in the collegium of the Augustales in Misenum in Italy, portrays the emperor (his face replaced by one of Nerva) in the spectacular act of attacking on a steep horse (fig. 6). It is likely that the Misenum horse was placed outside the *templum augusti* which held statues of his father and brother, both represented in heroic nudity copying the fifth century BC statuary type of the Greek hero/god Diomedes. The same statuary type was also used by Nero and later recarved into a portrait of Domitian early during his

---

20   See note 47. For a reconstruction of the statue, Coarelli 2009b. See Antony Augustakis & Emma Buckley in this volume.

21   For a reevaluation of the role of the *Equus Domitiani* in the forum Romanum, Muth 2010. For the colossal scale in portraiture, Ruck 2007.

22   Wolfsfeld 2014, 200 with fig. 6.

23   As the colossal acrolith emperor statues from the baths in Sagalassos, see Mägele 2008, Waelkens 2008.

father's reign.[24] While the military aspect of the Misenum Vespasian and Titus statues was indirectly referred to in the pose of the famous hero and his sword and in the statue support in the shape of a cuirass, Domitian's steep horse could not have expressed the emperor's military *virtus* more directly.[25] A number of headless cuirass statues and torsos might also have represented Domitian, and would have propagated the military aspect of his public image further.[26] While these statues would all have been displayed in public spaces, a relief fragment of a cuirass figure with mutilated face deriving from the area of Domitian's villa at Castel Gandolfo near Rome, seems to indicate that the military habit of the emperor was omnipresent.[27] This is endorsed by the two surviving life-size marble busts of Domitian: one shows him with a nude breast wearing either a *paludamentum* (military cloak) or an aegis on the left shoulder, the other with the *paludamentum* fastened on the shoulder by a landing owl and a *balteus* (sword belt) swung across the shoulder (fig. 7).[28]

The sophisticated reference made to Domitian's patron goddess Minerva by the landing owl fibula clarifies that the Emperor's double role as Rome's military leader and divine protector was as important in the intimate bust format as in the images set up for public viewing.[29] The only known three dimensional representation of the Emperor in full heroic nudity is a miniature bust resting on acanthus foliage, perhaps intended for posthumous veneration in a private shrine (fig. 3). The continuous emphasis on the military power in different portrait formats of Domitian is novel in the iconography of the Roman emperor. Earlier examples turn up during the late Julio-Claudian period. Caligula seems to have been the first living emperor to be represented in a cuirassed bust, and at least ten statues of Nero in cuirass have survived.[30] Before Nero, the cuirass statue was a format generally avoided by the emperor himself and almost exclusively used for the young crown princes.[31] It was Nero though who seems to have been balancing the military habit carefully with a continuation of the civic virtues of his predecessors. This development towards more emphasis on the emperor's military power was further promoted by Vespasian and Titus after their victory over Judaea. Domitian's victories over the Germans allowed him to continue and re-enforce the military aspect of imperial rulership, with which his ancestors had begun, by giving it stronger emphasis, more visual sophistication and by associating it with Minerva whose role was that of a guardian rather than aggressor.[32]

Catching the Viewer – Anchoring Tradition, Anchoring Innovation

Returning to the inevitability of reading biography into a face, how might a contemporary viewer have perceived the Domitian portrait? As the third (and last) member of the Flavian family dynasty to become emperor, Domitian and the styling of his portrait would inevitably have been seen against those of his two family forerunners. Anchored in the Republican tradition, his father Vespasian's first portrait type represents one of the most radical shifts observable in the self-representation of the Roman emperor as convincingly argued by R.M. Schneider.[33] With its cubic head, fat neck, toothless mouth, small scaly eyes mostly covered by wrinkled skin, broad furrowed forehead and near baldness, Vespasian's portrait breaks away from previous conventions in the emperor portrait. True, a similar even more expressive style and iconography was already seen in the portrait of Galba but here only attested in his small profile face on his coinage.[34] Due to his short and turbulent reign Galba's portraits were never widely distributed, and it seems that the effect of his image distinguished by extreme physiognomy, fatness and high age was never put to the test in life-size or over life-size three-dimensional sculptural portraits which have a much more powerful presence. A colossal head of Galba's rival the Emperor Vitellius clearly demonstrates the effect of such extreme physiognomy.[35] In all likelihood, the first Vespasian type was quickly replaced by a type showing a considerably rejuvenated Vespasian with more hair, fuller (not toothless) mouth and lips, and less wrinkles.[36] Did Vespasian's first portrait type break with established

---

24   It cannot though be excluded that the horse had fallen from the *summa cavea* of the adjacent theatre, see Fejfer 2008, 460, note 14 with references. For the Nero/Domitian statue in Munich, Glyptothek inv. GL 394, see Gliwitzky/Knauss 2017, 185-186, 367-368. For the Misenum complex Fejfer 2008, 79-81.

25   See also the cuirass statues of Domitian from the theatre in Vaison-la-Romaine, Musée Archéologique Théo Desplans 99054.22 and from the basilica in Velleia, Parma , Museo di Antichità 1952.827, in Wolfsfeld 2014, 198-9 figs. 3-4 with references.

26   On the increasing number of cuirass torsos dated to the Flavian period, see Wolfsfeld 2014, 203 with note 112.

27   As do also cameos. For the Castel Gandolfo fragment see Wolfsfeld 2014, 201 with note 102 on the reconstruction of the fragment.

28   According to Zanker it cannot be determined whether the Capitoline bust wore an aegis or a paludamentum, see Paul Zanker in Fittschen/Zanker 1985, 37, no. 33

29   For the Toledo bust, see Zanker 2018.

30   Wolsfeld 2014, 199. For the bust of Tiberius in cuirass from Ephesos as posthumous, Wolfsfeld 2014, 185.

31   Wolfsfeld 2014, 189.

32   According to Wolters/Ziegert 2014, 60, note 57 the coinage shows strong military interest during Domitian's early reign with the *Germania capta* motif disappearing in 90 in the bronze coinage.

33   Schneider 2003.

34   Gliwitzky 2017, 291.

35   Copenhagen, Ny Carlsberg Glyptotek I.N. 3167, in Johansen 1995, 24, cat. 1.

36   Bergmann/Zanker 1981, 334-335, Zanker 2014, 62.

decorum of what an emperor portrait was expected to look like? Was it too close to caricature or even too close to Vespasian's actual look becoming uncanny? In fact, both Titus' portraits and early portraits of Domitian are clearly related to that second Vespasian portrait type. As his sons were younger and had more hair, their portraits picked up the coiffure of the late Nero portrait (though condemned!), his luxurious long, well-trimmed and carefully groomed hairstyle with comma shaped locks across the forehead and a puffy, soft and spotless skin. Yet, the two sons show the same cubic heads, fat and short neck and fleshy cheeks as their father, and the knowledge about Vespasian's biography no doubt influenced the verdict of the portraits of the two sons. While Domitian's later portraits continue to show him with basically the same yet shorter hairstyle he became significantly slimmer and his short fat neck was replaced by a very long slim neck which intensified the now elongated shape of the head. His face was now portrayed without wrinkles except for the occasional presence of two softly modelled grooves across the forehead. Perhaps the longer and more engaging face compensated for a troublesome premature hair loss which was considered a disfigurement.[37] As noted by Zanker, none of the surviving bust portraits of Domitian show the pathos which can be observed in some late coin portraits – and in some luxury items in flat art which seem made after the coin portraits (see fig. 5).[38] In fact none of the surviving three-dimensional portraits of Domitian shows pathos which suggests that there is no one to one correspondence between the models used in three-dimensional art and those of the mint, a phenomenon which is not limited to the Domitian portrait but to imperial portraiture more generally.[39] Different media may follow different trajectories in the imperial representation. We do not know how Domitian's portrait of the *Equus Domitiani* and the *Palatinus colossus* looked, whether they showed the Emperor in a now lost pathetic three-dimensional portrait type. The surviving three-dimensional portraits of Domitian however, seem anchored in the styles preferred by his dynastic predecessors and earlier emperors. In fact, the older Domitian got the more his portraits became idealized. In doing so he reinvented the classicizing portrait tradition of the Julio-Claudian emperors and its appropriateness, a *decorum* to which later emperors continuously returned. Even if we accept the colossal head of Minerva in Budapest to have taken over Domitian's portrait features and thus referenced the Emperor's divinity, this practice was part of a long tradition, as was the privilege to portray emperors, heroes and gods in colossal size.[40] However, there was significant innovation and experimentation in luxurious materials and formats regarding the Domitian portrait. The few surviving busts of Domitian are of exquisite quality. They are not re-carved (perhaps they were hidden away or as the small bronze bust which was found in the Tiber, thrown away after his death?) and show the quality and virtuosity in the carving and in the styling of the emperor's portrait. They all represent him in the demi-nude or nude habit and sport a number of unusual features such as a possible aegis, a landing owl, a small index plate, a sword belt, and a foliage base, details which suggest that the best workshops were experimenting with new designs in the bust format and Domitian's portrait in that format.[41] A similar interest in new designs register also busts of *privati* during the late Domitianic and early Trajanic period.[42] And it was under Trajan's rule that the bust reached an iconic elegance with a high turned bust foot and the *pelta* shaped index plate which seems to make the bust almost floating. This careful balancing of the heavy bust against its radically reduced support of the index plate drew not only new attention to the name tag, but also to the virtuosity and sophistication in the craftsmanship needed to get this balancing aesthetically and technically right. I argue that in the Domitianic period Rome's workshops seem to have led the way and were encouraged to experiment with the bust format, a format that must have been used primarily for private settings and intimate viewing. Another exceptional image of Domitian is his black diorite statue from the sanctuary of Isis in Beneventum (see Versluys, fig. 4). It represents the emperor as a

---

37   Draycott 2018 on the Roman attitude towards premature hair loss and on Domitian's hair loss and his treatise *On the Care of Hair*.

38   Zanker 2018, 229.

39   Fejfer 2008, 411. In contrast to what scholars have usually argued I suggested on the basis of both numismatic evidence and sculpted portraits of a number of emperors, that we should accept that there is no one to one correspondence between coin types and sculptural types of the emperor and that we have to rethink how the system 'worked'. I suggested that it was the sculptural workshops which developed the prototypes suitable for replicating in high numbers whereas the mints usually but not always worked with separate prototypes.

---

40   Szépmüvészeti Múzeum inv. 34.7016, see Prusac 2016, 240, Hekster, 2015, 253-255. Borg 2019, 213-215 on deities with the features of members of the imperial house.

41   The sword belt is seen earlier as are the paludamentum and the simple index plate but none of these features become common before the Trajanic period, see Fejfer 2008, 236-261.

42   A bust in Villa Albani sports a cat skin in Bol 1994, 392-393, cat. 514 (R. Amedick), and a bust in the Glyptothek in Munich inv. 72 of Trajan wears an aegis and a sword belt, in Gliwitzky/Knauss 2017, 208, 373, cat. 76 while a bust likewise of Trajan in Copenhagen, Ny Carlsberg Glyptotek IN 1723 sports an aegis and a bust support at the back carved in the shape of a palmtree, see Johansen 1995, 102-103, cat. 36.

Fig. 7. Portrait Bust of the Emperor Domitian, about 90, marble, h. 23 7/16 in. (59.6 cm), w. 16 ¼ in. (41.3 cm), Toledo Museum of Art (Toledo, Ohio), Gift of Edward Drummond Libbey, and from the Florence Scott Libbey Bequest in Memory of her Father, Maurice A. Scott, 1990.30

striding figure with clenched hands in Egyptian style and insignia of Egyptian royalty, thus highlighting again the strong interest of this period in exploring uncommon formats, styles and materials.[43]

A variety of sources, material and written touch upon Domitian's religious innovations and divine ambitions: Statius comments on Domitian's divine look in the *Equus Domitiani*, as discussed above, other authors that he demanded to be addressed as *dominus* et *deus*.[44] There is evidence for the revival of genius cult of the Emperor,[45] the wearing of divine attributes in the coinage is significant, the transfer of the burial site from the mausoleum of Augustus to the imperial cult temple *Templum Gentis Flaviae*, focus on his divine ancestors, etc.[46] However, the styling of the known portraits of Domitian does not suggest a shift towards a new monarchic or autocratic emperor image.[47] They are rather anchored in the visual tradition of the dynasty to which he belonged, complemented by references to the Julio-Claudian portrait tradition. No imperial portrait type could capture all of what that emperor was or stood for, but by drawing on the visual traditions in the portraiture of his ancestors and the biographies associated with them, the anticipated reception and verdict rendered on Domitian's portrait was no doubt actively manipulated.

---

43   For the interest in luxurious materials and their sophisticated use under the Flavians, Schneider suggests that the Ny Carlsberg Glyptotek hippo inv. 1415 in red marble may date to the Flavian period (Schneider 2018, 274-276, cat. 173). For the Beneventum statue, Beneventum Museum inv. 1903, see Sara Cole in Spier et al. 2018, 264-265, cat. 165.

44   Bönisch-Meyer/Witschel 2014, 121.

45   Gradel 2002, 190-191.

46   Borg 2019, 213-214. On the buildings for his divine ancestors, Borg 2019, 244-245.

47   Nor does the epigraphic evidence suggest any shift towards a more divine status of the emperor, Bönisch-Meyer/Witschel 2014, 161. The use of colossal scale in portraiture had a long tradition, see Ruck 2007 and Cordes 2019. For an interesting re-evaluation of the *Equus Domitiani* and its colossal size in its setting, see Muth 2010.

Historical Reliefs and Architecture

Paolo Liverani

'Historical reliefs' are a sensitive indicator of the policy followed by the emperors and, therefore, they are particularly interesting from both the artistic and historical points of view.[1] Before discussing them in detail, let me begin by stating some general premises that should be made explicit since, although the term 'historical relief' is a traditional one in archaeology, it needs to be used with some caution. First of all, we should not think that this kind of relief constitutes an objective historical document, a sort of photograph of important events in the history of an emperor or of Rome, but it is instead the political and ideological representation of events or elements of the imperial program. For this reason, the term 'state relief' has often been the preferred technical term and, in the recent past, the even more neutral and generic term 'representational art' has been employed.[2] Secondly, we should stress that this type of representation was not necessarily the direct expression of the will of the emperor or of his court. First of all, in Rome there was no planned propaganda on the model of modern states with government departments dedicated to manipulating public opinion. Thirdly, although the patronage varied, the political message was always mediated. In the case of works commissioned by the emperor, the mediators were the message-makers who had the task of creating signs, symbols, speeches and laws. In the case of other patrons – such as the Roman Senate or another city – the works were the product of an implicit or explicit negotiation between the emperor formulating his policies and the subjects reacting, interpreting and implementing them.[3]

We can exemplify what is at stake by examining the decoration on the Arch of Titus *in sacra via*,[4] a monument whose construction was planned by the Roman Senate shortly before the premature death of Titus, but which had to be built and finished under his brother and successor, Domitian. The arch was placed across the path of the triumphal parade led by Vespasian and Titus in 71 to celebrate the conquest of Jerusalem (Levick, figs. 1-3). The two large panels that decorate the interior sides of the archway are well-known: in the northern one, Titus is crowned by a Victory on the triumphal quadriga and is accompanied by twelve lictors. A group of senators led by *Honos* follows him, while in front of the chariot stands Virtus. These two personifications represent key recurrent

---

1   For an overview on the historical reliefs of the age of Domitian cf. Koeppel 1984, Hölscher 2009.
2   Bergmann 2000, Hölscher 2015.
3   For this approach cf. Lenski 2016.
4   Pfanner 1983.

concepts of the Roman triumph. The panel on the southern side depicts the procession displaying the spoils captured in the siege of Jerusalem: two *fercula* (or, wooden stretchers) carry the seven-branched Menorah, the golden Table of Shewbread and the silver trumpets, passing through the *Porta Triumphalis*. Around the attic entablature on the exterior of the arch is located a frieze representing the same procession, this time carved in its entirety, albeit on a miniature scale. Finally, for the viewer who looks upward, the carved figure of Titus rises impressively overhead on the apex of the archway, appearing as *divus* ascending to the heavens on the back of an eagle.

For a better understanding of the arch's message, we have to consider that – although the honourand was Titus – the function of the monument fitted well with Domitian's program to strengthen his own legitimacy by showing as *divi* both his brother Titus and his father Vespasian. The latter was venerated in the temple he built at the foot of the Capitoline Hill, at the western end of the Forum Romanum. Vespasian's temple formed the perfect backdrop of Domitian's colossal equestrian monument in the Roman Forum. Although the *Equus Domitiani* has left no archaeological trace owing to Domitian's *damnatio memoriae*, we can have an idea of its position thanks to Statius' detailed poetic description.[5] It probably stood in the middle of the western half of the Forum, a position that let it been seen with proper perspective.[6] Finally, the Emperor reiterated the message about the Flavian dynasty and its *divi* when he built the *Templum Gentis Flaviae* on his birthplace on the Quirinal hill.[7]

The triumphal connotation marks another leitmotiv of the monumental program of Domitian. This element is evident in the Arch of Titus but was manifested even in a clearer way thanks to the arches erected in his honour throughout the city. They are mentioned in the sources,[8] but none of them survived the *damnatio memoriae* or the passage of time. Only one – perhaps the most important – has left some traces and probably could be seen until the seventeenth century – even if completely transformed: the *Porta Triumphalis*. This gate marked the crossing point of the pomerium, the sacred boundary of Rome delimiting the city from the *ager*, or the surrounding territory. Military weapons were prohibited inside this line, and a victorious Roman general with his army could enter the city only

during the triumphal ceremony after passing through this gate. During the Republic and the early imperial period, the gate stood on the southern side of the Capitoline Hill, but Vespasian extended the pomerium so that the crossing point had to be moved, too. Domitian built the new gate and commemorated it on sesterces of the year 95-96.[9] It was a quadrifrons arch crowned by two elephant quadrigae driven by the Emperor himself in the guise of a gilded statue. The same monument was enthusiastically described by Martial:[10]

> A sacred arch is there erected in memory of our triumphs over subdued nations.
> Here two chariots number many an elephant yoked to them;
> the prince himself cast in gold, guides alone the mighty team.

The elephant quadrigae were a characteristic feature of this arch, allowing us to recognize it in several historical reliefs of later periods.[11] We can probably identify the Porta Triumphalis with a late antique arch dedicated to Emperor Honorius around 400, which is conventionally called the Arco di Portogallo. The arch is documented in several drawings by Renaissance architects made before its demolition. It stood in Via del Corso, the ancient via Lata, the urban segment of the via Flaminia.[12]

Returning to the Arch of Titus, we have to consider the role of its patron: the Roman Senate. By erecting the arch and decorating it with this program, the Senate had a double purpose. First of all, it directed praises of Titus at the people of Rome, but it also indirectly honoured Domitian. The latter was, according to Goffman's terminology,[13] the 'unaddressed recipient': a recipient intended, but – so to speak – tacitly implied. In other words, the Senate expected the Emperor also to acknowledge the dedication. This second purpose, indeed, is almost more important than the first: in this way, the Senate intended to demonstrate its loyalty – a useful thing to do if we consider its difficult relationship with Domitian – but at the same time the Senate wanted to be recognized by both the Roman people and the emperor as the sole institution authorized to confer the status of *divus* on a deceased Emperor such as Titus. By doing so, the Senate also bolstered the legitimacy of the reigning Emperor, Titus' brother Domitian and gave him an incentive to be on his best behaviour, at least in his relationship with the senators.

---

5   Stat., *Silv.* 1.1-31, cf. *BMCRE* II, 406, no. 476.
6   I am not convinced we can identify the position of the monument in the eastern half of the Forum as Giuliani/Verduchi 1987, 118-122, no. 17 (very cautiously) proposed. Coarelli 2009b, 83 misinterpreted the meaning of the position of the *Equus* as sign of disrespect for the traditional places of the Republican power. Furthermore the inscription *CIL* VI, 1207 = 31263 = 36890 has no relation to Domitian: cf. Liverani 2016, 358-363.
7   See here contribution by Eric Moormann.
8   Suet. *Dom.* 13.2, Dio Cass. 68.1.1.

9   Carradice 1982, *RIC* 2.1, 796, p. 324.
10   Martial. 8, 65 (93 d.C.). Translated by Henri G. Bohm.
11   Liverani 2006-2007.
12   Liverani 2004, Liverani 2005, Liverani 2006-2007.
13   Goffman 1981, 133.

Fig. 1. Entablature representing the myth of Arachne. Rome, Forum Transitorium (courtesy Rome, Sovrintendenza Capitolina ai Beni Culturali).

A completely different program emerges from the decoration of the Forum Transitorium, the elongated plaza connecting the Roman Forum with the lower-class district of the Subura on the slopes of the Quirinal Hill. Domitian's architect struggled to find space for this new forum, which had to be squeezed between the pre-existing Forum of Augustus and the Templum Pacis. The Temple of Minerva, the goddess that Domitian venerated with particular devotion, stood on its northeastern end. Today, only the podium exists, but the southeastern wall of the forum, dividing it from the precinct of the adjacent Templum Pacis, survives with part of its figural decoration still intact. Above the Corinthian columns, the entablature is richly decorated by a frieze depicting myths connected with Minerva (fig. 1).

The main scene portrays the myth of Arachne,[14] a young woman highly skilled at using the loom, who dared to challenge Minerva herself. The goddess, in disguise as an old woman, tried in vain to dissuade Arachne from this mad course of action. Once the contest ended, Minerva was struck by the extraordinary beauty of her rival's cloth representing the loves of the gods. Furious, she destroyed

it, prevented the desperate Arachne from committing suicide, and punished the girl by transforming her into a spider eternally doomed to spin webs. The frieze continues with scenes depicting women weaving and spinning under the tutelage of Minerva. This is quite an unusual subject for a state relief, and probably a unique case, at least in Rome, of a mythological representation on an official civic monument. The choice, on the other hand, was counterbalanced but the subject of the panels decorating the attic above the frieze. Only one of them survives in place. It portrays an armoured female figure, which has been traditionally interpreted as Minerva. In 2000, the fragments of another female figure were excavated, and a more careful consideration of the two panels connected them with other examples of personifications on imperial monuments. The first parallel came from the well-preserved sculptural decoration of the Sebasteion in Aphrodisias, a sanctuary honouring the emperors.[15] Here the personification of the Pirusti, a tribe of the Illyricum (Dalmatia), is very similar from a typological point of view to the alleged 'Minerva'. The two panels, therefore, represent *gentes* or *nationes*, peoples (not provinces as

14   D'Ambra 1993.

15   Ungaro 2005, Del Moro 2007, 181-185.

Fig. 2. Cancelleria Relief, side A. Vatican Museums, Museo Gregoriano Profano ex Lateranense, inv. 13389-13391 (courtesy Governorato SCV – Direzione dei Musei, all rights reserved).

Fig. 3. Cancelleria Relief, side B. Vatican Museums, Museo Gregoriano Profano ex Lateranense, inv. 13392-13395 (courtesy Governorato SCV – Direzione dei Musei, all rights reserved).

usually understood) of the empire according to a motif widely employed in the imperial monuments of the Julio-Claudian period and also attested during the second century.[16] The earlier Forum of Augustus hosted a series of dedication from several *gentes*, according to the historical sources.[17] The Domitianic cycle, therefore, is quite traditional, alluding to the multifarious populations that made up the Roman Empire, grouped around the emperor as sign of unity.

The Cancelleria Reliefs are surely among the most famous figural monuments of the age of Domitian (figs. 2-3).[18] They consist of two reliefs of large dimensions, more than two meters high and respectively about five and six meters in length, but at least one slab for each of them is missing so that the original length must have been

more than seven meters. Rarely has a figural monument been so hotly debated by archaeologists, but, despite the extensive secondary literature, several points still remain uncertain. The reliefs were found between 1937 and 1939 under Palazzo della Cancelleria in Corso Vittorio Emanuele in Rome. The context was the deposit of an ancient marble workshop. Here the reliefs were in temporary storage after having been taken off the monument they originally decorated and while they were waiting to be reused on a new monument. But, as the archaeological discovery makes clear, such reuse never occurred.

In what follows here, it is only possible to give a brief summary of the extremely detailed and complex scholarly discussion, choosing among the most likely opinions, which, however, are not always to be considered as certainties. On the frieze A, the Emperor occupies the centre of the scene. Behind him stands the female personification of *Virtus* in Amazon dress; she gives encouragement to the Emperor. Next comes the Genius of the Senate and the

---

16   Liverani 1995.
17   Vell. Pat. 2.39.2, cf. *CIL* VI, 31267.
18   Magi 1945, Langer/Pfanner 2018.

Roman People followed by a group of soldiers. Several lictors, the winged figure of a Victory (missing for the most part), Minerva and Mars precede the Emperor and invite him to advance. The face of the Emperor was clearly recarved: the traits are those of Nerva but the hair has the typical Domitianic hairstyle (*coma in gradu formata*). The fact that this part of the relief was recarved is clear from a roughly carved stripe between forehead and the fringe, traces of the reworking owing to the *damnatio memoriae*, the destruction of the images and inscriptions of the Emperor decreed after Domitian's assassination. The lictors standing before the Emperor carry the fasces with axes, and on one of them we find small traces of red among the folds of his dress, the *sagum*.[19] All these elements are signs of the *imperium*, the military power of the Emperor, and therefore the lictors must be standing outside the pomerium. On the other side, in contrast, the lictors behind the Emperor carry fasces without axes. Thus, they are still inside the pomerium. This means that the Emperor is going to cross the boundary of the city in a *profectio* for a military expedition. Frieze B is divided in two halves by two lictors placed in the middle and depicted from behind. This is a typical figural device for dividing two scenes or groups. On the right side is Vespasian crowned by a flying Victory among lictors (without axes) and the Genius of the Senate and the Roman People. In front of him is a young togate figure, whose identity has been hotly debated. Many have proposed to interpret him as the young Domitian, but his traits are generic and he must rather be identified as a magistrate or a similar institutional personage. The left group consists of the Vestal Virgins, the priestesses of Vesta, with their lictor and a seated female goddess – probably Roma. Some more figures were portrayed on the missing slab in the middle of the group of the priestesses. The portrait of the Emperor is stylistically very different from the other heads and also a little smaller: there is the strong suspicion it, too, was reworked, even if in a more accurate and mimetic way than on frieze A. In this case, too, the original Emperor must be recognized as Domitian, but here he is portrayed performing an *adventus*, a ritual arrival into the city of Rome, not necessarily after a war.

The two reliefs are unanimously considered as pendants, originally part of the decoration for a Domitianic monument, recarved after the death of the Emperor and his *damnatio memoriae*, and rededicated to the successor, Nerva. Finally, not later than the Hadrianic period, the monument was dismantled. A number of hypotheses have been proposed about its identity, but considering the weakness of their foundation, we cannot take them too seriously as they are speculative exercises and, indeed, not very productive. Furthermore, the discussion about the program of the reliefs usually misses the point about the patronage, which is very relevant, as we have already seen in the case of the Arch of Titus. Therefore, we should not simply assume that the reliefs had imperial patronage rather than senatorial, and this detail might have some interpretive consequences. Summing up, we can try to draw some conclusions, notwithstanding the numerous uncertainties. The style of the reliefs – albeit with some evident differences between the two friezes due to different sculptors – is quite a classicizing one, recalling to some extent various Julio-Claudian monuments. The difference from the style of the Arch of Titus is more apparent than real, owing to the different states of preservation of the surfaces. The two friezes of the Cancelleria Reliefs complement each other: the military *profectio* and the civic *adventus* allude to the military virtues and good fortune of the Emperor. At the same time, they demonstrate the legitimacy of the Emperor's power displayed before one of the most prestigious priestly colleges of Rome, the Vestal Virgins, and before Rome itself.

The body of evidence we have examined up to this point constitutes the most important part of our documentation. Few other examples can be briefly considered, but they are less meaningful because of their fragmentation and lack of precise context. In 1901, a series of sculptural fragments were found during the building of the northern portico of Piazza della Repubblica in Rome, on the site of the great exedra of the Baths of Diocletian. They were stolen by the workers and arrived on the antiquarian market where Paul Hartwig acquired most of the marbles, donating them to the National Museum of Rome (Conlin, fig. 7). Some other fragments ended up in the Kelsey Museum of the University of Michigan. All of them were assigned to the Domitianic period on stylistic grounds and attributed to the *Templum Gentis Flaviae*. Impressive structures datable to the Domitianic period on the basis of brickstamps were found at various times under the areas occupied by the Planetarium, Via Parigi and Via Vittorio Emanuele Orlando, close to the findspot of the sculpture. The remains included a precinct and a podium that some scholars identified as the *Templum*.[20] The hypothesis is not without its problems because the Regionary catalogues – a list of monuments of Rome organized by the urban *regiones* (districts) and dating to the early fourth century CE – mention both the *Templum* and the Baths of Diocletian, but in this case it is difficult to imagine how the temple could have remained visible inside the area of the baths, which were built much later. Be that as it may, the sculptural fragments suggest that we should reconstruct an enclosure with a series of figures such as caryatids on the outside and with two relief panels,

---

19   Liverani 2014, 26.

20   Candilio 1990-1991, Paris 1994, La Rocca 2009, Coarelli 2014, 194-207. See Eric Moormann in this volume.

Fig. 4. 'Nollekens Relief'. St. Petersburg, Gatchina Palace (photo courtesy John Pollini).

one depicting a sacrifice in front of a temple, the other the Emperor Vespasian among soldiers and other figures.

Another interesting document is the so-called Nollekens relief, representing an imperial sacrifice (fig. 4).[21] After its discovery in 1722 in the imperial palace on the Palatine, the relief was extensively restored and transferred to the Gatchina Palace at St. Petersburg. Now it is in a poor state of preservation owing to damage and losses suffered during World War II, but some old photographs and eighteenth century drawings help us to identify the original parts now lost. In the middle Domitian is shown sacrificing on a little altar, to the right is the Genius of the Roman Senate and the personification of Rome with a young assistant for the sacrifice (*camillus*). To the left are two lictors carrying the fasces with axes, a flute player and a second *camillus*. Pollini, who rediscovered the lost relief, interprets the scene in connection with the triumph and considers it as the sacrifice performed by the Emperor in front of the Porta Triumphalis before entering the city. Setting aside some minor problem of his reconstruction connected with this gate,[22] the triumphal connotation is based on weak evidence and must remain hypothetical.

What appears interesting is the survival of Domitian's portrait in the imperial palace on the Palatine after his *damnatio memoriae*, but, unfortunately, we do not know the exact find spot and cannot solve the riddle.

More fragments pertaining to great friezes are preserved in the Antiquarium of Villa Barberini at Castel Gandolfo, discovered at various times in the area of the *Albanum Domitiani*, the huge imperial villa situated a few kilometers from Rome along the Via Appia. Some of these marbles were already documented in Piranesi's etchings, others came to light during the works converting Villa Barberini to a papal residence in the thirties of the past century. Among the first group is an imposing fragment with a pile of enemy weapons collected after a victory in battle, a trophy recalling the decoration on the base of Trajan's Column.[23] In the second group are other fragments of reliefs:[24] a badly damaged portrait of Domitian, originally crowned by a Victory, the shoulder of a togate figure and the bust of a soldier wearing a sophisticated type of cuirass: a mail shirt with small feather-like scales attached to the rings. Both the portrait of the Emperor and the bust of soldier present themselves in a frontal position, an uncommon characteristic in the relief of the first century, highlighting the importance of the figure portrayed in

---

21   Pollini 2017.
22   Pollini (2017) seems to be not aware of the discussion about the position of the Porta Triumphalis after the extension of the pomerial limits.

23   von Hesberg 2001, 246-247, fig. 3.
24   Liverani 1989, 17-18, nn. 1.3.

the act of addressing the beholder. Unfortunately, we cannot propose any hypothesis about the iconography or the context of the reliefs, but it is clear that the villa had strong public connotations. On its grounds was a theatre for public celebrations and artistic performances, and the fragments just described demonstrate the presence of one or more buildings exalting the military virtues and the victories of the Emperor, according to schemata and iconographies already known from the other triumphal monuments of the same Emperor.

The Image of the Emperor in Contemporary Epic Poetry

Claire Stocks

Much of what we think we know about Domitian's image is shaped by the memory sanctions applied after his assassination. Statues produced during his lifetime were destroyed or re-carved and authors such as Pliny (c. 61-110) and Tacitus (c. 56/58-120) went to great lengths to portray the man as despotic and unpredictable in an effort to contrast him with the emperors who followed him: Nerva and especially Trajan.[1]

Not everything from Domitian's reign was destroyed, however, and in the case of the literary sources, we have a wide body of material – especially poetic material – that refers directly or indirectly to the Emperor and that was produced during his lifetime. These sources are consistent in the type of Emperor that they portray: benevolent to his people yet set above them; a god on earth, specially favoured by the goddess Minerva and the chief deity in the pantheon, Jupiter. Yet not all of this praise is sycophantic. The poets Statius (c. 45/50-96) and Martial (c. 38/41-102/4) clearly had enough freedom with respect to their literary output that they were not afraid to compare Domitian to a king[2] – something of a taboo in Rome – or to make humorous comparisons between the Emperor and the gods.[3] It is possible that even later literary sources, which are notorious for their negative depiction of Domitian, show the Emperor in his youth as being capable of cracking a joke, if we can assume that the story of Domitian's self-authored literary pamphlet on hair-loss was a witty nod to his own baldness.[4] Domitian it would seem could appreciate a joke, and possibly even at his own expense, as long as he was the one making it.[5]

---

1   See especially Antony Augoustakis & Emma Buckley in this volume for more on the literary sources on Domitian's reign.

2   Statius, *Silvae* 4.2.

3   E.g. Martial *Ep.* 9.3, 9.34, 9.36.

4   Suet. *Dom.* 18.2. With thanks to Peter Heslin for pointing out the possibility that Suetonius depicts Domitian making a learned joke at his own expense. Southern 1997, 119, citing a poem (5.49) by Martial in which he jokes about the baldness of a certain Labienus, observes that the book in which this poem features was dedicated to the balding Domitian: 'thus the fact that Martial was not invited to go and live somewhere a long way from Rome indicates that Domitian could accept the change in his appearance with resignation and some humour.' See here Jane Fejfer, p. 80 note 37.

5   See Henriksén 2012, xxviii on Martial's humorous poems in which he depicts Domitian as the envy of Jupiter "such jokes involving the emperor (but naturally not made at his expense) could not have been made unless Martial was sure about Domitian's reaction." In the case of Statius, Newlands 2002, 272 notes that whilst the poet enjoyed Domitian's patronage, the social distance between them remains evident in his poems.

Certainly Domitian took a keen interest in the literary production of his day, evidenced not only through the authorial aspirations of his youth, but from his continued interest in poetry and the arts throughout his time as Emperor, which included the institution of several literary competitions as part of his *Capitolia* games in Rome and also the Alban Games in honour of Minerva, which were held annually at his villa in the Alban Hills.[6] The poet Statius, at least, took part in both – winning the victor's crown at Alba and suffering a painful defeat at the *Capitolia*.[7]

Literature, therefore, not only bears much of the responsibility for how we remember Domitian, but it was a prominent feature of his reign. It is not surprising, therefore, that we should find reflected in these literary sources, some of the key messages of Domitian's principate, that is the 'image' of the Emperor.

The Image

As numerous papers in this volume show, Domitian, like many emperors before him, paid close attention to the shaping of his image. This was an Emperor who, during his lifetime, carefully crafted his public persona through (among other things) coinage, building works, and literary production, all of which are illustrative of his desire to follow in the footsteps of Rome's first Emperor, Augustus.

Poets writing under Domitian appear to show a similar penchant for the Augustan era, notably the writers whose works show more than passing intertextual engagement with the epic poetry of one of the most famous Augustan poets, Virgil:[8]

> uiue, precor; nec tu diuinam Aeneida tempta,
> sed longe sequere et uestigia semper adora.

Live, I pray; and essay not the divine Aeneid, but ever follow her footsteps from afar in adoration.

This quotation, from the end of Statius' epic *Thebaid*, which focuses on the war of the seven against Thebes, implies a reverential approach to Virgil's famous epic, the *Aeneid*, but it masks one of the key features of Flavian poetry and society at large: reinvention. Statius, like Domitian, was anchoring his output to an Augustan precedent, but at the same time reinventing epic as Rome knew it. His take on fratricidal war offers a darker, more violent approach to epic warfare and serves as a reminder of the civil war of 68-69 that brought the Flavian Emperors to power.[9] Yet at the same time there is more direct praise of the Emperor than we see in Virgil's poem: Domitian is heralded at the start of the epic, and appealed to again at the end: *iam te magnanimus dignatur noscere Caesar* ('now great-hearted Caesar deigns to know you').[10] In terms of the Emperor's image, at least, Domitian is the light amid the dark of the *Thebaid*'s familial conflict, with the word *magnanimus*, a standard heroic epithet in Roman epic, casting the Emperor in the role of an epic hero akin to the great Aeneas himself.[11]

In general, Roman epics written under the early Caesars, whilst their subject matter was often distantly historical or mythological (with the exception of Lucan's *Bellum Civile*), were nonetheless political, and all four surviving epics[12] that were produced by the poets of Domitian's day refer to the ruling Flavians at some point in their works. The references are invariably flattering, and regardless of the truth of such descriptions, the *image* is suggestive of an imperial household that was not only benevolent to inspiring authors, but worthy of comparison to the gods.

Yet this poetry of praise also often comes with a disclaimer – about the text that the author dare not write. We see this again with the opening of Statius's epic *Thebaid*:[13]

> limes mihi carminis esto
> Oedipodae confusa domus, quando Itala nondum
> signa nec Arctoos ausim spirare triumphos
> bisque iugo Rhenum, bis adactum legibus Histrum
> et coniurato deiectos uertice Dacos   20
> aut defensa prius uix pubescentibus annis
> bella Iouis. tuque, o Latiae decus addite famae
> quem noua maturi subeuntem exorsa parentis
> aeternum sibi Roma cupit (licet artior omnes
> limes agat stellas et te plaga lucida caeli,   25
> Pliadum Boreaeque et hiulci fulminis expers,
> sollicitet, licet ignipedum frenator equorum
> ipse tuis alte radiantem crinibus arcum
> imprimat aut magni cedat tibi Iuppiter aequa
> parte poli), maneas hominum contentus habenis,   30
> undarum terraeque potens, et sidera dones.
> tempus erit, cum Pierio tua fortior oestro
> facta canam:

---

6   See Nauta 2002, 328-329. On the *Capitolia* see van Onno Nijf, Robin van Vliet & Caroline van Toor in this volume.

7   *Silvae* 3.5.31-33.

8   Statius, *Thebaid* 12.816-817. All translations from Statius' works by Shackleton Bailey (2004).

9   In addition to engaging directly with Virgil's *Aeneid*, Statius also looked to the epic poet Lucan, writing under the emperor Nero, whose epic poem *Bellum Civile* on the civil war between Caesar and Pompey sets the tone for violent and visceral epic thereafter.

10   Statius, *Thebaid* 12.813. Domitian at the start: 1.22-31.

11   Cf. *Aen*.1.260.

12   Valerius Flaccus' *Argonautica* (unfinished), Statius' *Thebaid*, Statius' *Achilleid* (unfinished), and Silius Italicus' *Punica*.

13   Statius, *Thebaid* 1.16-33.

Let the limit of my lay be the troubled house of Oedipus. For not yet do I dare breathe forth Italian standards and northern triumphs – Rhine twice subjugated, Hister twice brought under obedience, Dacians hurled down from their leagued mountain, or, earlier yet, Jove's warfare warded off in years scarce past childhood. And you, glory added to Latium's fame, whom, as you take on your aged father's enterprises anew, Rome wishes hers for eternity: though a narrower path move all the planets and a radiant tract of heaven invite you, free of Pleiades and Boreas and forked lightning; though the curber of the fire-footed horses himself set his high-shining halo on your locks or Jupiter yield you an equal portion of the broad sky, may you remain content with the governance of mankind, potent over sea and land, and waive the stars. A time will come when stronger in Pierian frenzy I shall sing your deeds.

When Statius switches to his description of the epic he would have written, if only he had felt up to doing so, he begins with the word *limes*, which here means 'limit', but it also refers to a threshold and hence to the liminal boundary that Statius does not (yet) feel able to cross. The image of the Emperor that he then presents stresses his greater-than-human aspects: not only is he the mighty warrior who has conquered the Germans and the Dacians, but he was protected by Jupiter in his youth (*i.e.* in the fire on the Capitol in 69) and now marked-out for divinity (although Statius prays that he will not leave earth just yet…). Nonetheless there is tension here, a concern that if the poet spends too long on extolling the Emperor's virtues – and the image he presents – he risks usurping the Emperor's authority in the control of that image. This *recusatio*, which is essentially a disclaimer, is also a feature of Statius' other (unfinished) epic the *Achilleid*, where once again he apologises to the Emperor for the poem he is *not* writing):[14]

At tu, quem longe primum stupet Itala uirtus
Graiaque, cui geminae florent uatumque ducumque 15
certatim laurus – olim dolet altera uinci–,
da ueniam ac trepidum patere hoc sudare parumper
puluere: te longo necdum fidente paratu
molimur magnusque tibi praeludit Achilles.

But you, the wonder of Italy's and Greece's manhood first by far, for whom the twin laurels of bards and captains flourish in rivalry (one of the twain is long since sad to be surpassed), give me good leave; suffer me in my eagerness to sweat awhile in this dust. On you I work in long and not yet confident preparing, and great Achilles is your prelude.

Here Statius alludes not only to an Emperor who was a warrior and a poet (in his youth) but also hints at the way in which Domitian was beginning to cast himself as Emperor – not only a leader for Rome, but also for Greece, as illustrated by his addition of the *Capitolia*, games in honour of Jupiter, held every four years in Rome and which included a series of Greek *agones* (games), held in the stadium that he had built for the purpose. Later literary sources condemn Domitian for his over show of 'Greekness' in hosting these games, but their popularity is clear: unlike Nero's *Neronia*, Domitian's games survived beyond his lifetime. Moreover, Statius' praise for Domitian here implies an admiring audience that consisted of Italians and Greeks, alluding to the cosmopolitan image that Domitian was cultivating at home and across the empire.

Further reflections of Domitian's image as Emperor can be seen in the epic poem of Silius Italicus (c. 25-c.101) on the Second Punic War. These lines of praise do not feature in the proem to the epic, but in a prophesy by the god Jupiter concerning the future of Rome, in which Domitian is presented as the culmination to the Roman's future greatness (much as Virgil's *Aeneid* presents Augustus).[15]

quin et Romuleos superabit uoce nepotes
quis erit eloquio partum decus. huic sua Musae
sacra ferent, meliorque lyra, cui substitit Hebrus   620
et uenit Rhodope, Phoebo miranda loquetur.
ille etiam, qua prisca, uides, stat regia nobis,
aurea Tarpeia ponet Capitolia rupe
et iunget nostro templorum culmina caelo.
tunc, o nate deum diuosque dature, beatas   625
imperio terras patrio rege. tarda senectam
hospitia excipient caeli, solioque Quirinus
concedet, mediumque parens fraterque locabunt:
siderei iuxta radiabunt tempora nati.'

In addition, he will surpass with his voice all descendants of Romulus talented in eloquence. To him the Muses will bring their sacred gifts: he will be better in music than him who made Hebrus stop and Rhodope come to him; he will sing more wonderfully than Phoebus. He will build a golden Capitol on the Tarpeian rock, where, you see, our old plane stands, and he will join the top of my temple to the sky. Then, son of gods and father of gods to be, rule the lands blessed with paternal sway. The house of heaven will receive you in old age and Quirinus will yield his throne to you, as your father and brother place you in their midst: and the temple of your starry son will gleam next to you.

---

14   *Achilleid* 1.14-19.

15   Silius *Pun.* 3.618-629. Translation by Augoustakis & Buckley in this volume, p. 161. Cf. *Aen.*6.791-795 and *Aen.*8.678-679.

By having Jupiter foretell Domitian's future godhood, Silius gives divine backing to the Emperor's image as a god-in-waiting. Moreover, this prophesy serves as a reminder to the reader of the close relationship that Domitian cultivated with Jupiter, which is then affirmed by the reference to the golden temple that the Emperor will build on the Capitol. The contrast that Jupiter draws between his 'present' (the second Punic War) and the 'future' of Rome under Domitian allows Silius to suggest that the Emperor's rule was pre-ordained. It also allows him to draw a direct line between the ancient, physical, city of Rome and the city as it now appears under the Flavians, with the temple that Domitian will build marked as the successor to Jupiter's 'ancient palace' (*prisca...regia*). The Flavians were a new imperial family for Rome, but such texts as these, which incorporate Domitian into the Rome's history, create an image of the Emperor as the legitimate successor to the city's past.

Also, by stressing Domitian's status as master builder, Silius presents him as a successor to Augustus, and in a manner that clearly echoes Virgil's Augustan epic. In the *Aeneid*, Virgil similarly draws a comparison between the 'Rome' of Aeneas' day and the golden buildings of the Capitol that Augustus will institute:[16]

hinc ad Tarpeiam sedem et Capitolia ducit
aurea nunc, olim siluestribus horrida dumis

from here [Evander] leads him to the Tarpeian dwelling and Capitol, now golden, once thick with woody thickets.

The contrast is not just between past and present here, but in the type of landscape Rome enjoys: in the past these hills were rough and untamed, in the Augustan present they are 'golden'. It is a contrast subtly implied by Silius' text too, with the word for 'ancient' (palace), *prisca*, also suggestive of something primitive: Domitian, like Augustus before him, has made Rome better than it was...

In the *Aeneid*, it is the poet who makes the comparison between past and present; Silius, in having his Jupiter echo Virgil's words raises the stakes by having the god himself celebrate the changes wrought to his earthly seat. A further parallel with Augustus is also suggested by the reference to Domitian as a second Quirinus, the divine identity of Rome's legendary founder, Romulus. Like Augustus before him, therefore, Domitian is heralded as another founder for Rome and more than this, one who emulates Romulus in his path to divinity. The reference to Quirinus may even be suggestive of Domitian's birthplace on the Quirinal hill, and where he had established a temple to the Flavian *gens*, an apt association in a passage which states that Domitian will follow his father and brother in ascending to the stars. The image is not straightforward praise, however. Whilst Silius suggests a scene of familial harmony, the association with Quirinus is also a reminder of that god's earthly identity as Romulus, the legendary founder of Rome who killed his twin brother Remus in an argument over the city's walls. This fratricidal conflict is often cited in Roman imperial literature as one of the causes for Rome's propensity for civil war. It is not too great a leap, therefore, for the educated reader to see in this positive image a hint also of the civil war that brought the Flavians to power, and perhaps also a hint of the rumoured conflict between Titus and Domitian over the succession to Vespasian.[17] In the above passage, Silius says that Domitian will be placed in heaven *between* (*medium*, 3.628) his father and brother, implying his superiority to them both.

Conclusion

The greatest surviving body of epic works from the first century of Rome's principate come from Domitian's reign, but the literary output of this period was far greater. Beyond the epics, we have the epigrams of Martial, the rhetorical works of Quintilian, the *Natural Histories* of Pliny the Elder, and the *Stratagems* of Frontinus, among others. Much of this material alludes to Domitian and his world directly or indirectly, offering a contemporary snapshot of the Flavian era. When thinking about the image of Domitian in literature, however, perhaps the most important 'take-home' fact is this: although later writers invariably portray Domitian in a negative light, some of these same authors – notably Pliny the Younger and Tacitus – owe their political careers in no small part to him. Their eagerness to compare the present times they were enjoying as writers under Nerva and Trajan with the supposedly dark days of Domitian masks their own complicity in his reign. Were they truly suppressed under Domitian? May be. But what matters for the discussion here is the Emperor that they and other writers present. Essentially, these representations fall into two categories: Domitian before and after his assassination. As the other papers in this volume show, careful consideration is needed with both of these versions of the Emperor, but we need not struggle

---

16   Verg. *Aen.* 8.347-348.

17   The stories about the tension between the brothers Titus and Domitian, who were ten years apart in age, occur in later sources (e.g. Suet. *Titus* 9.3 and *Dom.* 2.3), but the imperial imagery prevalent during the Flavians' reign is one of fraternal harmony, with Titus and Domitian, like the Julio-Claudian fraternal pairings before them, compared to mythic twins Castor and Pollux. On this see especially Stocks 2018, 267-269.

to determine which is more truthful than the other, because truth is not the issue. The *image* of the Emperor – how he is presented and how he was perceived is what matters. Viewed in this light, the literary sources at our disposal offer an entire spectrum of different 'Domitians', each one competing for our attention. Viewing these representations simultaneously, rather than separately, allows us to view Domitian's reign and its memory holistically, offering many different pieces for the bigger puzzle of how we interpret this Emperor and his legacy.

Imperial Women and the Dynamics of Power. Managing the Soft Power of Domitia Longina and Julia Titi

Lien Foubert

The imperial *domus* was a crowded meeting-place. It was the residence of the emperor, many of his relatives, their slaves and members of staff. They interacted on a daily basis with members of the equestrian and senatorial elites.[1] The relationships between all these people were based on balances of power: each individual consciously or unconsciously strove to strengthen his or her position vis-à-vis others so as to optimize his or her quality of life. The more bargaining power one had, the stronger one's position in the relationship. Rank, friendship, social networks, property, dynastic role, personality, access to the emperor were among the many factors that continuously influenced these balances of power. When one of these factors changed, the relationship needed to be renegotiated. Women took part in these dynamics. The so-called peacock coins that were issued by the Domitian court in 88, figuring his wife Domitia Longina and his niece Julia Titi, illustrate how the emperor tried to control these mechanisms of power (figs. 1-2).[2]

A Court with Two *Augustae*

When Domitian accessed the throne in 81, the stage of the imperial *domus* already contained one *Augusta*. Flavia Julia, referred to by modern historians as Julia Titi (daughter of Titus) to distinguish her from other Julias, was awarded the title of *Augusta* around 79. She must have been between fifteen and eighteen years old and was the sole living offspring of the then reigning Emperor Titus. Domitian, brother and heir to the throne, had not yet conceived a child who survived the precarious early years of childhood. It must have been clear to Roman society that the conferral of the title *Augusta* marked Julia as an essential agent in the continuity of the *domus Augusta*, the imperial household.[3] She appeared in official documents as *Iulia Augusta*, the same official name

---

1. Acton 2011.
2. *RIC* II² *Domitian* nos. 678-684.
3. During the Julio-Claudian period, *Augustae* had either been matriarchs of the imperial family or mothers to imperial heirs. See esp. Flory 1998.

borne by Livia, Augustus' wife, a coincidence that would hardly have escaped the attention of their social peers.

Julia's bargaining power, however, drastically changed when her father suddenly died and her uncle accessed the throne. Domitian had been married for eleven years to Domitia Longina, daughter to the popular and successful general Gnaeus Domitius Corbulo who was forced to commit suicide by the emperor Nero.[4] Her father's fate and his popularity with the Roman people would have added to Domitia's prestige and aura. It has also been argued that Domitia may very well have been a direct descendant of Augustus, giving her the most prestigious lineage thinkable.[5] When her husband accessed the throne, Domitia, who was in her early thirties, was awarded the title of *Augusta*. In theory, this equalled Domitia to the other *Augusta*, Julia Titi, as both were now marked as essential to the welfare of the dynasty. As the wife of the reigning emperor, however, Domitia would have had easier access to the emperor's ear. On the other hand, Julia was younger and, hence, her chances to secure heirs to the throne larger. Since Domitian deified his brother, Julia could also call herself daughter of the divine Titus. In short, those who interacted with these women – including the emperor himself – needed to reassess their relationships, as all of these factors could have impacted on their own social position. The presence or absence of a mutual understanding or friendship between Domitia and Julia, moreover, could have facilitated or complicated the courtiers' decision as to whom they owed their loyalty.

Unfortunately, reconstructing the nature of the relationship between the two *Augustae* is impossible. The post-Domitianic literary tradition created the portrait of a cruel and excessive tyrant, to which the characterizations of Domitia and Julia needed to contribute. According to that literary tradition, Domitian had seduced his niece, both when Titus was alive and afterwards. When she became pregnant with his child, he compelled her to commit an abortion which resulted in her death in the last months of 89.[6] The ancient writers claim that Domitia was an adulterous woman, who fell in love with Domitian when she was still married to another. But even after their union, rumour had it that she had an affair with Titus and later with the well-known pantomime actor Paris. The latter love affair supposedly resulted in Domitian divorcing her, but because the Roman people demanded her return, so the sources tell us, he took her back and reinstalled her as empress of Rome.[7] Scholars have tried to entangle both women's portraits from the ancient

writers' anti-Domitianic bias. Though it remains possible that Julia died due to complications of pregnancy, it has been convincingly argued that Domitian was nowhere near Julia to father a child nor to force her to abort the foetus. And as to Domitian's relationship with Julia and his divorce from Domitia, it has been pointed out that dynastic motives might have been behind these decisions, for it is not unreasonable to think that Domitian sought to rearrange his marital status in the hope to secure an heir to the throne.[8]

To what extent these stories were based on truth remains impossible to tell. It is also not clear whether these rumours already circulated in Roman society during Titus' and Domitian's reigns or whether they were invented afterwards because they fitted the image of Domitian. At the very least, we can say that in the minds of the ancient writers – and presumably in the minds of their respective audiences as well – it was conceived plausible that the presence of two *Augustae*, especially when it was debatable which one of them should (and could) provide an heir to the throne, could cause anxiety due to shifting allegiances and conflicting ambitions of everyone involved. Their public appearance on Domitian's imperial coinage seems to tap into such dynamics of power.

The Peacock Coins of Julia Titi and Domitia Longina

Around 88, after his reconciliation with his wife and before Julia's death, Domitian issued *aurei* to honour both Domitia Longina and Julia Titi. Considering the denomination, the main target audience of these coins must have been the Roman aristocracy, *i.e.* the elites who tried to come to terms with the changes in the bargaining power of these women. In many ways, Domitia and Julia are presented as equals. Their dress and hairdo is very much alike and both of them are identified as *Augusta*. The legend identifies Julia with a simple 'Iulia Augusta' (fig. 1), while Domitia is identified with a lengthy 'Domitia Augusta, wife of Imperator Domitianus Augustus Germanicus' (fig. 2; see also fig. 3). The reverses of both their coins contain an image of a peacock, the symbolic bird of Juno, the goddess of birth. Julia's coins bear the reverse inscription 'daughter of Divus Titus', while Domitia's coins read *concordia Augusta* ('imperial harmony') which may be intended to emphasize the restored connection between the emperor and his wife. The poses of the birds set them apart: Julia's is faced frontal with the train spread, while Domitia's appears in profile with the train folded.[9]

---

4   Levick 2002.
5   Chausson 2003.
6   Suet. *Dom.* 22, Plin. *Ep.* 4.11.6-7, Juv. 2.29-33.
7   Suet. *Tit.* 10.2, *Dom.* 3.2 and 10.1, Dio Cass. 65.3.4 and 67.3.1-2, Aur. Vict. *Caes.* 11.11.
8   Vinson 1989, Wood 2010.
9   *BMCRE* 2.250 and 2.350. Wood 2010, Wood 2016.

Fig. 1. *Aureus* of Julia Titi, daughter of Titus and niece of Domitian, 88-89 (?). London, British Museum, inv. 1864,1128.45 (courtesy The Trustees of the British Museum).

Fig. 2. *Aureus* of Domitia Longina, wife of Domitian, 88-89. London, British Museum, inv. 1864,1128.50 (courtesy The Trustees of the British Museum).

Domitian's choice to issue coins to honour both women at the same time in an almost identical way at a moment when he had just reconciled with his wife is a peculiar one. After all, there can only be *one* empress, so why not just emphasize the return of the marital bliss in the imperial household? The emperor's strategic manoeuvre can be explained when one takes the age difference between the women into account. It could not be excluded that Domitia would still produce an heir. If not, there was always the possibility for Domitian to adopt one of Julia's potential children, if she were to remarry

and become a mother. A hypothetical untimely death of Domitia would also leave open the way for Domitian to marry his niece, which was not considered incestuous anymore since the Emperor Claudius had legalized this marital bond so that he could marry his niece Agrippina the Younger. There were enough scenarios to be conceived, in other words, that necessitated an almost equal social and public standing for the two *Augustae* in order to allow Domitian the largest possible elbow room to ensure dynastic continuity. Moreover, Domitian's balanced public treatment of the women made it more difficult for members of the elite to choose sides. The nature of Julia's and Domitia's respective bargaining power differed, which could potentially lead to party formation at the imperial court. These coins could be understood as an attempt by the emperor to control such dynamics of power. All of which proved to be of no avail as Julia must have died shortly after these coins were issued, leaving only one *Augusta* for the courtiers to come to terms with.

Fig. 3. Chalcedony cameo carved with an image of the empress Domitia Longina carried by a peacock. London, British Museum, inv. 1899,0722.4 (courtesy The Trustees of the British Museum).

PART IV

The World of Domitian

Living Like the Emperor: A Portrayal of Domitian in his Villas and on the Palatine

Aurora Raimondi Cominesi & Claire Stocks

Introduction

What does it mean to live like an emperor? The source material at our disposal paints a conflicting picture. Typically, those emperors who are remembered as good, such as Augustus, acquired a reputation for living a frugal lifestyle: men who lived to serve the state and who kept their personal affairs private. In contrast, those emperors who are remembered negatively, or who suffered memory sanctions after their deaths, such as Caligula, Nero, and Domitian, are portrayed as blurring the lines between the public and the private: conducting business behind closed doors, or living a decadent lifestyle. Suetonius, in his *Lives of the Caesars*, tells us that Nero, for example, turned Rome into his personal playground through the construction of his colossal Golden House (*Domus Aurea*) and committed the ultimate taboo for a member of the political elite, by performing on stage.[1]

The reality, in so far as we can determine what that was, is far more nuanced. As first citizen (*princeps*) of Rome, Augustus was not just a man of the people, he stood in *loco parentis*. In 2 BC he was given the title *pater patriae* ('father of his country'), making him simultaneously a 'father' for Rome and his own family; in the same year his daughter Julia was accused of adultery and her private indiscretion resulted in a very public punishment – exile to the small island of Pandataria (now Ventotene) off the Italian coast.[2] Augustus' promotion of new laws on morality, instigated in 18-17 BC, made him disinclined to listen to appeals for clemency and he, rather than the senate, appears to have decided Julia's punishment.[3]

Augustus' domestic woes, played out as they were on a public stage, illustrate the problem posed – even for a supposedly 'good' emperor – in negotiating the boundary between public and private life. Finding that balance remained a challenge for all of Rome's emperors in the first century, and it is a problem perhaps best exemplified by the

---

1   Suet. *Nero* 20.1.
2   See Suet. *Aug.* 65, Vell. Pat. 2.100.2-5, Dio Cass. 55.10.12-16, Sen. *Ben.* 6.32.1-2. The exact circumstances of this exile and whether adultery was the *real* reason for Julia's exile remain subject to debate. See, for example, Cohen 2008.
3   Tac. *Ann.*3.24, Sen. *Clem.*1.10.3.

Fig. 1. Palatine Hill, view of the triclinium of the Domus Flavia (so-called *Cenatio* Iovis) (akg-images / Eric Vandeville).

Fig 2. Reconstruction of the Domus Flavia on the Palatine (akg-images / Peter Connolly).

double-function of the imperial residence. The emperor's *domus* on the Palatine was the *locus* for imperial business and public banquets, but it was also the place where the emperor would eat and sleep when in Rome. Outside of the city, the imperial villa offered a retreat from the noise (and heat in summer) and an opportunity for the emperor to enjoy some down-time (*otium*, leisure), but here, too, emperors would conduct public business by taking the imperial court with them (the *consilium*), and – in the case of Domitian – even hold court cases there or public events such as the Alban games.

Domitian's Palaces and Villas

The Palatine, from which we derive the word 'Palace', is the area of Rome most closely associated with the emperor. Here, emperors from Augustus onwards had made their home, with each one adding to the imperial complex, beginning with Augustus' supposedly humble dwelling that was situated close to site where Romulus, Rome's legendary founder, was said to have had his house. By the time of the Flavians, the imperial Palace complex had incorporated the structures built by Tiberius, Claudius, and Nero and included most of the Palatine hill. Domitian was responsible for much of the new building work and, following a pattern set by Nero with respect to the *Domus Aurea*, he divided his new Palace complex into a public area (the *Domus Flavia*), a private residence (the *Domus Augustana*) and gardens, which was partially built over Augustus' former residence.[4] The public area of the *domus* was approached from the Forum, using the new *clivus* built by Domitian which probably started by the Arch of Titus and included two additional arches (one of Vespasian and one of Domitian himself) (see the relief from the Tomb of the Haterii, here Moormann, fig. 2). The poet Statius would likely have taken this route up to the public area of the *domus*, when he was invited to feast with the emperor in Domitian's elaborate dining room, the *Cenatio Iovis* ('dining room of Jupiter'), built over the rest of one of Nero's private, panoramic dining rooms (known today as the nymphaeum of the *Domus Transitoria*):[5]

Regia Sidoniae conuiuia laudat Elissae,
qui magnum Aenean Laurentibus intulit aruis;
Alcinoique dapes mansuro carmine monstrat,
aequore qui multo reducem consumpsit Vlixem:
ast ego, cui sacrae Caesar noua gaudia cenae   5
nunc primum dominaque dedit consurgere mensa,
qua celebrem mea uota lyra, quas soluere grates
sufficiam? non, si pariter mihi uertice laeto
nectat odoratas et Smyrna et Mantua lauros,

digna loquar. mediis videor discumbere in astris   10
cum Ioue et Iliaca porrectum sumere dextra
immortale merum.

He praises the regal banquet of Sidonian Elissa, he who brought great Aeneas to the Laurentine fields, and he who presents the feast of Alcinous with immortal song wore out Ulysses in his return over the vast tracts of sea. But I, to whom Caesar has granted for the first time the novel delights of his sacred dinner, and has given me the privilege of not rising at my master's table, with what lyre do I celebrate my devotion, what thanks can I find sufficient to express? Not if both Smyrna and Mantua were to wind scented laurels about my happy head should I utter something worthy. I seem to recline amid the stars together with Jupiter and to take the immortal wine offered by the Ilian hand.

Statius begins with a reference to the 'regal banquet' of the legendary Carthaginian Queen, Dido, but the word *regia* also means 'the house of a king' (*rex*), a word with potentially negative – and monarchical – connotations.[6] For a moment, therefore, Statius appears to be steering a risky course as he tricks his reader into thinking that he is calling Domitian's *domus* the residence of king. Yet despite these word games, Statius' poem stresses the honour he feels in dining with the Emperor 'among the stars'. It also highlights the double-function of the emperor as both a public and private figure: Domitian is there, visible, but aloof – presented as a Jupiter-like figure who remains at a distance. Later in this same poem, Statius makes reference to his victory in the Alban games, which were likewise presided over by Domitian.[7] These games, held almost annually in honour of Domitian's patron goddess Minerva, took place at another of Domitian's imperial residences, his villa at Albanum, known today as the Castel Gandolfo, the summer retreat of the Pope.

In addition to the villa in the Alban hills, there are at least five other private villas with possible links to Domitian: at Tusculum, Antium, Caieta (Gaeta), Circeo (at Circeii), Anxur (Terracina) and Baiae. To this we should add those properties which were part of the imperial inheritance, the family house on the Monti Sabini and the numerous private properties of Domitia Longina, Domitian's wife, who inherited them from her father. Only the one at Circeii has been identified with certainty, and its remains can be visited (with difficulty) in a nature reserve by the Lago di Paola to the North of Naples. From the excavations that have taken place there, we know that there was a bath complex, probably dating to the late

---

4   Zanker (2002) 107. See also Natasja Sojc in this volume.
5   Stat. *Silv.* 4.2.1-12. Translation adapted from Newlands (2002), 278.

6   See Newlands, 2002, 265.
7   Stat. *Silv.* 4.2.64-67.

1st century, with the rest of the villa dating from the late 1st to early 2nd century. These excavations also uncovered the remains of high-quality sculptures, indicating that this was an elite residence, although these are difficult to date. There is also a large villa at Antium, which has yet to be explored fully, but the dating for this is controversial (with remains there attributed both to Hadrian and Domitian). Whilst the vestiges of a large number of villas have been discovered at the popular bathing resort of Baiae, there is no evidence at the moment to attribute any of these to Domitian, and nothing at all has been found at the other sites.

Where the archaeological remains are lacking, we rely predominantly on the literary material. For the villa at Baiae, we have a reference in Martial's *Epigram* 4.30, telling us that Domitian had tame, 'sacred', fish (*sacribus piscibus*, 4.30.3) at his villa that would lick their master's (*dominus*, 4.30.4) imperial hand, suggesting the Emperor's mastery over nature, a recurrent theme in the works of Flavian poets and also a recurrent theme in works on the Roman country villa and its environs. It is Martial again who mentions the villas at Anxur (with its health-giving waters, *salutiferis candidus Anxur aquis*) and Circeo,[8] but for the latter we also have an inscription from Spain dating to 91, the *Lex Irnitana*, which concludes with the statement that it has been dictated by Domitian 'at Circei', indicating that Domitian also conducted official business at this villa as he did at his Alban villa and in Rome.[9] This tendency of Domitian to use his private villas outside of Rome as places of business, instead of merely exploiting them for *otium*, shows once again the increasing difficulty, for Roman emperors, to draw a clear line between private and public affairs. As with Tiberius' official 'retirement' in his villa on the island of Capri, from where he conducted all his imperial duties, Domitian's use of his villas was not always viewed favourably.

Living Like an Emperor: Domitian and His Alban Villa

Of all Domitian's villas, it is his Alban retreat that has attracted the most attention, not only because of the extensive archaeological remains and multiple literary references, but because this was the location that served as a focal point for much of the condemnation of Domitian's reign after his assassination. Presented as the *Albana arx* ('Alban citadel') by Tacitus, with the word *arx* used here to refer to a tyrant's citadel,[10] this villa was remembered by writers after Domitian's death as the site of executions behind closed doors, kangaroo courts,[11] and the home of an Emperor who suffered from increasing bouts of paranoia. But it was also the scene of public events and parties, notably the Alban games, celebrated by Statius among others during Domitian's lifetime. The villa *Albanum*, therefore, offers a fascinating insight into the life of an Emperor who was praised for his generosity during his lifetime and condemned for his brutality after death.

Domitian's association with the Alban Hills began at an early age and it is likely that he used the villa of Pompey at Albanum prior to building his own. Cassius Dio writes that he went there in his youth because he was afraid of his father's disfavour (65.3.4), and spent time there – as a true despot-in-the-making would – stabbing flies with his stylus (65.9.42). Even if Domitian *did* spend a large amount of time at this villa during the early part of Vespasian's reign, he was hardly a recluse: numismatic evidence from the 70s indicates that he held six consulships (five as suffet) during this time, demonstrating that even if he was a junior partner in the Flavian dynasty, he was still visibly present in Rome. Tacitus infers that he had taken up residence on the Palatine, for a brief period of time over the years 69-70, having been given 'the seat and the name of Caesar'.[12] In 70, we see him moving back to his family house on the Quirinal, where he was born ('at the Pomegranate', *ad malum Punicum*,) (Suet. *Dom.* 1.1) and an area which he would later turn into a public monument (a temple) to the Flavian gens, just as Augustus had monumentalized his birthplace by building the Meta Sudans.[13] With the death of Titus, Domitian established himself once more on the Palatine.

The remains of the villa itself are sparse, but based upon what was left of a staircase, Giuseppe Lugli, the first scholar to study the villa in-depth, concluded that it was built over three stories and faced west toward the sea and Ostia.[14] We can be reasonably certain that there were three *atria* and a bath complex, and lead pipes have been found bearing Domitian's name. Lugli also found the remains of a path, leading out from the villa, with four nymphaea en route with trace remains of statues. This pathway ended in an open space that contained a theatre cut partly into the hill, and which was most likely the location for the recitations and other events that marked the Alban Games. Much work has been done by F. Magi (1968-1976) and H.

---

8   Mart. *Ep.* 5.1.6 and 11.7.3-4.

9   On the *Lex Irnitana* see González/Crawford 1986, and on the 'goodbye' message from Domitian at the end of this legislation see Mourgues 1987.

10   Tac. *Agr.*45.1. For the specific meaning of *arx*, see *OLD* s.v. arx, 1c.

11   Pliny (*Ep.* 4.11.6) talks about Domitian using the Alban villa to conduct the trail of the Vestal virgin. See Jones (1992), 28.

12   Tac. *Hist.* 4.2. See Darwall-Smith 1994, 148.

13   Suet. *Dom.* 1.1 and 2.1. See Eric Moormann in this volume.

14   Scholars today still rely heavily on the surveys published by Lugli from 1913 through to 1920: Lugli 1912, 1914a-b, 1917, 1918, 1919a-b, 1920. In more recent years, excavations at the villa were taken up by Henner von Hesberg, see in particular von Hesberg 1978-1980, 1981, 2005, 2006, 2009. See additionally Darwall-Smith 1994 for a comprehensive summary of the excavation work that had taken place at the Alban Villa up to that moment.

von Hesberg (1978-1980) among others in reconstructing the space and its decoration, which we know included a frieze of animals with floral motifs as well as another nymphaeum nearby with a frieze of Venus, Cupids, and Priapi.[15] Extant fragments from a passageway at the back of the theatre depict the Muses and mythological scenes. Brickstamps found in this location appear to be Domitianic.

The type of imagery displayed in these public areas of Domitian's villa is reflective of artistic styles of the time, but also of a desire by emperors – and Rome's elite in general – to surround themselves with scenes, and heroes, from myth, especially the Trojan cycle. This popularity is reinforced by Roman authors from the late republic onwards who, like Statius at the start of *Silvae* 4.2 (above), frequently make use of imagery associated with heroes such as Aeneas and Odysseus (also known as Ulysses). In the main villa complex, there were images associated with Aeneas as well as Venus,[16] and down by the lake there was a cave, which Domitian had turned into a grotto (the so-called 'Ninfeo Bergantino'), where the torso of Polyphemus was located. Studies of this grotto have revealed niches in the walls (probably for statues), a circular pool and an island in the centre. There were mosaics around the edge, copies of which were recorded during the excavations of 1841, displaying mostly marine subjects, including a Medusa, a quadriga, Tritons and Nereids.[17] The remains of other statues and imagery indicate that the decoration of this grotto was firmly linked to the myth of Odysseus and his travels back to his home on Ithaca after the Trojan war.

The use of such imagery in a nymphaeum by the coast was far from unique, and we have several other examples from coastal villas showing the popularity of Odysseus and Polyphemus as the subject matter for these grottos, which also functioned as dining rooms.[18] The grotto at Albanum, however, appears to have had a specific model, namely the grotto at Sperlonga which is almost identical in layout. Sculptures found here from the excavation in 1950 also show scenes from Odysseus' journey including another Polyphemus, a Scylla, the capture of the Palladium with Diomedes, and Odysseus carrying back the body of Achilles. This association is particularly apt, because the cave at Sperlonga has strong connections to the Emperor Tiberius and may in fact be the same cave/grotto mentioned by Tacitus at 'Spelunca'.[19] We have other evidence to suggest that Domitian, in his role as master builder, sought to emulate Tiberius, including possibly naming the *Domus Tiberiana* on the Palatine in his honour.[20] Certainly Tiberius set a precedent for the imperial villa complex, with his building work on Capraea (Capri) consisting of 12 villas according to Tacitus including the famed *villa Iovis* ('villa of Jupiter') and a series of gardens, grottos, and nymphaea.[21] Similarly, both Tiberius and Domitian would be remembered as reclusive emperors who spent too much time in *otium* at their villas.

Literary references to Domitian's Alban villa paint a colourful picture of an Emperor enjoying his time away from Rome in a mixture of business and pleasure pursuits. The Alban games feature prominently, with the poet Statius – in addition to *Silvae* 4.2 – describing how he won the poetry competition there and received a gold wreath from the Emperor himself.[22] These games are also described by Cassius Dio, who tells us that the competitions consisted of grand contests for poets, orators, and gladiators; Suetonius tells us that Domitian celebrated these Quinquatria at his Alban estate every year in honour of Minerva (*celebrabat et in Albano quotannis Quinquatria Minervae*).[23] In addition, Dio refers to youth games that took place at the villa and describes a particular incident during one festival of youth (*Iuvenalia*) where the consul Glabrio, as a result of Domitian's jealousy of the man's fighting prowess, was summoned to the Alban estate and required to dispatch a lion in the arena, which he duly did.[24] This was not enough to save him; he was later executed, in part on the charge of fighting as a gladiator with wild beasts. Juvenal too, in a *Satire* that parodies Domitian dragging the imperial court with him to Alba, also refers to wild beast hunts that took place in the theatre/arena.[25]

According to the biographer Suetonius, Domitian was not averse to hunting himself when at his Alban estate, and whilst the author is rather disparaging of the Emperor's lack of interest in 'real' weapons (*arma*), he depicts him as being adept with a bow, killing 100 wild beasts of different sorts and with such precision that he could shoot two arrows into their heads to give the impression of horns. In similarly disparaging tones, Pliny – whilst praising the Emperor Trajan – notes that Domitian was no sea man and was afraid even of the sound of oars when taking a boat out on the Lake Nemi at Alba.[26]

---

15 Magi 1968-1969, 1973-1974, 1976, von Hesberg 1978-1980 and 1981. See Claudia Valeri in this volume.
16 See Neudecker 2015, 396.
17 On the details of this grotto see also Darwall-Smith 1994.
18 Neudecker 2015, 394-395, writes that by using such imagery the diners (or 'symposiasts') "were not only transported into a mythological world, but were reminded of the negative consequences of overindulging at the same time, given that Polyphemus was ultimately blinded in his drunkenness."
19 Tac. *Ann.*4.59.

20 Darwall-Smith 1994, 156.
21 Tac. *Ann.* 4.67.
22 Stat. *Silv.* 3.5.28-31.
23 Dio Cass. 67.1.2, Suet. *Dom.* 4.
24 Dio Cass. 67.14.3.
25 Juv. 4.99-101.
26 Suet. *Dom.* 19, Plin. *Pan.* 82.

Conclusion: Public vs. Private in Elite Villas

Domitian's imperial complex on the Palatine, as well as his villa at Alba, with their public and private areas illustrate the problem posed to emperors who wished to enjoy their *otium*, whilst also maintaining their position as first citizen. Enjoying leisure time was not a problem in itself, in fact it was a celebrated part of Rome's elite culture and even the great Augustus enjoyed time away from Rome. References to elite villas, for example, are frequent in literary works of the time, including the letters of Pliny, in which he describes in detail the decorations and delights of the Roman villa and Statius' *Silvae*, which praises the peaceful setting of Manilius Vopiscus' home from home.[27] Elite villa culture was also enjoyed by those citizens who spent very little, if any, time in Rome, such as Pollius Felix who was from the Campanian region.[28] Statius describes a welcome visit to Felix's villa on the coast, noting the building's connection with nature (in some rooms showing mastery over the natural world, in others allowing natural forces – such as the noise of the sea – to come inside), and referring to Pollius Felix as the 'master' of this dwelling, using the same word, *dominus*, used elsewhere of Domitian.[29] All these examples show that the celebration and enjoyment of villa life was not limited to the Emperor.

Yet time spent enjoying the pleasures of one's villa is frequently used as a means of condemning supposedly 'bad' emperors after their deaths, illustrating that the problem was not pleasure in itself, but the perceived excess of that pleasure. Tiberius was remembered as being too much of a recluse, Domitian was remembered for worse; it was not the time that he spent at his Alban retreat, his Alban *arx* (see above), that was the problem, but what he allegedly did there: passing judgement on the very elite who shared in that same culture of *otium*. How Domitian utilised his public and private space – how he lived as emperor – has attracted so much attention because, as was the case with the emperors before and after him, it was used as a tool by Rome's authors for assessing his memory. Thus, whilst the design and content of his Alban villa appear to differ very little from that of those enjoyed by his successors, notably Hadrian's large villa at Tivoli, that villa became a symbol for the hatred attached to Domitian and his memory after death.[30] Proof for these authors, if proof were needed, that Domitian had abused the delicate balance between the public and private worlds of the imperial residence. An abuse that his successors promptly used for their own propaganda, because as they pour their condemnation on Domitian's *arx* in the countryside, they also made sure to advertise the positive transformation of his *arx inaccessa* on the Palatine into a communal space.[31] After all, i.e. as is written by the poet Kaveh Akbar, 'There are no good kings. / Only beautiful palaces' – and these are always worth reusing and innovating by the next ruler.

---

27   Plin. *Ep.* 2.17 and 5.6, Stat. *Silv.*1.3.
28   See Newlands 2002, 154.
29   Stat. *Silv.* 2.2, esp. 2.2.45.
30   Darwall-Smith (1996), 161, shows the importance of memory, and how it was applied to Domitian's imperial residences, when suggesting a reason for why the Alban villa was loathed by posterity, but Domitian's buildings on the Palatine persisted without comment: "There was, however, a crucial difference. Nerva and Trajan had to use his buildings in Rome: the Palatine had become the official imperial residence, and Trajan certainly moved in there. The Alban Villa was more disposable: no emperor need use it again. Therefore it became, so to speak, the architectural scapegoat for Domitian. It was no House of Horror, but simply unlucky in its association with its creator."
31   Pliny *Pan.* 48-49.

Between Magnificence and Misery: Living Conditions in Metropolitan Rome

Nathalie de Haan

Rome Rises from its Ashes

Reading the poetry of Martial and Statius, we are told that Rome regained its grandeur as Capital of the world, thanks to the large scale building activities under Domitian. Martial compares Rome to a phoenix rising from its ashes.[1] The ashes should be taken literally here, since the fire of 80 created the need for Domitian to rebuild a number of public buildings, right after his accession to the throne. The devastating fire provided him with the space to rebuild part of Rome's centre on a grand scale, adorning the city's public spaces with lavishly decorated buildings in full pomp and splendour. But poets like Martial confront their readership with the less attractive aspects of living in first-century Rome as well: poor and expensive housing, vermin and diseases, criminality, floods and fires were the kind of problems that any 'ordinary Roman' had to face. The satirical works of Martial and Juvenal have often been dismissed as exaggerated, and we should keep in mind that their remarks do not necessarily reflect the hardship of *every* Roman who was not a member of the senatorial elite or the imperial court. But we should also remember that whilst the satirical aspects of Martial's and Juvenal's poetry often centre on the exaggerated suggestion that a poet's life in Rome was one of hardship, this does not mean that such hardships did not exist. Careful use of these and other written sources as well as material remains show both the magnificence and misery, the splendour and squalor of the immense Capital that was Rome under Domitian.

In Augustus' Footsteps: Imperial *Munificentia* and *Magnificentia*

"...So now has a new Rome thrown off her ancient length of days and taken the countenance of her ruler" wrote Martial in his fifth book of epigrams in the late 80s.[2] The grand scale restoration and building projects under Domitian were changing Rome's cityscape dramatically in those years.[3] The regained grandeur of the Capital, after disastrous fires in 64 and 80, reflected the long term ambitions and self-confidence of the Flavian dynasty

---

1   Mart.5.7.1-2: *Qualiter Assyrios renovant incendia nidos / una decem quotiens saecula vixit avis.*

2   Mart. 5.7.3-4: *taliter exuta est veterem nova Roma senectam / et sumpsit vultus praesidis ipsa sui.*

3   See the contribution of Eric Moormann in this volume.

Fig. 1. Marble tomb relief, early second century, depicting a crane on the left for the construction of the Haterii family tomb, shown in the centre. The Haterii brothers were contractors, active during the Flavian period. Vatican Museums, Museo Gregoriano Profano ex Lateranense, inv. 9998 (courtesy Governorato SCV – Direzione dei Musei, all rights reserved).

in their own days, and the material remains still visible today are the tangible legacy of a crucial period of the Principate. Crucial, because Flavian rule was successful in implementing a number of administrative, monetary and military reforms that had a major impact upon successive dynasties, whilst being safely anchored to the government of Rome's first Emperor. As many scholars have observed, Flavian building projects emulated those of Augustus in scale, splendour and refinement. In sharp contrast to Nero, and following the example of Augustus, all three Flavian Emperors invested in the magnificence of Rome's public space and in amenities for the people, rather than for the emperor himself, as Martial's famous line "Rome restored to herself" reminds us.[4] This was at least part of the rhetoric that accompanied the Flavian restorations and rebuilding of parts of Rome. Moreover, Martial's remark offers a glimpse into Roman mentality of the first century in terms of what an emperor's subjects apparently expected him to provide. Yet despite classing Domitian as a 'good' emperor *because* of the public amenities he constructed, Martial still manages to condemn Domitian's predecessor Nero in spite of his ability to provide outstanding public baths: "What was worse than Nero – but what is better than his baths?!"[5] Even 'bad' rulers, it would seem, could (sometimes) meet the expectations of the people.

Few emperors built on a larger scale than Domitian did during the fifteen years of his reign.[6] As a consequence, the centre of Rome still bears the imprint of the buildings that were restored, completed or initiated under the last Flavian. The lengthy list of buildings he commissioned or restored in Rome after the fire of 80 was recorded in later ancient and medieval sources, despite Domitian's bad reputation after his death.[7] Some of these buildings were intended to demonstrate his loyalty towards the gods and his family, for example those commemorating the *gens Flavia* which included the temple dedicated to the deified Vespasian and Titus. On the Capitoline Domitian rebuilt the temple of Jupiter Capitolinus that had recently been restored after the fire of 69 but suffered from conflagration again in 80. The importance of this key project can be read from the fact that the new temple, lavishly decorated, was dedicated as early as 82. As *pontifex maximus*, the responsibility for Rome's most important sanctuary rested on Domitian's shoulders. Moreover, both Jupiter and the site of the Capitoline Hill had a special meaning for Domitian, who had safely escaped from there during the Vitellian siege in 69.

The adornment of Rome's public space was one of the expectations any emperor had to meet. This is the essence of Martial's famous lines on Rome under the Flavians: "Rome has been restored to herself, and under your rule, Caesar, the pleasures that belonged to a master now belong to the people."[8] Public buildings included those for government and administration, such as the Curia, the completion of the baths of Titus and buildings for leisure and entertainment (the Stadium and Odeum, and, of course, the completion of the Colosseum). Moreover, the food supply was facilitated by Domitianic (re)buildings such as the Horrea piperataria and the Porticus Minucia Vetus.

His palace, designed by architect Rabirius and built between 81 and 92, was of enormous dimensions. It occupied most of the Palatine and was lavishly decorated with coloured marbles.[9] This was far removed from Augustus 'modest house' on the Palatine, a residence that was in part built over by Domitian's palace. Here lies one of the keys to understanding at least part of Domitian's post-mortem black reputation: his palace was regarded as an expression of *privata luxuria*.

Building projects required manpower and thus they must have created job possibilities. The employment of *opus caementicium*, a building technique that reached its perfection in the Flavian age, required a large amount of unskilled labour. The transport of all the material to building sites was a huge logistical operation and it would have needed a lot of animals, manpower and planning to get the right amounts of building materials (stones, sand, lime, wood, brick and tile, travertine and marble, and paint) to the right spot at the right time. Porters and assistants were needed for the bricklayers working high up on the scaffolding. Moreover, manpower was needed to operate cranes (fig. 1). A telling anecdote can be found in Suetonius' *vita* of Vespasian. A mechanical engineer, who presented his invention to the Emperor for the transport of big columns up to the Capitol was rewarded but sent away with Vespasian's statement that he needed the chance to employ ("feed") the common people.[10]

Only the woodworkers who created the timber frames for concrete vaults and cupolas were highly skilled workmen, as were experienced contractors and architects. In any case, major building projects meant work for many people, a blessing for the many who worked as day-labourers and depended on daily wages. But there was a downside as well. First of all, the noise caused by the ongoing building projects must have been at times unbearable. Moreover, the continuous supply of building

---

4   Mart. *Spect.* 1.2.11-12: *reddita Roma sibi est et sunt te praeside, Caesar, / deliciae populi, quae fuerant domini.*

5   Mart. 7.34.4-5: *Quid Nerone peius? Quid thermis melius Neronianis?*

6   For the buildings commissioned or finished under Domitian see Blake 1959, 99-124 and Darwall Smith 1996, 101-252. Cf. Frederick 2003.

7   E.g. Chronographer of AD 354, Jer. *Chron.* (*Ab Abr.*) AD 85-90 (216th and 217th Olympiad).

8   Mart. *Spect.* 1.2.11-12. See quotation in note 4.

9   See the contributions by Claire Stocks & Aurora Raimondi Cominesi and Natascha Sojc in this volume.

10   Suet. *Vesp.* 18.

materials, day and night, must have kept many from sleep. The amount of material needed was enormous, and only a steady supply ensured the swift progress of the building activities during daylight. A remark in Martial is revealing here: "(...) and I am scarcely able to break through the long trains of mules and the marble blocks you see hauled by many a rope."[11] The lines were written in the late 80s, when building activities were booming. We do not read about accidents during building activities, but risks were certainly involved. Compared to modern grand scale projects around the globe today, we could expect that there would have been a number of injured – some fatally – people per project. Records are missing here, also due to the fact that at least part of the heaviest and most dangerous work was done by prisoners of war and other persons who received little to no attention in the sources.

Dangers, Diseases and Death

No matter how magnificent public spaces in Rome could look, the living conditions for many of its inhabitants were quite miserable. Rome was a shiny metropolis in the praise of many an author, but a sordid city behind that façade.[12] Smaller backstreets were dirty and muddy if unpaved, as was the case with many smaller streets that had no sidewalks.[13] Complaints about mud and filth in the streets can be found in Martial and Juvenal.[14] Seneca mocks dainty people who demand spotless silver plate, polished coloured marbles and expensive woodwork in their homes, but have no problems at all outside "when facing filthy and muddy backstreets, where the majority of passers-by is dressed in dirty clothes and the subsiding walls of apartment buildings show damage and cracks."[15] Dumping trash on the streets was the order of the day. Roman law provides

us with a series of stipulations connected to prohibitions on throwing litter or objects out of the windows onto the street, in order to protect pedestrians walking below.[16] These prohibitions, repeated time and again, indicate that such behaviour was clearly a problem. Vespasian seems to have been blamed by Caligula for failing to fulfil one of his responsibilities as *aedilis*, namely the sweeping of the streets (*cura verrendis viis*).[17] Since the time of Caesar the *aediles* in Rome were assisted by *quattuorviri viis in urbe purgandis* (or *quattuorviri viarum curandarum*), who were responsible for taking care of the streets within the city walls. The office of *quattuorvir* was normally held by a young senator as the first step in the *cursus honorum*, prior to an aedileship; the actual work of cleaning and sweeping was done, of course, by state slaves. The collection of refuse was most probably also a task for the *aediles*, but our source material is scarce. The *Tabula Heracleensis* mentions carts for the collection of manure that were allowed to leave Rome during daytime.[18]

It was common practice to throw refuse and rubbish into the Tiber or into the sewers that eventually debouched into the river. For that reason, Augustus had the bed of the Tiber widened and cleared from debris and waste in order to prevent floods, whereas Nero, according to Tacitus, "had the grain for the populace – which had been spoilt by age – thrown into the Tiber as proof that the corn-supply was not a matter for anxiety."[19]

Street life would be lively and noisy, with vendors and beggars, and pavement dwellers at night time. Martial comments in one of his epigrams on an edict issued by Domitian in 92, in which the Emperor forbade shops from occupying parts of the streets.[20] He concludes: "Now it is Rome, it used to be a big shop." Literary sources are usually silent about homeless people, but it is likely that a fair number of people would have lacked permanent shelter and have lived on the streets for most of the time.[21]

---

11 Mart. 5.22.7-8: *Vixque datur longas mulorum rumpere mandras / quaeque trahi multo marmora fune vides.* Cf. Juv. 3.232-238 (noise at night) and 254-261 (accidents during transport of building materials). Interesting in this respect is the remark by Pliny the Younger that Rome's buildings (under Trajan) are no longer shaking caused by the transport of immense blocks of stone for building: Plin. *Pan.* 51: *Itaque non, ut ante, immanium transuectione saxorum urbis tecta quatiuntur.*

12 The seminal study for this subject is Scobie 1986. See Koloski-Ostrow 2015a for an excellent overview and analysis of hygiene and sanitation in Roman Italy, discussing both archaeological remains and written sources.

13 Holleran 2011, 248.

14 Juv. 3.247-248, Mart. 3.36.4, Mart. 5.22.5-6 (on the muddy *Alta semita*), Mart. 10.10.8, Mart. 12. 29 (26).8. The "morning mud" (*matitunum lutum*) here refers perhaps to the fact that at night more overflow water from public fountains would wash over the streets then during day time, when people would come to get water at these fountains.

15 Sen. *De ira* 3.35: *aequissimo animo foris et scabras lutosasque semitas spectant et maiorem partem occurrentium squalidam, parietes insularum exesos rimosos inaequales.*

16 *Dig.* 9.3: *De his, qui effuderint uel deiecerent.* See also Juv. 3, 268-277.

17 Suet. *Vesp.* 5.3, cf. Dio Cass. 59.12.3: "Later he caught sight of a lot of mud in an alley, and ordered it to be thrown upon the toga of Flavius Vespasian, who was then aedile and had charge of keeping the alleys clean."

18 *CIL* I 593: *plostra ... stercoris exportandei caussa.* "It is not the intent of this law to prevent ox wagons or donkey wagons that have been driven into the city by night from going out empty or from carrying out dung from within the city of Rome or within one mile of the city after sunrise until the tenth hour of the day" (transl. from Johnson/Coleman-Norton/Bourne 1961, 93-96, n.113).

19 Suet. *Aug.* 30.1, Tac. *Ann.* 15.18.2.

20 Mart. 7.61.

21 Martial and Juvenal are the exceptions. Martial speaks about bridges as places where people looked for shelter: 10.5.3, 12.32.25. Both authors refer to the clivus Aricinus (on the Via Appia, south of Rome) as one of the places where beggars gathered: Mart. 2.19.3, 12.32.10, Juv. 4 117.

The stench of so many persons and animals living together in busy neighbourhoods must have been overwhelming.[22]

Cramped in small apartments with few facilities for personal hygiene, people would suffer from the presence of all sorts of vermin like lice, flies, fleas, bugs, mice and rats. The rooms, cold and damp in winter, and hot in summer would in many cases not offer much comfort. This is not to say that *everyone* owning or renting an apartment in an apartment building (*insula*) lived in miserable circumstances. The source material, both written sources and material remains in Rome and Ostia, shows a wide variety in size and quality.[23] Already in the second century BC, high rents were charged for lofty apartments in luxurious *insulae*. Location mattered, of course: living up-hill, catching more sunlight on clear winter days, and the afternoon breezes in the heat of summer, was definitely better than a place in the lower areas of the city. But still, many inhabitants of Rome, especially newcomers, had to face a harsh reality and lived in low-quality buildings in the less attractive and densely populated areas of the Urbs.

All sorts of diseases, contagious or not, could afflict people living in such crowded neighbourhoods, and even Rome's well-to-do citizens were not immune to infections and plagues. It was a fact of life, as Celsus reminds us, that living in a city was less healthy than elsewhere.[24] Livy mentions plagues during the early years of the Republic and he reports at length about a contagious disease, first afflicting cattle, then humans as well, in Rome's countryside and the city itself for the years 181-179 BC. It was a plague "so violent in the city, that Libitina could scarcely supply the requisites for burying the dead."[25]

For the first century, a number of plagues were recorded in the sources, but in reality their number would likely have been higher. A plague in the year 80 was reported to be a pestilence (*pestilentia*) "the like of which had hardly ever been known before."[26] Suetonius mentions another plague under Nero that caused the death of 30,000 people in a single autumn (65).[27] In such extreme circumstances, proper burials were impossible and many corpses would have been thrown in huge grave-pits, or cremated together with other bodies.[28] From the Augustan period onward communal pyres were the fate of the poor, whose relatives could not afford a funerary ceremony. Public slaves took care of the bodies of those who had been left on the street, or thrown into the Tiber or a sewer; with an estimated death-rate of more than eighty deaths a day in Rome under normal circumstances, these slaves would have had to remove carelessly dumped bodies often.[29] Martial offers a glimpse of this practice when referring to four branded slaves "bearing a corpse of low degree like a thousand that the pauper's pyre receives."[30] Still, stories such as the one about a stray dog that dropped a human hand under Vespasian's breakfast table make clear that even a cremation on a communal pyre could not be taken for granted for the indigent people.[31] Martial confirms this with a vivid depiction of a beggar's fear for his last hour, hearing already the wrangling of dogs and flapping his rags to chase away noxious birds.[32]

Diseases or even plagues were sometimes the result of a preceding catastrophe: floods of the Tiber. In areas affected by floods the stagnant water must have harmed the supply of fresh drinking water and caused the kind of diseases that accompany floods even today.

Inundations caused by the Tiber were indeed a recurrent problem. In the first century AD, at least six major floods caused trouble, deaths and material damage.[33] Tacitus offers a vivid picture of the damage caused by a major flood in the year 69:

> Yet the chief anxiety which was connected with both present disaster and future danger was caused by a sudden overflow of the Tiber which, swollen to a great height, broke down the wooden bridge (the Pons Sublicius) and then was thrown back by the ruins of the bridge which dammed the stream, and overflowed not only the low-lying level parts of the city, but also parts which are normally free from such disasters. Many were swept away in the public streets, a larger number cut off in shops and in their beds. The common people were reduced to famine by lack of employment and failure of supplies. Apartment houses had their foundations undermined by the standing water and then collapsed when the flood withdrew.[34]

---

22   Koloski-Ostrow 2015b, Morley 2015.

23   Priester 2002 offers an extensive overview of the written sources. Cf. De Haan 2016.

24   Celsus *Med*. 1.2.1: "The weak, however, among whom are a large portion of townspeople, and almost all those fond of letters, need greater precaution, so that care may re-establish what the character of their constitution or of their residence or of their study detracts" (transl. Loeb edition). Cf. Nutton 2000.

25   464 BC: Livy 3.6.2-4. 181-179 BC: Livy 40.19.3, 41.21.3-7.

26   Suet. *Tit*. 8.3 *item pestilentia quanta non temere alias*. Possibly, this is the same plague as the one reported by Jerome for the year 77: Jer. *Chron*. (*Ab Abr*.) AD 77 (214th Olympiad): "A massive plague happened at Rome, so that for many days about 10,000 men were listed in the daily register of the dead." (*Lues ingens Romae facta, ita ut per multos dies in ephemeriden decem millia ferme mortuorum hominum referrentur*.)

27   Suet. *Ner*. 39.1, Kyle 1998, 121 with note 67.

28   Bodel 2000, 133-134.

29   Bodel 2000, 129.

30   Mart. 8.75.9-10.

31   Suet. *Vesp*. 5.4. The exact location and date are not mentioned by Suetonius, but presumably Vespasian was having breakfast in his *domus* on the Quirinal or in the suburban villa of the Flavians.

32   Mart. 10.5.9-12.

33   Based on Aldrete 2007, appendix 1, 242-243.

34   Tac. *Hist*. 1.86 (translation Loeb).

Plutarch mentions this devastating flood in his biography of Otho as well, and adds that the grain market was flooded, resulting in food shortages for many days.[35] In another passage, reporting a flood in 15, Tacitus briefly states that the subsiding of the Tiber from the flat areas of the city (*plana urbis*) caused the destruction of buildings and death of people (*aedificiorum et hominum strages*).[36] He also tells that Tiberius refused to have the Sibylline Books consulted, because he preferred to keep human and divine affairs secret, yet ordered that Ateius Capito and Lucius Arruntius should find a solution for controlling the river (*remedium coercendi fluminis*). It perfectly fits the negative way of depicting Tiberius that Tacitus makes a negative remark about Tiberius first, before mentioning the *remedium* this Emperor was looking for. Conversely, when Pliny writes about a flood of the Tiber during the reign of Trajan he mentions a spillway (*fossa*) that had been built by this Emperor, thanks to his excellent foresight.[37] Despite the care of Trajan, however, continuous storms and heavy rains resulted in inundations of Rome's hinterland caused by the Tiber and Anio. "Many people have been maimed, crushed, and buried in such accidents, so that grievous loss of life is added to material damage."[38]

Another risk that was always present were fires. The scale of the fires in 64 and 80 was perhaps exceptional, but the phenomenon of fire itself was not. A passage in Aulus Gellius' *Attic Nights* speaks volumes:

> (...) as we were on our way up the Cispian Hill, we saw that a block of houses, built high with many stories, had caught fire, and that now all the neighbouring buildings were burning in a mighty conflagration. Then someone of Julianus' companions said: "The income from city property is great, but the dangers are far greater. But if some remedy could be devised to prevent houses in Rome from so constantly catching fire, by Jove! I would sell my country property and buy in the city."[39]

Vitruvius deplores the widespread practice of building walls of wattle work (*opus craticium*), for whilst it was a cheap and quick construction, such walls "[were] like torches ready for kindling."[40] The dangers of fires are addressed by Martial and Juvenal and despite the fact that their poems are satirical, there must have been a lot

of truth in these expressions of fear, otherwise the comic working would not have been convincing.[41] Building communal walls between buildings had been forbidden since the time of Augustus, but it is not entirely clear to what extent this rule was followed. A re-issue of this prohibition under Nero suggests that the observance of this rule had not been very strict.[42]

Fire walls that should protect public spaces were lacking in 64 according to Tacitus, and probably also in 80, given the size of the areas that burnt.[43] Both Suetonius and Tacitus mention measures taken by Nero after the devastating fire of 64 that raged for six days and seven nights, destroying an immense number of apartment buildings, the *domus* of former leaders and temples and "whatever else interesting and noteworthy had survived from antiquity."[44] According to Suetonius Nero paid for porches in front of houses and apartment buildings, so that firemen could fight fires from the flat roofs of these porticoes.[45] Tacitus reports the same and gives a lengthy description of other measures as well,[46] but his comment in the chapter that follows is that "neither human help, nor imperial munificence, nor all the modes of placating Heaven, could stifle scandal or dispel the belief that the fire had taken place by order."[47]

Crises and Care

Soon after his ascension to the throne, in the fall of 81, Domitian received the honorary title *Pater Patriae*.[48] As a father of the fatherland, he was supposed to take good care of his subjects and to meet the expectations that came with this position, just as his predecessors had had to respond to immediate problems for the populace of Rome and elsewhere. Titus' track record during his short but eventful reign had been positive: the sources report favourably on the relief programmes he initiated after the eruption of Mt. Vesuvius in 79[49] and his concern during the plague of 80.[50]

Essentially, however, many actions by the imperial authorities in Rome and elsewhere seem to have been immediate reactions to upcoming threats and responses to existing problems rather than long-term planning

---

35 Plut. *Otho* 4.5.

36 Tac. *Ann.* 1.76.

37 Plin. *Ep.* 8.17. The date of this flood is not exactly known, but most probably in 107 or 108. Cf. Aldrete 2007, 29.

38 Plin. *Ep.* 8.17.5: *Multi eius modi casibus debilitati, obruti, obtriti; et aucta luctibus damna* (transl. Loeb).

39 Gell. *NA* 15.1.2-3 (transl. Loeb).

40 Vitr. *De arch.* 2.8.20: *quod ad incendia uti faces sunt parati* (transl. Loeb).

41 Juv. 3.197-202.

42 Wallat 2004, 140-143.

43 Cf. Tac. *Ann.* 15.38.2: *Neque enim domus munimentis saeptae vel templa muris cincta aut quid aliud morae interiacebat.*

44 Suet. *Ner.* 38.2.

45 Suet. *Ner.* 16.1.

46 Tac. *Ann.* 15.43.

47 Tac. *Ann.* 14.44.

48 Kienast/Eck/Heil 2017, 109.

49 Suet. *Tit.* 8.3. Moreover, Suetonius stresses the fact that Titus had paid for the relief and support from his own money (*opitulando quatenus suppeteret facultas*).

50 Suet. *Tit.* 8.4.

or policies for prevention. But food supply was a major concern of Roman emperors, because shortage of food would undoubtedly result in the discontent of the people and possibly affect his authority in a negative way.[51] High prices would cause poverty for too many, and hunger would end in riots. The corn dole was an important instrument for the emperor to show the populace of Rome his care for their well-being. Even Tiberius, who allegedly had stated "let them hate me, as long as they fear me," ordered the Senate to regulate the prices of foodstuff yearly.[52]

True policy-making for the long term, however, for housing the population of Rome and for public health care, seems to have been absent. This had never been the concern of the senatorial elite during the years of the Republic and Roman emperors, from Augustus onward, continued this trend.

As for housing, rules to ensure safety existed, as the measures taken by Nero after the fire of 64 show. Also, restrictions to the height of apartment buildings should have guaranteed more safety for the inhabitants.[53] But we never read about housing programmes for the poor or comparable measures initiated by the authorities. As in many other areas of life, the imperial authorities followed essentially the line of non-interventionist policies, and building houses was left to private parties: real estate developers and contractors.

People who could afford it would hire a doctor in case of need, but programmes to prevent diseases or to control the safety of building-sites or public space in general did not exist. The building of baths was booming from the second half of the first century onward, in Rome and elsewhere in the Empire.[54] But even the public baths, clearly an expression of Roman awareness that bodily hygiene and personal health were interconnected, could hardly be regarded as hygienic places: disinfectants were unknown and the heating of warm water was time- and energy-consuming, so bathers would share the warm water in communal pools with many other persons.[55] Likewise, Roman public latrines were not hygienic *per se*, despite clear ideas about cleanliness and the need to get rid of dirt and bodily excrements.[56]

The Water Supply

Together with food, the supply of sufficient quantities of drinking water of good quality was one of the main concerns. We are relatively well-informed about water management and technical details of Rome's public water supply systems, thanks to Frontinus' treatise. Sextus Iulius Frontinus, *curator aquarum* under Nerva from 97, was a contemporary of Domitian, who had served as an officer in Domitian's military campaigns.[57] Frontinus kept a low profile during the last years of Domitian's reign. After his appointment by Nerva, a position that brought him back into the centre of power, his criticism on the policies of Nerva's predecessors is sharp. According to Frontinus, water was a public commodity and presenting himself as a zealous civil servant of the Roman state, he was fighting unnecessary waste of water and the abuse of water rights.

Frontinus provides a detailed overview of the quantities of water that were at the disposal of Rome's inhabitants on a daily basis in around 100.[58] Nine aqueducts supplied the city with ca. 500,000 cubic metres of water, or 500 million litres per day. These figures were approximately the same during Domitian's rule, since the last two aqueducts built in Rome (under Trajan and Septimius Severus respectively) were only built after Frontinus had written down his estimations of the delivery of each aqueduct. Part of this enormous amount of water was destined for bath buildings in Rome, both the imperial *thermae* and the numerous smaller public bathing complexes. The *horti* were another important consumer of water, just as the private citizens, all members of the elite, who had running water in their homes, thanks to a private connection to the tap water system, which was a *beneficium Caesaris*.

Most citizens however, did not enjoy such a privilege and had to get their water at public outlets or fountains (*lacus* or *salientes*). The number of street fountains (*lacus*) was according to Frontinus 591.[59] Very roughly speaking, some 1400-1600 persons would make use of each of these public fountains. The real number, however, must have been lower, since apart from the private connections, people would also draw water from other public facilities such as *munera* (*nymphaea* and ornate fountains). Archaeological evidence from Ostia can shed some more light on this matter: here it seems, the inhabitants of one apartment building would dispose of a *lacus* in the courtyard, allowing for several hundred people to use the water.

---

51 For the supply of food in imperial Rome Peter Garnsey's study (1988) is still most useful. Paul Erdkamp offers an excellent chapter on this subject in the volume edited by the same author (Erdkamp 2013).

52 Suet. *Tib.* 34.1.

53 According to Strabo (5.3.7) under Augustus the maximum height was 70 feet; under Trajan this maximum was lowered to 60 feet (*Epitome de Caes.* 13.13). Cf. De Haan 2016, 725.

54 Fagan 1999, 74.

55 The water could be kept warm for several hours by technical installations such as *testudines* (*alveorum*). See for an excellent overview of water-related technical details and water management in bath buildings Manderscheid 2000. For hygienic conditions in public baths see Fagan 1999, 176-188.

56 Jansen 2011, Koloski-Ostrow 2015a.

---

57 Peachin 2004, *Die Wasserversorgung im antiken Rom* 2013 and De Haan 2013 with bibliography.

58 Frontin. *Aq.* 67-80 provides the numbers of delivery of each aqueduct in *quinaria* and explains the distribution of water; for modern calculations for the daily delivery based on Frontinus see Bruun 2013 (in *Die Wasserversorgung im antiken Rom*).

59 Frontin. *Aq.* 78.3.

Frontinus also discusses the necessary inspections and maintenance of the system, making clear how in cases of repair or maintenance the supply would be secured and how the illegal drawing of water both outside and inside the city were monitored. Moreover, he speaks about *commentarii*, including those kept by his predecessors. This suggests a high grade of organisation and the existence of some kind of archives. More importantly, with 67 litres per day per capita, as modern calculations show, Rome's water supply was abundant.

A Thin Line: Imperial *Munificentia, Magnificentia Publica* and *Privata Luxuria*

Restoring and rebuilding devastated areas was exactly what his subjects would have expected from any Roman emperor. After all, since the Late Republic Rome's leading men had taken the lead in initiating major building and infrastructural programmes, providing the city of Rome and its surroundings with temples, *basilicae, horrea,* aqueducts and roads. From Augustus onward, building in the city of Rome was both a privilege and a duty for the members of the imperial family. The spoils of war were meant to beautify the city of Rome in order to glorify Rome's power, embodied by the emperor. The Flavians had continued this line, with Augustus as their example and via Augustus they referred back to an even more remote past, the Roman Republic.

Moreover, building for the gods and building for the people was the kind of munificence that was appreciated in Roman society, a mentality that was deeply anchored in the Republic. Hence, all investments in the public space, such as temples, altars, baths, and buildings for entertainment and leisure for the common people were highly appreciated. The infrastructure of the Capital (roads, sewers, aqueducts, the banks of the Tiber) were perhaps less associated with imperial pomp and splendour, but crucial for the quality of life for Rome's inhabitants and thus of equal importance. Malfunctioning public facilities, the water supply first and foremost, would undoubtedly have had a negative impact on any ruler's reputation.

Still, the dividing line between magnificence and extravagance was thin, and easily transgressed. The danger of being blamed for *luxuria* (luxuriance) was always looming. In Domitian's case the reproach was certainly there, at least after his violent death. Grand scale building in the public sphere was one thing, but commissioning a palace with the dimensions and opulence in decoration such as Domitian's residence on the Palatine was another. The unconcealed splendour of his private dwelling showed from a far distance already that he was no longer the *princeps civium* but rather *dominus et deus*. In such a light, Domitian was easily blamed for the excessive costs of his building programme. More than twelve thousand talents of silver alone (some HS 288 million) were spent on the gilding of the temple of Jupiter Capitolinus, and the columns of Pentelic marble were imported from Athens.[60] This extravagant rebuilding of the Capitoline temple became suspect after Domitian's death, for by then it was easy enough to doubt his loyalty towards the gods. In his *Life of Publicola* Plutarch has the Greek poet Epicharmus enter the scene who addresses Domitian and reproaches him for his spendthrift: "You to be sure, are neither pious nor magnificent. You have a disease – your insane desire to build – just like Midas, wishing that everything for you would turn into gold or stone."[61]

Pliny the Younger also joins in the condemnation for Domitian's approach to building work, criticising him for his lavish building programme and unbridled greed, and the number of golden and silver statues of Domitian in the temple of Jupiter Capitolinus and its precinct.[62]

In the end, despite Domitian's extensive investments in the public sphere, emulating the Augustan example, his post-mortem fate in the decades following his murder was that the comparison with Nero prevailed. But unlike Nero's Golden House, Domitian's buildings were not teared down and still belong to the tangible legacy of his fifteen years of rule.

---

60 Plut. *Publ.* 15.3. Plutarch adds to his remarks about the columns that they had been reworked in Rome and "did not gain as much in polish as they lost in symmetry and beauty, and they now look too slender and thin."
61 Plut. *Publ.* 15.5. Translation from Frederick 2003, 200.
62 Plin. *Pan.*51 (building activities) and *Pan.* 52 (golden and silver statues of Domitian).

Entertainment and Spectacles during Domitian's Rule

Daniëlle Slootjes

Three times I gave gladiatorial shows in my name and five times in the names of my sons or grandsons. In these gladiatorial shows about 10,000 men fought. Twice I presented to the people in my name the spectacle of a contest of athletes summoned from every side and for a third time in the name of my grandson. [...] I gave beast hunts to the people of wild animals from Libya in my name or that of my sons and grandsons in the racecourse or in the forum or in the amphitheatre twenty-six times, during which nearly 3,500 animals were slaughtered.[1]

Introduction

'Bread and Circuses' have become inextricably connected to our understanding of the Roman world in which emperors took care of their subjects by organizing games and providing (free) grain in order to obtain the loyalty and support of the people of Rome.[2] The first emperor Augustus proudly stated in his testament, as cited above in the passage of his *Res Gestae*, that he gave gladiatorial shows, athletic contests and beast hunts, both in his own name as well as in that of his family. By the end of the first century, it seems to have become common practice that – while *aediles* continued to be responsible for most of the smaller scale entertainment in the city as they had been during the Republic – emperors now organized the grandest and most extraordinary public events in the city. For the relationship between an emperor and his subjects, the games and entertainment had turned into an expression of their close bond. For many people these public events were occasions at which they could physically see their ruler and share an experience with him and the imperial family. Emperors knew that if they were able to answer to the people's expectation of entertainment by way of games, spectacles or theatrical performances, this would be helpful in becoming accepted as ruler and developing a popular image with the people of Rome. Apart from seeking the backing of their fellow senators and loyalty of the army, emperors were often eager to look for the support of the people of Rome who were also important for the legitimization of a stable imperial rule.[3]

---

1   Augustus, *Res Gestae* 22, translation Cooley 2009.
2   There is an extensive bibliography on this topic; to mention only a few here: Veyne 1976, Wiedemann 1992, Köhne/Ewigleben/Jackson 2000, Fagan 2011.
3   Flaig 1992.

This article presents a two-fold analysis of the way in which the Emperor Domitian was presented as an organizer and spectator of games and public entertainment. The first part will offer an examination of Suetonius' twelve biographies, starting with Julius Caesar and ending with the Emperor Domitian.[4] A comparison between Suetonius' descriptions of the various emperors and their involvement in entertainment will demonstrate the importance of an emperor's organizing of and presence at public shows in Rome, although it seems not to have been one of the decisive factors in forming Suetonius' overall assessment of an emperor's rule. Second, a brief examination of the magnificent Amphitheatrum Flavium, better known as the Colosseum, which ended up a joint project by the Emperor Vespasian (69-79) and his sons Titus (79-81) and Domitian (81-96), will zoom in on one particular venue for mass entertainment. It will illustrate how an imperial dynasty refurbished a public location in order to emphasize their own legitimacy and express their imperial power, ostensibly under the guise of offering the people games and entertainment.

Suetonius on Roman Emperors and their People at Entertainment

In his biographies of the twelve Caesars, Suetonius gives fairly detailed descriptions of the actions, behavior and life style of the emperors of the first century.[5] In each life he explains how the emperors dealt with their main support groups: the senatorial and equestrian elites, the army and the people of Rome. Donations of money or grain and the organization of games and entertainment were the most important gifts that an emperor had to offer to his people. The more donations and the grander the entertainment presented by an emperor, the better the chances of obtaining a positive assessment of one's rule, at least with the people. Suetonius' descriptions of the involvement of the various emperors in games and entertainment show that it is not merely their organization that was valued but imperial presence and personal attention at these spectacles that made them beneficial for the emperors' relation with his people.

While Suetonius' description of Julius Caesar's organization of public shows remains fairly matter-of-fact, it is in Augustus' life that the audience obtains a more lively and perhaps also ideal image of how an emperor should

be interested in spectacles. Augustus not only "surpassed all his predecessors in the frequency, variety, and magnificence of his public shows," but "whenever he was present, he gave his entire attention to the performance, either to avoid the censure to which he realized that his father Caesar had been generally exposed, because he spent his time in reading or answering letters and petitions; or from his interest and pleasure in the spectacle, which he never denied but often frankly confessed."[6] Augustus is said to have set up guidelines for participants and seating arrangements at shows, by which Suetonius illustrated that the emperor tried to regulate games and entertainment fairly but also to make them accessible to as many people as possible in an orderly way.[7] Furthermore, Augustus was not only concerned with the experience of the audience, but he also "honoured with his interest all classes of performers who took part in the public shows."[8]

A comparison with the narratives of the later Caesars shows that Augustus is given a long positive description of his involvement in entertainment. Apart from Tiberius who stood in sharp contrast with Augustus, as Tiberius "gave no public shows at all, and very seldom attended those given by others, for fear that some request would be made of him"[9] and no mention of entertainment at all in the accounts of the very short ruling Caesars Galba, Otho and Vitellius, Suetonius devoted one or more sections to games and spectacles in each life of the other Caesars. In most lives, these entertainment sections are part of the first half of the lives in which typically the positive features of the emperors are being discussed. In the earlier sections of the lives of Caligula and Claudius, for instance, Suetonius explained how these two emperors enjoyed shows and organized many different types of them.[10] However, in the second half of their lives, Suetonius seemed to have seized the opportunity to emphasize these emperors' cruelty and unpredictability during gladiatorial shows.[11] Perhaps surprisingly, in Nero's life there are many examples of his harsh and brutal behavior towards others, but in the descriptions of his involvement in games and entertainment Suetonius focuses more on listing Nero's various types of shows and the Emperor's own wishes to perform.[12]

Suetonius' account of the Flavians demonstrates a notable development in the narratives of Vespasian, Titus and Domitian. Most of Vespasian's story is taken up by the military challenges he faced before eventually

---

4   The analysis will deliberately focus mostly on Suetonius, as a contemporary to Domitian, even though other ancient authors such as Cassius Dio have written about Domitian as well but they are further removed in time and less clear on their sources.

5   Wallace-Hadrill 1983, Power/Gibson 2014. For studies on the imperial ideal and virtues in Suetonius' work, see Bradley 1973 and 1991.

6   Suet. *Aug.* 43, 45.

7   Cf. Rose 2005, 100-102.

8   Suet. *Aug.* 45.

9   Suet. *Tib.* 47.

10   Suet. *Calig.* 18-21, *Claud.* 21.

11   Suet. *Calig.* 26-27, *Claud.* 34.

12   Suet. *Nero* 11-12, 21-22.

securing the imperial throne. Suetonius briefly describes Vespasian's public works, with a strikingly brief and uninspired reference to the building that within one or two decades was to become one of the most eye catching public buildings of Rome: "an amphitheatre in the heart of the city".[13] Vespasian indeed started the construction of the Amphitheatrum Flavium, the largest amphitheatre the Roman world had ever seen, but died before it was finished. His son and successor Titus completed it and celebrated its opening with hundred days of games which must have been an amazing occasion for the inhabitants of the city who must have had various opportunities to go to different spectacles during this extended period.[14] Remarkably, Suetonius' account is very factual on the opening and festivities:

> At the dedication of the amphitheatre and of the baths which were hastily built near it he (=Titus) gave a most magnificent and costly gladiatorial show. He presented a sham sea-fight too in the old naumachia, and in the same place a combat of gladiators, exhibiting five thousand wild beasts of every kind in a single day.[15]

The brevity of the description is all the more striking, because in several of his other lives of the Caesars Suetonius offered more detail to enliven the accounts about spectacles, which must have been much shorter and less spectacular.[16] Especially, when one takes into account that the new Amphitheatrum was the largest venue of its kind and must have triggered spectators' excitement for the opening games, Suetonius' meagre reference is remarkable. Furthermore, it also stands in stark contrast with the much more intense images of such celebrations in Martial's *De Spectaculis* or in Cassius Dio's more extensive and detailed account of the various types of games during these hundred days.[17]

Whereas Vespasian and Titus are given a favorable portrayal, Suetonius' tone in Domitian's narrative changes as he presents the emperor as a tyrannical and cruel man. One needs to keep in mind that to Suetonius – writing only shortly after Domitian's rule – a negative portrayal of the last emperor of the Flavians would seem quite appropriate. Domitian seems to have liked public spectacles as he "constantly gave grand and costly entertainments, both in the amphitheatre and in the Circus, where in addition to the usual races between two-horse and four-horse

chariots, he also exhibited two battles, one between forces of infantry and the other by horsemen; and he even gave a naval battle in the amphitheatre. Besides he gave hunts of wild beasts, gladiatorial shows at night by the light of torches, and not only combats between men but between women as well."[18] Notably, Domitian was personally engaged by being present even "amid heavy rains," by presiding at competitions or by showering the people with gifts.[19] Similar to the case of Augustus, personal imperial engagement and an attentive attitude of Domitian towards the audience and performers seems to have been presented and valued as an advantageous characteristic of a ruler. Moreover, comparable to the description of Nero whose negative image does not so much emerge in the description of his involvement in games and entertainment, the overall unfavorable judgement of Domitian by Suetonius is not expressed in these sections either.

This overview of the way in which Suetonius presented the first twelve Caesars and their organization of public spectacles has shown that the emperors used it in particular to offer the people of Rome pleasant and even spectacular performances in various venues as an expression of their relationship with their subjects. As the last of Suetonius' Caesars, Domitian was presented in this respect in similar fashion as his predecessors. He behaved as an emperor was supposed to act in his attempt to secure his subject's respect and loyalty. Even more, his personal attention and interest at public shows gives the reader the impression that he was particularly good at showing his people his commitment to them.

The Flavian Colosseum: Imperial Monumentalization of Entertainment

During the Republic and the early Empire, Rome had seen the construction of various public and in some cases large venues where crowds could come together for exciting shows and spectacles, for instance in the theatres of Pompey or of Marcellus, or the amphitheatre of Statilius Taurus (destroyed in 64), or for awesome chariot races in the Circus Maximus (with its impressive capacity of over 150,000). In the year 70, after a dreadful period of several emperors trying to establish their power, Vespasian managed to stabilize his imperial position. He started the construction of the Amphitheatrum Flavium, financed as we now know by revenues from the Siege of Jerusalem.[20] The emperor seems to have deliberately chosen to build

---

13 Suet. *Nero* 11-12, 21-22. See Welch 2007, 132.

14 Elkins 2019, 86-116.

15 Suet. *Titus* 7. On aquatic entertainment in the early empire, see Coleman 1993.

16 Suet. *Julius* 39, *Calig.* 18 and 27, *Claud.* 21 and 34, *Nero* 12.

17 Dio Cass. 67.25.1-5. Cf. Welch 2007, 145-147, and Buttrey 2007 for discussion on whose games – of Titus or of Domitian – Martial was describing.

18 Suet. *Dom.* 4. Cf. Statius, *Silv.* 1.6.51-56, *Kalendae Decembres*. For a modern study on female gladiators, see McCullough 2008.

19 Suet. *Dom.* 4.

20 On financing the Colosseum, see Alföldy 1995. On the construction and functioning of the Colosseum more generally, see Coleman 1993, 58-60, Rose 2005, Beard/Hopkins 2005, Welch 2007, 128-161.

Fig. 1. Groundfloor level, interior showing the entrances to the Colosseum (photo Alinari 28836, late 19th century).

Fig. 2. View towards the arena of the Colosseum (photo Alinari 128837, late 19th century).

the largest and most extravagant stone amphitheatre ever as a public statement of his newly acquired power. Its capacity would allow an enormous crowd to watch games and gladiatorial combat together which must have changed the spectators' experience from previous decades when crowds at these events would have been smaller.

Recent modern analyses have emphasized that Vespasian and his successors Titus and Domitian consciously attempted to erase Nero from the physical landscape of the center of Rome.[21] The area where Nero had built his *Domus Aurea* and in particular the artificial lake that had been dug on the imperial domain was taken over by the Flavians for the construction of the Amphitheatrum. Although scholars believed for a long time that this zone had been full of shops of the middle classes of the city, recent ideas indicate that Nero had probably

confiscated this particular area from the wealthy who had had their large city houses there.[22] However it may be, Martial presented the construction of the Colosseum as an act of giving back to the people: "Rome has been restored to herself, and under your rule, Caesar, the pleasances that belonged to a master now belong to the people."[23]

Furthermore, with their (building) activities, imperial policies and representation the Flavians deliberately placed themselves in line with the good emperors of the Julio-Claudian dynasty, in particular Augustus and Claudius.[24] In his description of Vespasian's public works, Suetonius referred to his construction of the Colosseum as "a plan which he learned that Augustus had cherished."[25] Notably, the hierarchical seating arrangements of the Colosseum bring back memories of Suetonius' account of Augustus who – fed up by the "disorderly and indiscriminate fashion of viewing the games" – had come up with a strict ordering of seating reflecting the social hierarchy within Roman society.[26] In the newly built Amphitheatrum these old arrangements

---

21 One might argue that Domitian continued his predecessors' plan to replace Nero's public legacy. While Nero had set up new festivals, the so-called *Iuvenalia* and *Neronia*, Domitian started to organize a new festival named the *Capitolia* for which he built the new Stadium and Odeum near the Campus Martius and a festival honoring Minerva which was organized at the emperor's Alban villa (Suet. *Dom.* 4). Notably, while having been a poet himself, Domitian did not compete in his own festivals as Nero had done. Hardie 2003. On the *Capitolia*, see Onno Van Nijf, Robin van Vliet, & Caroline van Toor in this volume.

22 Welch 2007, 128-161, Elkins 2019, 11-21.
23 Mart. *Spect.* 2. Welch 2007, 147-161.
24 Elkins 2019, 64-75.
25 Suet. *Vesp.* 9.
26 Suet. *Aug.* 44.

seem to have been reinstated again, or as according to Elkins, the Colosseum "was a public building for the enjoyment of all, although it reasserted social order through its strict segregation of classes in its seating arrangements."[27]

Vespasian did not live to see his ambitious building project completed, but his son Titus finished most of it and celebrated hundred days of Games as the official opening in 80.[28] Within a year after the grand inauguration, Titus passed away and Domitian obtained the imperial throne. During his rule, he probably transformed the fourth level of the Colosseum that might have been constructed in wood by Titus into a stable stone level and he added a substructure below the ground level which might have impeded future naval battles to be organized there because it would no longer have been possible to fill a basin with water.[29] As mentioned in the section on Suetonius' presentation of Domitian, the Emperor liked to organize games, and the Colosseum offered a grand venue for such occasions. As Elkins has argued, its construction should be seen as part of a larger Flavian building and reconstruction program which also consisted for instance of the Temple of Jupiter Optimus Maximus or the Aqua Claudia, and in general the areas of the Caelian and the Esquiline Hill. In other words, entertainment venues were not only locations where emperors and subjects would meet for a fun day of shows, but they were part of a larger ideological framework of imperial representation. Domitian understood how his personal attention at public spectacles was part of his imperial legacy.

---

27   Elkins 2019, 20. Cf. Rose 2005, 100-102.
28   Welch 2007, 131, Elkins 2019, 1-4, 86-116.
29   Cf. Suet. *Dom.* 4, which indicates that Domitian gave naumachia at another location close to the Tiber where he had dug an artificial pool. Elkins 2019, 21 and 71-73, Coleman 1993, 58-61.

Domitian and the Capitolia

Onno van Nijf, Robin van Vliet & Caroline van Toor[1]

Introduction

A striking grave monument on the Via Salaria in Rome (fig. 1) stood testimony to one of the most remarkable initiatives of Domitian: the institution in 86 of the *Capitolia*, a Greek-style contest with athletic, musical, equestrian and literary competitions.[2] The monument shows a young boy dressed in Roman toga, holding a scroll. On the same monument Greek and Latin texts were inscribed.[3] His name was Quintus Sulpicius Maximus. He participated at the tender age of 11 with a Greek composition in the third edition of the contest; he did not win, but he received an honourable mention.[4] The Capitolia were not a children's game, however. Famous poets like Statius and Florus competed, but failed to win (causing the latter to leave Rome in disappointment). The effort may have been too much for Sulpicius as well, as he died from exhaustion after "having spent his mornings and nights on his meditations on the Muses," thus spoiling the hopes of his freedmen parents.[5] Sulpicius' monument gives a good impression of the remarkable mixture of Greek and Roman ingredients that constituted the Capitolia.

Greek and Roman Elements in the Capitolia

The Capitolia were a clever piece of bricolage mixing Greek and Roman elements.[6] Intended for an empire-wide audience, they referred simultaneously to the Olympic traditions and to the traditional significance of Jupiter and the Capitolium for the preservation of imperial Rome – and the Flavian dynasty.[7] The festival was dedicated to Jupiter Capitolinus, the Roman counterpart of Olympian Zeus, with whom Domitian

1   The authors wish to thank Ruurd Nauta, Jitse Daniels and the members of the Groningen Ancient History group for their help and discussion. The research was carried out in the double framework of the Oikos Anchoring Innovation Initiative and the NWO funded project 'Connecting the Greeks': www.connectingthegreeks.com.
2   Suet. *Dom.* 4.4, Robert/Lianou/König 2010. The most comprehensive discussion in: Caldelli 1993 and Rieger 1999, 171-203.
3   Greek and Latin: IGUR 3, 1336, ILS 5177 has only the Latin text.
4   Garulli 2018, Nocita 2000, see SEG 50, 1060, Döpp 1996.
5   Οὔτε γὰρ ἠοῦς, οὐκ ὄρφνης μουσέων ἐκτὸς ἔθηκα φρένα (IGUR 3, 1336, C 3-4).
6   Heinemann 2014 offers a good discussion of the balancing of Greek and Roman ingredients.
7   Hardie 2003, 130.

Fig. 1. Funerary monument of Quintus Sulpicius Maximus. Rome, Musei Capitolini, Centrale Montemartini, inv. MC 1102/S (courtesy Rome, Sovrintendenza Capitolina ai Beni Culturali; photo Zeno Colantoni).

their crowns. Like the Emperor, they were all dressed as Greek agonothetes (festival presidents).[9]

The typical Greek-style characteristics of the programme stand out. The contest followed the traditional threefold model of the Greek games, with musical, equestrian and gymnastic events, in the traditional age-categories of the paides (boys), ageneioi (youths), and andres (men).[10] They were held every four years, probably between late April/ early May and June.[11] Like the Sebasta they were inserted in the Greek festival circuit. However, Roman elements were also in view. The horse races were held in the Circus Maximus, itself a particularly Roman setting very different from the Greek hippodrome. Moreover, the races followed a Roman model,[12] with the charioteers recruited from the factions of the Whites, the Reds, the Greens and the Blues.[13] The most strikingly Roman element were the Latin literary contests, perhaps specifically designed to attract participants from the Western provinces.[14] Contests in Latin oratory – mentioned by Suetonius – do not seem to have survived Domitian's reign, but poetry competitions lasted until the fourth century. An innovation was the inclusion of races for unmarried girls, that may have been inspired by the example of the Sebasta of Neapolis, but no names of victors have survived.[15] The prize for all these contests, as with the other Greek contests, was a crown, which in Rome was made of oak leaves. The oak was of course associated with Jupiter, but it would have brought up associations with the traditional Corona Civica that was traditionally awarded to benefactors of the Roman people.

Moreover, the festival had a distinct impact on the urban landscape requiring the construction of Greek building types that had not existed in Rome. Central on the Campus Martius, Domitian ordered the construction of a huge roofed odeum that seated between 5000 and 10,000

was frequently compared.[8] The festival opened with a procession of the delegations from the festival sites on the Campus Martius to the newly restored temple of Jupiter on the Capitol, where joint sacrifices may have taken place for the Capitoline triad and the Emperor. The Emperor's appearance was a carefully stage-managed mix of Greek and Roman elements. He presided over the games seconded by the priest of Jupiter, the Flamen Dialis, and by the collegium of the Sodales Flaviales Titiales, the priests responsible for the cult of the Flavians, who bore Domitian's own image in

---

8   This suggested that the supreme rule of Jupiter over the cosmos was mirrored in Domitian's rule over the oikoumene. Sulpicius' Greek poem shows that at least some Romans picked up the reference. Nauta 2002, 328-335.

9   Suet. *Dom.* 4.4: *Certamini praesedit crepidatus purpureaque amictus toga Graecanica, capite gestans coronam auream cum effigie Iouis ac Iunonis Minervaeque, adsidentibus Diali sacerdote et collegio Flaualium pari habitu, nisi quod illorum coronis inerat et ipsius imago.* "He presided over the contests wearing boots and dressed according to Greek fashion in a purple toga, and on his head, he wore a golden crown with an image of Jupiter and Minerva. By his side were seated the priest of Iupiter and the college of the Flavian priests, similarly dressed."

10   Caldelli 1993, 32-34.

11   Caldelli 1993, 57-59.

12   Rieger 1999, 183-188.

13   Rieger 1999, 185-186, with reference to inscriptions listing Capitolia victors also known from the Green and the Blue stables: CIL VI, 10058, 100800.

14   Hardie 2003, 129. See below, for an overview of the origins of the known participants.

15   Suet. *Dom.* 4: *Certabant ... in stadio uero cursu etiam virgines.* "In the stadium ... even unmarried girls competed in the footrace." For the Sebasta: SEG 14, 602 (Seia Spes); a race for parthenoi at the Sebasta of Neapolis: SEG 64, 860. Female athletes in the Isthmia, Nemea and Corinth: *Corinth* VIII, 3, 153, FD 3.1, 534.

spectators for the musical and literary competitions. A stadium – whose contours are still visible in the Piazza Navona – was built for the athletic events.[16] In the fourth century these were still reckoned among the main "perennial adornments of the city" (*haec decora urbis aeterna*).[17] They served a Greek style festival, but stylistically they had more in common with Roman spectacle buildings like the Colosseum than with their counterparts in Greece.[18]

Greek Contests in Rome

Domitian was not the first Roman emperor to set up Greek-style games, nor would he be the last. Augustus had celebrated his victory over Mark Antony by founding a new city Nikopolis (Victory city) and raising the local Actian games to panhellenic status.[19] In this respect he stood in a long tradition: since the second century BC Greek cities had been organising Greek contests for individual Roman generals, or for the new goddess Thea Rhomē (Roma) whose cult followed closely on the stages of progressing Roman rule.[20] There had been some Greek style games in Italy – mostly organised by victorious Roman generals, but these remained incidental.[21] Augustus was the first to organise Greek style games on a regular basis on Italian soil. In 2 he instituted the Augustan Games (the Sebasta) in Neapolis (Naples), as a counterpart to the 'Romaia Sebasta' that had been set up for him by the province of Asia in Pergamon.[22] They were to have equal status to the Olympic games, as we learn from an inscription set up at Olympia that records the programme, but they were anchored in a long local tradition, as Neapolis was part of Greek-influenced southern Italy.[23] The games were a great success, and were repeated every four years until the fourth century. Of Augustus' immediate successors, Nero was the first to set up a Greek style contest in Rome itself, the Neroneia, which he founded after his return from a successful (in his own eyes at least) agonistic tour through Greece.[24] No victors are known, however, and the games were abolished after Nero's death.

The new Flavian dynasty invested heavily in properly Roman types of spectacle and entertainments to boost its popularity, but the adoption of Greek style contests had to

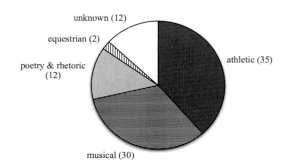

Fig. 2. Recorded victories in the Capitolia (chart by authors).* *Cf. Caldelli 1993, 121-163. This chart is based on the data we have collected for www.connectedcontests.org. This project aims to collect prosopographical data on all Greek athletes and performers.

be handled with care.[25] Domitian was careful not to repeat Nero's mistakes: the festival was not named after himself, he did not participate himself, nor did he force Roman nobles to compete.

We can only surmise why Domitian set up the Capitoline games. Personal tastes may have played a part. Growing up under Nero he shared the contemporary fashion for Greek style performances among the young men of the Roman elite.[26] Such personal interests were also pursued in his villa in the Alban hills where he organised literary contests in honour of Minerva that were not continued after his death.[27] But it is also likely that he sought to emulate Augustus, which is supported by his strong personal involvement in the Sebasta of Neapolis. We know now that he served as agonothete, competed in chariot races and oratory (with an encomium on Divus Titus), and was himself the object of encomiastic poetry competitions.[28] It has also been suggested that he meant the games as a gesture towards his Greek subjects – Nero's antics had certainly hit a chord in Greece.[29] Whatever his intentions, the long-lasting effect of the new foundation was to offer entertainment to the Roman people and to link the city of Rome firmly to the Greek festival network that was flourishing in the eastern provinces. In fact, his reorganisation of the festival calendar and the urban landscape would have established Rome as a Greek city, the proper capital of a Greco-Roman Empire.[30]

16   Suet. *Dom.* 5.
17   Amm. Marc 16.10.4. Rieger 1999, 192-194.
18   Heinemann 2014. See also Daniëlle Slootjes in this volume.
19   Zachos, 2008, Pavlogiannis/Albanidis/Dimitriou 2009.
20   Greek Games in honour of Roman generals: Thériault 2012. For the Romaia contests see Van Nijf/Van Dijk 2020.
21   Lee 2014, Mann 2014.
22   Robert/Lianou/König 2010, 123, cf. IGR 4, 454
23   IvO 56. For the Sebasta see now Miranda de Martino 2014 with references to earlier literature. Cf. SEG 64, 859-62.
24   Suet., *Nero* 12,3. On Nero's tour: see Alcock 1994.

25   For Roman attitudes to Greek athletics, see: Mann 2014, Lee 2014.
26   It is possible that he was partly inspired by the Neroneia, although a Neronian inspiration is very unlikely in other aspects of his reign, Nauta 2010.
27   Nauta 2002, 329. See on this villa, Aurora Raimondi Cominesi & Claire Stocks and Claudia Valeri in this volume.
28   Miranda De Martino 2014.
29   Hardie 2003, 127.
30   For the expression: Veyne 2005.

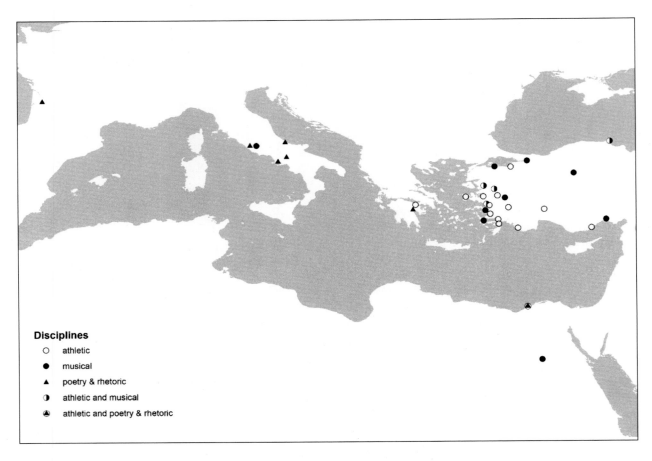

Disciplines

○　athletic
●　musical
▲　poetry & rhetoric
◑　athletic and musical
◓　athletic and poetry & rhetoric

Fig. 3. Map recording the origins of the known participants in the Capitolia.

If Domitian wanted to turn Rome into a centre of empire-wide agonistic activity he certainly succeeded. When in the second century a successful athlete wanted to present the global reach of his athletic career he stated that he had been "successful in contests from the Capitolia in Rome to those in Syria."[31] He was not the only one: an overview of the known victors shows that they came from all regions of the Roman Empire. Most of these were renowned athletes and musicians from the Greek provinces. The first known victor – at the Capitolia of 86 – was the runner Titus Flavius Metrobios of Iasos in Western Asia Minor, a periodonikes; *i.e.* he had been victorious at all the great Greek contests.[32] He may have owed his Roman citizenship to his victory at the Capitolia.[33] Later editions continued to attract the greatest champions: from the second century we learn that M. Aurelius Damostratos Damas from Sardeis,

one of the greatest athletes of the era, and perhaps of all times won twice, in 174 and 178, as did father and son M. Aurelius Demetrios and M. Aurelius Demetrios Asklepiades (probably in the 180's) from Hermoupolis in Egypt.[34] All were high-ranking members of the Empire-wide athletic association. The participants in the equestrian and literary competitions came predominantly from Italy and the western provinces.

The Capitolia were star-studded events that attracted not only participants, but also sports fans from all over the Empire, such as Q. Iulius Miletos, "who had left his hometown of Tripolis in Lydia to watch the contest that was presided over by the Emperor Severus".[35] As this was written on his epitaph in Rome, it seems that his trip cost him his life.

Not everybody may have been equally positive about this flourishing of Greek agonistics on Roman soil – and

---

31　IGR 4,1636.

32　I.Iasos 107, 108. His fatherland honoured him also with an inscription: SEG 48, 1333, cf. I. Iasos 109.

33　Two other victors shared the privilege: T. Flavius Artemidorus and T. Flavius Hermogenes. See www.connectedcontests.org.

34　Damas: Sardis 7.1, 79; for a full dossier see: Strasser 2003. Aurelius Demetrios (IGUR II, 239) Asklepiades (IGUR II, 242), with a discussion by Strasser 2004.

35　IGUR IV, 1567, with Strasser 2001.

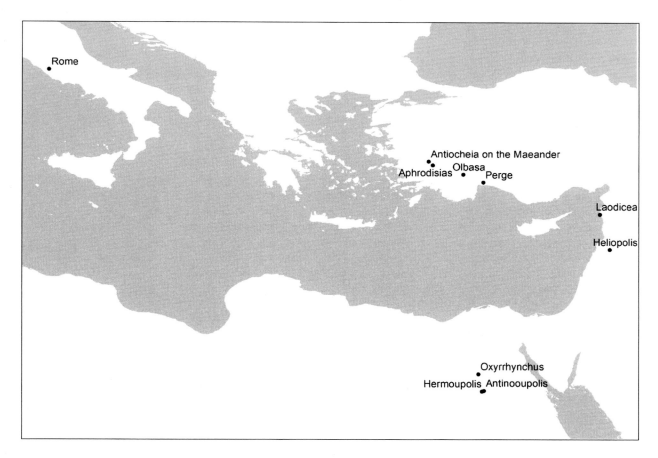

Fig. 4. The location of Capitolia and Isocapitolia (map authors).

critics arose especially after Domitian's death.[36] In one of his letters, Pliny approvingly quotes the comments of an old curmudgeon, Junius Mauricus, who upon hearing that Greek-style contests had been abolished in Vienne (Gaul) wished that they could also be abolished in Rome itself.[37] Such criticism does not seem to have had an effect on the Capitolia, however, nor on the popularity of Greek athletics in Rome. The Capitolia not only continued, but were actively supported by later emperors, as were other athletic contests. Hadrian rearranged the 4-year Greek festival calendar, and confirmed a fixed position of the Capitolia between the Hadrianeia of Athens and the Sebasta of Neapolis.[38] His main concern appears to

have been the opportunities the festivals offered for the propagation of imperial rule. Antoninus Pius praised the African city of Barca-Ptolemais for sending a delegation to the Capitolia to join in the sacrifices that were held for the Emperor.[39] Marcus Aurelius and his successors used the contest as a public stage to offer Roman citizenship to successful athletes,[40] which shows another way in which Greek cultural events could be used to push a Roman political agenda. We know that Severus organised a successful edition, which was celebrated by his coinage.[41] The Capitolia continued to be celebrated through the third and fourth centuries, and seem to have maintained their relatively high status. An edict of the Emperors Diocletian and Maximian limits the entitlement to freedom from liturgies to athletes who had obtained at least three crowns, among which at

36 For Roman views on Greek athletics: Mammel 2014.

37 Plin. *Ep.* 4.22.

38 SEG 56,1354, 63-65: ὁ δ' ἐν Τάραντι ἀγὼν μετὰ Ἁδριάνεια ἀγέ-|σ<θ>ω τοῦ Ἰανουαρίου μηνός, ἀπὸ δὲ Καπετωλείων, ὡς μέχρι νῦν ἐπετελέσθη, ἀγομένων ἐν Νεαπόλει ἀγώνων· εἶτα Ἄκτια ἀρχόμενα μὲν τῇ πρὸ θ' καλ(ανδῶν)| Ὀκτων(βρίων), συντελούμενα δὲ ἐν τεσσαράκοντα ἡμέραις. "The contests in Tarentum must be held after the Hadrianeia in the month January, The contests in Neapolis must be held after the Capitolia, as they have been until now. Then the Actia must start before the Kalends of October, and conclude within 40 days."

39 SEG 28, 1566.

40 They were building on a precedent set by Domitian: Strasser 2004, and note 34 above.

41 RIC 260 = BMCRE 216, 319, Damsky 1990, with Strasser 2001, 131-135.

least one crown in Rome or Old Greece.[42] But the Roman events continued too: the last known victor was a Latin poet: Attius Tiro Delphidius, who was successful in the Capitolia of 338 or 342.[43]

Anchoring and the Capitolia

The Capitolian games were not only themselves anchored in Greek and Roman traditions, but they also provided an anchoring place for innovations elsewhere. Caldelli suggests that their foundation promoted a taste for Greek style agonistics even in the western provinces including Gallia Narbonensis, as most known athletes from that region postdate the institution of the Capitolia.[44] More secure signs of anchoring strategies are found in the eastern provinces, where several cities organised their own versions of the Capitoline games. No Capitolia were founded on proper Greek soil, but we find Capitolia and Isocapitolia (i.e festivals that claimed the same kind of rewards for their victors) in cities like Aphrodisias[45] and Antiocheia on the Maeander (Caria),[46] Perge (Pamphylia),[47] Olbasa (Pisidia),[48] Heliopolis[49] and Laodicea[50] (Syria) and Oxyrhynchus,[51] Antinoopolis,[52] and Hermoupolis[53] (Egypt), as well as an unknown city in Bithynia (fig. 4).[54] Not all these cities had a long Greek pedigree, but they may have wanted to use the festival culture to underline their claim to a Greek identity, while also signalling their allegiance to Rome. The Capitolia offered them a very Roman way to express their Greek identity and vice versa.

Domitian's Capitolia were a remarkable event. They succeeded where Nero had failed, in staging in the heart of Rome Greek style contests that reached out to an Empire-wide audience. Thus, Rome became a true 'assembly place for all the world'.[55] After Domitian's death and despite the *damnatio memoriae*, they were continued by Trajan and his successors for centuries and they may well have been Domitian's most successful innovation and longest lasting achievement.

---

42   C.Just 10.54.1: *coronis non minus tribus certaminis sacri, in quibus uel semel Romae seu antique Graeciae* (no less than three crowns in a sacred contest, among which at least one in Rome or Ancient Greece).
43   Caldelli 1993, 112 and no. 64, Rieger 1999, 201.
44   Caldelli 1997.
45   Roueché/de Chaisemartin 1993, 179-182 nos. 56-57.
46   Nollé 2009, 43-44, n. 231.
47   I.Perge 334, 336.
48   *IGR* 3, 411-4 +1493 with SEG 48, 1534.
49   Caldelli 1993, 117, Aliquot 2019.
50   Ziegler 1985, 147-151.
51   P.Harr I, 97, P.Oslo 3, 85 = P.Agon 89, P.Oxy 3135, 3116, 4080.
52   P.Agon 10 = P.Oxy, 3116.
53   SB 28, 16959, I.Side 130.
54   Moretti 1953, 87.
55   Cens. 18.5: *in illo orbis terrarum conciliabulo.*

Archaeological Evidence from Domitian's Palatine

Natascha Sojc

Archaeological Sources and the Domitian Palace[1]

Archaeological research concerning Domitian's palace has always focused on questions of the dating of the individual palace wings, which should allow a connection to the various emperors. For the Flavian period in general, and for the period roughly equivalent to the reign of Domitian, the archaeological sources have proven to be quite reliable. The palace's predominantly brick architecture shows *bipedales*, *i.e.* especially large bricks in the size of two Roman feet, at regular intervals in the layered masonry or on the relief arches above doorways and windows, often bearing a producer's stamp (fig. 1). The chronological order of these stamps has now been so well researched that it is possible with their help to assign various groups of rooms to Domitian's reign. In a further step this enables us to pose questions about the use and function of the palace architectures. However, since the luxurious furnishings of marble, gilding, mosaics and frescoes have mostly not survived, it is only possible to examine in a general sense which rooms would have served as the space in which Domitian conducted the business of Empire. For the interactions between Emperor and aristocracy at court, written sources mention above all banquets (*convivia*), morning audiences (*salutationes*), imperial rulings and counsels. For Domitian's palace architecture, therefore, a multitude of different uses of space must be assumed. Their function can nowadays only be derived from the architecture itself and will therefore always remain hypothetical. Moreover, it is also no longer possible to clarify which rooms were used by the Emperor himself or only by members of his family or court.

1   The author wishes to express her thanks to the Soprintendenza Speciale per i Beni Archeologici di Roma. Much appreciation and gratitude goes to the directors of the Netherlands Institute in Rome. I would like to express my particular gratitude to the German Archaeological Institute in Rome for its technical support. For their productive discussions I further wish to thank Evelyne Bukowiecki, Aurora Raimondi Cominesi, Léon Coret, Lisa Götz, Janet DeLaine, Pia Kastenmeier, Richard Neudecker, Alice Poletto, Andrea Schmölder-Veit, Hanna Stöger (†) and Clemens Voigts. For fruitful cooperation I wish to thank the Architekturreferat of the German Archaeological Institute, above all Ulrike Wulf-Rheidt (†) as well as Adolf Hoffmann, Jens Pflug and Dörthe Blume. A special debt of thanks is due to the Gerda Henkel Foundation, which financed and supported my study of the Domus Flavia.

	location	description	stamp	CIL	date
	room 525	brick type: bipedalis stamp shape: rectangular	CN DOMITIVS [palm twig] ARIGNOTVS·F	1094h	c. AD 75-100

Fig. 1. Example of brickstamp produced in the Flavian period found in situ in the walls of the Domus Flavia allowing a Domitian dating of the room. Rome, Domus Flavia (courtesy Léon Coret).

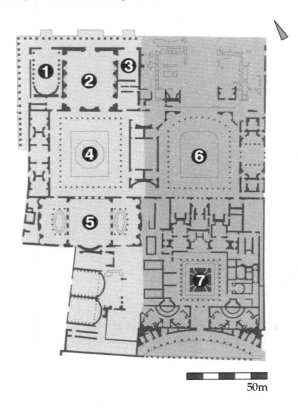

Domus Flavia
Domus Augustana

❶ Basilica
❷ Aula Regia
❸ Lararium
❹ Peristyle with fountain
❺ Cenatio Iovis
❻ Peristyle courtyard
❼ Sunken peristyle courtyard

Fig. 2 Overview of the nucleus of Domitian's palace with names given to individual wings and rooms by archaeological research for better orientation, but with no correspondence to ancient terminology. Rome, Palatine (A. Rheeder after instructions of the author).

50m

Multifunctional Palace Spaces for Courtly Interaction

The nucleus of Domitian's palace was formed by the adjoining wings of the so-called Domus Flavia and Domus Augustana which were arranged on one level,[2] expanding in some places to a basement level some 11 m below it or to a first storey above (fig. 2: i).[3] In research, the Domus Flavia is often interpreted as the public space of the emperor's palace and the Domus Augustana as his private area and retreat, because its ground plan appears subdivided into smaller spaces and conveys a secluded impression. However, the outstanding features that both wings have in common is their multifunctionality and their adaptability to a variety of occasions and interactions.

2   For the main level of circulation in the palace see Hoffmann/Wulf-Rheidt 2000, 293-298.
3   The naming of these wings does, as well as of individual rooms, e.g. 'Aula Regia' not correspond to an ancient terminology but archaeological jargon for orientation on the Palatine.

Fig. 3 Tribunal seen from the North c. 1870. Domus Flavia, so-called Basilica (ADA-F-000409-0000, Archivi Alinari, Firenze).

Domus Flavia

The most famous architectural structure from the Domitianic period in the Domus Flavia is most likely the so-called *Cenatio Iovis* that can be interpreted as a dining room (fig. 2): thanks to its floor plan, the internal position of the columns and the large openings on three sides, it can be recognized as a Cyzican oecus, a type of dining room described by Vitruvius.[4] In the north of the Domus Flavia three halls were identified as early as the eighteenth century by Francesco Bianchini, with their proposed functions still cited in the majority of research.[5] The excavator interpreted the so-called Basilica (fig. 3) as a room for imperial jurisdiction due to the tribunal, the so called Aula Regia (fig. 4: 531) as a reception hall and the Lararium (fig. 4: 532), due to its altar-like structure, as an entrance area of the palace.[6]

The Aula Regia and Basilica, together with movement divider 534, staircase 533, portico 515 and the Lararium, form a group of rooms opening onto the peristyle 516. The placement of the entrances is solely aimed at a regular design of the façade; *i.e.* the different dimensions of the

rooms were not visible from the outside and because of height difference in the terrain of more than 6 m there was no direct access from the north, from where the Domus Flavia appeared to sit elevated on a *basis*, (*i.e.* a platform). In the east, the group of rooms can only be reached after traversing the adjacent areas, whereas in the south they open onto the peristyle portico. The three halls, which are connected by two enfilades, differ in the size of their floor space,[7] in their furnishings but above all, in their accessibility. The Aula Regia, the central hall, could be entered through seven doorways, so that it was directly connected to all surrounding rooms, the movement divider to the upper storey, the north portico and the peristyle. It therefore offered more possibilities for different uses on different occasions than the Basilica with five or the Lararium with two entrances. If one uses the model developed by Mark Grahame for the evaluation of the degree of 'public' Roman architecture to interpret this characteristic difference, the Aula Regia proves to be a particularly easily accessible space and also appears as the central distributor within the three halls.[8] One can

---

4   See Gibson/DeLaine/Claridge 1994.
5   Cf. Bianchini 1738, 225.
6   Cf. footnote 3.

7   Aula Regia: approx. 1180 sqm, Basilica: approx. 620 sqm and Lararium: approx. 200 sqm.
8   Grahame 2000.

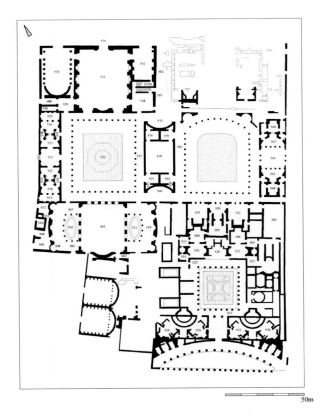

Fig. 4. Overall plan of the Domitian period with room numbers. Rome, Domus Flavia and Domus Augustana (A. Rheeder and M. Knechtl after instructions of the author).

imagine that the Aula Regia was probably used not only for a collective *salutatio* or a large-scale banquet but also for the reception of delegations, as the various entrances were suitable for regulating the flow of visitors. Furthermore, the Aula Regia – if Grahame's classification is applied further – could have served as the palace's internal equivalent of a square, perhaps as a meeting place for members of the court, which provided space for several groups' gatherings at the same time. The outstanding size and decoration of the Aula Regia, with columns in coloured marble, including pinkish *pavonazzetto* and yellowish *giallo antico*, and the 3.50 m high statues in green basalt, now in Parma, make it the most elaborate room of the imperial palaces on the Palatine known today. The hall also seems to have set new standards in comparison with public buildings existing in Rome at Domitian's time as it was only later surpassed in terms of size and splendour when the Basilica of Ulpia was built in Trajan's Forum.

Domus Augustana

In the Domus Augustana's 'sunken peristyle' a suite of rooms had been erected already in the Early Flavian period which were integrated into a further area of rooms on the main palace level and connected with a marble staircase during Domitian's reign (fig. 2). The assignment of this architecture to the Domitianic period had already been suggested by the excavator Alfonso Bartoli at the beginning of the twentieth century.[9] Documentation work carried out in the area since 2006, including a statistical study of the brickwork and brickstamps, has shown the dating to be largely correct. The elongated rooms, which due to their size should in some instances rather be addressed as halls,[10] opened with wide intercolumniations onto the peristyles and could have been used for the reception of delegations, or because of their characteristic layouts, also for courtly banquets (fig. 5). At the end of the first century the two peristyles and the fountain-atria might have been a novelty for the diners,[11] and the simultaneous dining on two floors must have impressed the visitors as an extraordinary sophistication (fig. 5). Against this luxurious background, various social interactions may have been staged, similar to those in the Domus Flavia. Also, the rooms of the Domus Augustana show a number of interconnections: they could be entered via an enfilade and also through a hall, *e.g.* 501.[12] To reach the southern area of room ensembles such like rooms 520 or 540, one was led through narrow corridors and had to pass either a guard standing in a niche or a door. The possibilities to control these accesses will perhaps not have been used for all occasions; for example, one can imagine all the doors of the Domus Augustana to have been thrown open for certain visitors.

Domitian's Palace – Spatial Structures in Comparison

In comparison to both the Neronian Domus Aurea on the Esquiline hill and the earlier palace constructions on the Palatine the Domitianic constructions in the Domus Flavia and the Domus Augustana seem to have aimed at a wide range of possibilities for differentiation of interaction through the architectural structures. The accessibility, visibility and permeability could be manipulated in various ways. Receptions, audiences and banquets could be staged according to the occasion or the wishes of the imperial host. For example, Domitian – or even one of his representatives or family members –

9   Cf. Bartoli 1929, Bartoli 1938.
10   Cf. room 551 with approx. 160 sqm.
11   For the fountain rooms 514 and 522 cf. Schmölder-Veit 2016.
12   Hall 501 measures approx. 200 sqm.

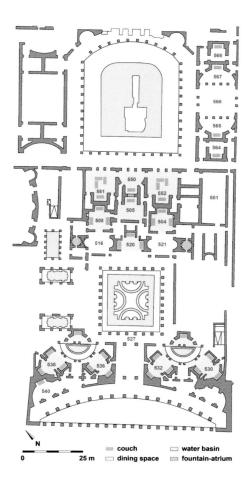

Fig. 5 Domus Augustana, hypothetical reconstruction of dining spaces for the Domitian period (C. Voigts and M. Knechtl after instructions of the author).

might have either greeted the persons gathered in the rooms collectively, or one after the other, if they were walking along the enfilade before him, while he reclined on a centrally placed couch. Just as well, for the purpose of a pre-selection according to status, the waiting people could have been received by a secretary in one of the rooms and from there they could have either been led forward or dispatched. Moreover, the spatial structures of the Domus Augustana and Domus Flavia would have lent themselves easily for the distinction of certain guests by their positioning near the god-like emperor surrounded by exquisite tokens of wealth, as well as being equally suitable for the harassment of aristocrats, by imposing on them long labyrinthine routes and long waiting times behind closed doors.[13]

---

13   Suggestions for further reading: Winterling 1999, Zanker 2002, Malmberg 2003, Bukowiecki 2008, Sojc 2012.

'Albanum Domitiani', Domitian's Villa in Castel Gandolfo

Claudia Valeri

A little over a century ago, Giuseppe Lugli, the first scholar to take an interest in the *'Albanum Domitiani'*, described the place as holding "a configuration so peculiar and so unlike any other in the Roman countryside, that it requires its own special set of rules to be studied".[1] What remains of the imperial villa lies today almost entirely within the confines of the papal property known as Villa Barberini;[2] in antiquity, however, the villa was at the center of a much larger property most likely starting at the Via Appia and extending towards the summit of the caldera and the borders of the lake which had been formed within. To the north, its limits would have coincided with the current center of Castel Gandolfo; to the south, with those of the town of Albano Laziale.

According to the literary sources, already Domitian's predecessors, the first having been Tiberius, and with the sole exclusion of Claudius, had frequented a residence known as *Albanum*. We are thus informed that an imperial property existed in the area, even though it remains uncertain how much of it coincided with the Domitianic complex. Since centuries, the area of the Alban Hill had already been dotted with residential complexes intended for the *otium* of the Roman *nobilitas*. To name only the most famous residents, Pompey, Lucullus, Cicero, Clodius, all had villas here. The *ager albanus* held many sources of attraction, amongst which we can count its proximity to Rome, only a mere 20 km away, as well as the beauty of its landscape, the scenery of the mythological deeds of the first

---

1   Lugli 1917, 29. Besides the work here cited, Lugli wrote numerous contributions on the topic still largely valid: Lugli 1914a-b, 1915, 1918, 1919a-b, 1920. Most recently, the imperial villa was the object of in-depth studies by Henner von Hesberg and his equipe, see especially von Hesberg 1978-1980, 1981, 2005, 2006, 2009. A monograph on the architectonic evolution of the villa is currently under preparation by Karolina Manfrecola: *Die Villa des Domitian am Albaner See. Bauforscherische Untersuchungen der antiken Überreste in und um die vatikanischen Gärten von Castel Gandolfo*, PhD Technische Universität Cottbus-Senftenberg, 2018-2019. The preliminary results of her research were kindly shared with the author and are presented here. See additionally Manfrecola 2020. Evidence of frequentation of the villa prior to Domitian is discussed in Di Giacomo 2020, through an in-depth analysis of epigraphic and literary sources.

2   With its extensive gardens, Villa Barberini at Castel Gandolfo is the most prominent of the Pontifical Villas. In accordance with the Concordat of February 11, 1929 between the Holy See and the Italian State, the property, once owned by the Barberini family, was assigned to the Vatican City State as an extraterritorial area to be added to the two pontifical properties of the Apostolic Palace and Villa Cybo. The complex had been a holiday retreat for the Pope since the seventeenth century; see Bonomelli 1953. In March 2014, by will of Pope Francis, the Apostolic Palace and Villa Barberini at Castel Gandolfo were made accessible to the public.

Fig. 1. Corbel from the theater in Domitian's villa. Castel Gandolfo, Antiquarium Barberini, Vatican Museums, inv. 59275. (courtesy Governatorato SCV – Direzione dei Musei. All rights reserved).

Latin peoples. On one side, the eye could rest on the crater lake of Albano and the surrounding hills, in particular Monte Cavo, once home to the federal sanctuary of the Latin League, dedicated to *Jupiter Latialis*. On the other, the sight would extend towards the broad stretch of the magnificent plain across the Via Appia, embracing almost entirely the coastal areas of the Tyrrhenian Sea south of Ostia. The mythological origins of the area indeed played a role in its later fortune. Statius calls it the *Dardanus ager*,[3] and other Flavian poets hardly pass on the chance of emphasizing the proximity of Domitian's residence with the ancient Trojan foundation of *Alba Longa*, home to the progeny that would one day make Rome.[4]

Nowadays, the hillside accommodating the gardens of Villa Barberini, which includes the ridge of of Lake Albano and the slope descending south-west towards the sea, is still divided in the same three large terraces, supported by two monumental substructures, of Domitian's residence. Its appearance today still bears the mark of the great work accomplished here by the architects and engineers of the emperor, among whom we should reasonably count the talented Rabirius. Cited by Martial in connection to the building enterprises on the Palatine, Rabirius likely took part in the planning of other architectural endeavors commissioned by the emperor. Even though the project of Domitian's villa must have included previous residential clusters within its plan, as proved by the remains resurfacing in various sections of the villa,[5] the plan remains one of absolute originality, characterised as it is by a series of building units of great enterprise distributed over a large area. Unfortunately, the absence of methodical excavations to cover the entire area left many questions open regarding the versatile features and the connections between these units.

On the upper terrace, large cisterns collected the rain water and, due to their high position, were able to supply all the edifices in the imperial residence. It is now believed that the central terrace – the largest and most complex structure, delimited uphill by the so-called 'avenue of the nymphaea', with a length of almost one kilometer and a width of one hundred meters – would have accommodated the actual residential quarter, as well as the more monumental buildings.

The Theater and its Findings

This vast terrace was characterised by the presence of a small theater, where no more than five hundred viewers could be seated. It was the place were poetic competitions and various spectacles took place, such as the March festivities sacred to Minerva (*Quinquatria Minervae*), a deity Domitian was particularly devoted to. A proof of this devotion is visible in a number of corbels in yellow marble (*giallo antico* from Numidia, modern Tunisia), possibly belonging to the decoration of this monument, adorned with owls with their wings spread (fig. 1).

The stage of the theater has not yet been completely excavated, while the area of the *orchestra* and a large portion of the stepped seats for the public (*cavea*) are clearly visible. Whereas its small size is comparable to that of other stage buildings from Roman villas, absolutely exceptional is its marmoreal decorative apparatus,[6] quite well reconstructed despite the large dispersion of material inflicted on the Domitianic complex by the phenomenon

---

3   Stat, *Silv.*5.3.228-229.

4   Stat. *Silv.* 5, 2, 168, Mart. *Epigr.* 5, 1-2. See also the contribution by Aurora Raimondi Cominesi & Claire Stocks in this volume.

5   These remains consist mostly of façade wall in *opus reticulatum*, the majority of which has been found in the central, residential unit of the villa. See most recently Manfrecola 2020.

6   Magi 1973-1974, von Hesberg 1981, 2005, 2006.

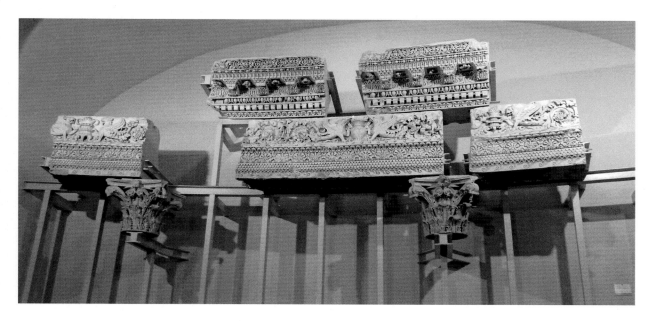

Fig. 2. Reconstruction of the *porticus in summa cavea*. Castel Gandolfo, Domitian's villa (courtesy Governatorato SCV – Direzione dei Musei. All rights reserved).

of reuse since Late Antiquity. The columned portico crowning the theater steps (*porticus in summa cavea*), was particularly elaborate and sumptuous, being enriched by a series of small nymphaea lavishly decorated in *opus sectile*. The richness of its decoration can be appreciated today by looking at the reconstruction of a small portion of the portico in the Antiquarium at Villa Barberini[7] featuring a series of capitals surmounted by fragments of the architrave and decorated with acanthus leaves and the well-known motif of two griffins flanking a crater (fig. 2-3). All these elements find a comparison with decorations of the late Domitianic period from Rome and Ostia.

Elements of the *frons scaenae* are on display in the same room at the Antiquarium. Its structure has been sufficiently well reconstructed at least for the first order; the appearance of the second is more uncertain, presumably its façade was punctuated by slender pilasters with statues to the forefront. At the center of the upper level a more elaborate entablature may have framed a statuary group of greater importance.[8] The entire monument was richly decorated: the ornaments of the pulpit appear to have been particularly intricate, with the insertion of large panels in *opus sectile*. The steps were covered with slabs of *giallo antico*, also used for the corbels, and Phrygian *pavonazzetto* marble was used for the balustrades, decorated with figures of actors wearing masks and dolphins.[9] Finally, the monumental parapets at the base of the *cavea* were adorned with scenes

Fig. 3. Corynthian capital from the theater of Domitian's villa. Castel Gandolfo, Antiquarium Barberini, Vatican Museums, inv. 36934 (courtesy Governatorato SCV – Direzione dei Musei. All rights reserved).

of *venationes* or griffins with cornucopias.[10] The ambulatory of the theater presented sophisticated stucco revetments of which some examples survives on the vaults. On the walls, the decorations were framed by architectural partitions and displayed mythological scenes, only a few of which survive today, with references to the themes and the characters that would have been found on stage in the theater.

7   Liverani 1989, 23-30.
8   Liverani 1989, 30-33.
9   Liverani 1989, 33-36, nos. 11-13.

10   Liverani 1989, 36 no. 14, 41 no. 17, fig. 17, 43-44 nos. 18.8-9.

Fig. 4. Panoramic view of one of the nymphaea. Castel Gandolfo, Domitian's villa (courtesy Governatorato SCV – Direzione dei Musei.

The Residential Buildings on the Central Terrace

Of the residential buildings placed on the central terrace, four large rooms with exedrae are still visible (fig. 4). In antiquity, the exedrae would have been richly coated with marbles and decorated with sculptures, and they would have accommodated water games. At approximately the center of the terrace an underground walkway, still usable, leads to the opposite side of the rim of the crater: from here, the emperor could have looked out and enjoyed the view on the Lake Albano, which could almost certainly also be reached on foot. At the end of the 'avenue of the nymphaea' the remains of the so-called 'imperial palace' are still visible. The area is little known today and even less understood. It appears to have been organised around various columned courtyards, and the remains of a ramp are still visible. Located at the outer margin of a multilevel construction, the ramp would have insured the connection between the middle and the upper storey.

The most significant of the surviving structures is the monumental cryptoporticus (fig. 5) carved into the substructure between the central and the lower terrace.

It is the most outstanding Roman edifice preserved today, even though it already partly collapsed in antiquity. Originally, it was likely divided in different sections, reaching a linear stretch of a little more than a thousand Roman feet (ca. 340 m), a height of 35 feet (a little over 10 meters), and a width of 25 feet (slightly less than 8 meters).[11] The southernmost section, already cut in the rock in antiquity to be used as quarry, was made more regular for about seventy meters, receiving light from a series of large windows opened in the intrados of the smooth vault. The remaining section that is still visible today was an independent structure taking light from large openings into the garden. Its vault displayed a coffered stucco decoration; stud prints on the walls point towards a marble revetment, most certainly in various coloured marbles. At the southern end, a staircase takes up the entire width of the edifice, and leads to a platform located ca. five m above ground level: we should imagine that the emperor Domitian would appear here to welcome his *clientes*

---

11   von Hesberg 2009, 327.

Fig. 5. View of the Cryptoporticus. Castel Gandolfo, Domitian's villa (courtesy Governatorato SCV – Direzione dei Musei.).

for the *salutatio*. For some time now the cryptoporticus has been considered to be a giant *aula* placed in direct communication with the entrance of the villa along the via Appia, with the function of directing guests towards the innermost part of the villa, the one reserved to the residential quarters. In this way, a central part of the imperial ceremonial came to be performed in the heart of the private residence, in a dialectic relationship between new sets of rules and daring architectonic designs, with two major consequences: the transformation of an *otium* villa into a sort of temporary seat of government and the abysmal distancing between the emperor and his subjects, not unlike the one existing between men and gods.[12]

The Lower Terrace

More elusive remains the appearance of the cluster of buildings downhill of the central terrace, among which is the so-called 'hippodrome', more likely a large,

monumentalised garden-space with a function similar to that of the Palatine stadium. From this area come a series of sculptures found during excavation works in the 1930s, currently mostly preserved in the Antiquarium at Villa Barberini. The findings, together with the material unearthed from the seventeenth century onwards, testify vividly to the quality of the sculptural decoration. The first mention of statues coming from the villa concerns four replicas of Praxiteles' Pouring Satyr found in 1657 in the vicinity of the theater.[13] It is easy to imagine, however, that more sculptural works have emerged during the renovation of the villa by the Barberini family.

It is not easy – and this may not be the place to do so – to try to reconstruct the decorative programmes unfolded in Domitian's villa, since its mobile furnishings have suffered an even more serious dispersion than its

---

12   von Hesberg 2009, 333.

13   The four statues, currently spread between Dresden, London and Malibu, were recently reunited on the occasion of an exhibition held at the Fondazione Prada in Milan, see S. Settis, *Serial/Portable Classic*, Milano 2015, 216-217.

Fig. 6. Statue of the 'Westmacott Ephebe' type. Castel Gandolfo, Antiquarium Barberini, Vatican Museums, inv. 36420 (courtesy Governatorato SCV – Direzione dei Musei. All rights reserved).

Fig. 7. Statue of Polyphemus in pentelic marble. Castel Gandolfo, Antiquarium Barberini, Vatican Museums, inv. 36410 (courtesy Governatorato SCV – Direzione dei Musei. All rights reserved).

architectonic material.[14] A few clusters of themes can nonetheless be discerned, as for example the depiction of athletes, testified by the discovery of a number of replicas of Classic Greek masterpieces. Among the most renowned is the beautiful head of the 'athlete Amelung', replica of a bronze sculpture attributed to Myron.[15] A copy of the Westmacott Ephebe (fig. 6),[16] is one of various replicas of

works created by the famous Polycletus, just like other pieces unfortunately found in a more fragmentary state.[17] The wonderful basanite torso of an athlete of the 'Ephesus type', derived from a late classical original attributed to the Polycletean school, can undeniably compete with bronze copies from the same original.[18]

The imperial villa was further enriched by a series of structures along the bank of the lake that functioned as summer triclinia and must have been equally richly decorated. Among these, the Bergantino nymphaeum deserves a special mention: originally a tuff quarry, the nymphaeum was remodeled with masonry coverings into a grotto of large dimensions, with alcoves organised around a large circular basin – nearly 13 meters in diameter – and a layout seemingly inspired by Tiberius' grotto in Sperlonga. As in Sperlonga, the surviving sculptural decorations refer to the adventures of Ulysses: a statue of Scylla in *bigio* marble emerged from the middle of the circular basin, while the episode of Polyphemus' blinding was set at the back of the cave. Of this group, in Pentelic marble, various fragments survive,

---

14   A comprehensive work on the topic is still wanting. A first attempt to round up the sculptural findings belonging to Domitian's villa dates to Lugli 1920; the work, however, fails to discern between the material actually coming from the villa at Castel Gandolfo and the material transferred from Rome or other residences to decorate the Barberini property (see Liverani 1993, 123-125). A group of finds pertaining to Domitian's villa is presented in Neudecker 1988, 139-144.

15   Castel Gandolfo, Villa Barberini, Antiquarium, inv. 36409, Picozzi 1975-1976, Liverani 1989, 62-63.

16   Castel Gandolfo, Villa Barberini, Antiquarium, inv. 36420, Liverani 1989, 55-58, 1993, 120-123.

17   Castel Gandolfo, Villa Barberini, Antiquarium, invv. 36407, 36408, 36406, Liverani 1989, 63-68.

18   Liverani 1989, 59-60, Belli Pasqua 1995, 78, no. 18, figs. 21-22. On the recent occasion of an exhibition on large Hellenistic bronzes, the Castel Gandolfo torso has been successfully compared to bronze replicas, see Daehner/Lapatin, 2015, 270-281.

among which is the Cyclops, depicted lying on a rock, drunk and immersed in sleep after having devoured some of Ulysses' companions (fig. 7).[19]

The Bergantino nymphaeum, which is open in the margin of the crater below the village of Castel Gandolfo and faces the lake, has all the characteristics of the *antra cyclopis*. This type of nymphaea, specifically used to accommodate the summer *triclinia* in the imperial villas, often reveal common features: their layout, the kind of lightning, which tends to be indirect or shielded, lending itself to evocative and imaginative effects, and, finally, the presence of sumptuous statuary decorations, in the context of which the saga of Ulysses, and in particular the adventure with the Cyclops Polyphemus, holds a place of honor. Domitian appears not to have given up on this crucial motif typical of the *otium* villas, thus recreating on the shores of Lake Albano a characteristic setting of the maritime residences located along the Thyrrenian coast of southern Lazio (Sperlonga) and the Phlegraean Fields (Baiae).

---

19   Castel Gandolfo, Villa Barberini, Antiquarium, inv. 36410, Magi 1968-1969, Liverani 1989, 71-80. To the group with the blinding certainly belongs the statue of a ram in Pentelic marble (inv. 36411), Liverani 1989, 79, no. 28. The identification of the subject is less certain for the fragment of a left male foot (inv. 59251), similarly found inside the Bergantino nymphaeum during the 1841 excavations by Giovanni Merolli.

PART V

Man and God

Domitian and Religion

Frederick G. Naerebout

Domitian and his contemporaries would not have been able to appreciate the phrase 'Domitian and religion' because in their fundamentalist world view the supernatural and man's relations with the supernatural (which is what I here roughly equate with the concept of 'religion') were omnipresent: for the Romans religion is not something that is there in addition to other aspects of life, but something that underlies all those aspects. Consequently, the study of Roman religion should be integrated into the study of Roman society at large. In Domitian's reign too, religion is everywhere: there is no politics or social life or whatever without religion playing a part. Nevertheless, there is nothing to keep us from paying special attention to what we would label as the specifically religious aspects of that reign – after all, neither politics nor economy in the way we conceive of those concepts were used by Romans to make sense of their society, but we could hardly do without them.[1] If only we keep in mind this fundamentalist nature of ancient religion: Domitian will not have thought, or done anything without in some way considering the supernatural as well as the human world and both worlds' responses.

Did Domitian also consciously *use* religion to further whatever goals he had as an emperor? If religious considerations were underlying all of his actions, as argued above, the answer must be affirmative. He did use religion, because everyone did: people in the ancient world were not primarily religious for the fulfilment of their *metaphysical* needs, but because they hoped the supernatural would address their *physical* needs and help them to survive, literally and figuratively, in a very harsh environment. For most of them, that was very much an individual thing. Those in a position of power, however, would have had rather more opportunities to make a difference beyond their own private destinies, by either propagating or counter-acting specific collective religious behaviours. To do so is manipulative, but it is not a cynical appeal to the supernatural by those who are in fact disbelievers; it rather shows the believers' trust in having the gods at their side. In the extremely hierarchical society of the Roman Empire, it is obvious that the gods would side with the powerful – who would be closer to the divine world anyhow, at least for as long as it lasted. Of course, the supernatural might desert one, something which everyone will have feared; the manipulators too, or even more so: the powerful have more to lose.

---

1   This should be enough to put a stop to the silly idea that we cannot use our concept of 'religion' when speaking of societies where the world is conceptualized in more or less different ways. Which does not mean that one should not have to worry about anachronisms and prejudices. Cf. Nongbri 2013, with the extensive review by Broucek 2015.

That Domitian took religion into consideration as a matter of course does not mean that he followed a religious policy. Roman emperors cannot really be said to have had any policy at all, and certainly no religious policy. *Religionspolitik*, which in essence is about the enforcement of adherence to a particular religious belief system, seems very much related to exclusive religions or religious denominations. It is hard to see how in the open, amorphous polytheism of the ancient world rulers could seek, or should even think of, influencing the religious convictions of their subjects.[2] However, in addition to individual and personal beliefs and choice, ancient religion is also about collective mythology and collective ritual. There, obviously, we find management, on all levels. But such management is about keeping things going according to the rules and regulations, not about prohibitions. When things are banned, we usually will find that this is not for religious reasons, for having "the wrong kind of religion", but because religion is supposed to be misused for, or functions as the cover for, seditious political activities.[3]

So, forget about 'policy' and let us move on to those of Domitian's deeds that might show us something of his religious convictions and which will have impacted to some extent the religious life of others. Here we have to deal with the fact that our sources for Domitian's reign are in large part produced after his murder by a palace cabal and after his symbolic erasure from collective memory (*damnatio memoriae*) by the Senate. The 'black legend' was intended to enlist Domitian amongst the 'bad emperors' and to maximize the contrast with his successors. Its existence means that we have plenty of anecdota and rather less hard facts than we would like to have.[4]

We can, however, certainly characterize Domitian as autocratic: pushing the emperor's power at the expense of the Senate.[5] He was also suspicious and ruthless: those who were a threat to his power, or were seen to be so, had to fear for their lives. But so-called 'good emperors' were just as ruthless. Domitian was not the 'blood-thirsty tyrant' that the black legend made him out to be (with lasting success). Above all, he was a micromanager, involving himself in the minutiae of running the Empire. He must have been extremely busy – as any emperor who took his role at all seriously, let alone an emperor like Domitian who took that role very seriously.

Domitian considered himself to be a *curator morum et legum*, protector of customs and laws, as Augustus before him.[6] In his quest for a traditional Augustan *pietas*, "doing one's duty", as in several other aspects, it might seem as if he wanted to turn the clock back to Augustan days. That is too simple. Domitian is a conservative in as far as all Romans were conservatives, that is to say, they embrace a conservatism of a quintessentially Roman kind, looking back to an idealized past, speaking of restoration and renovation, and at the same time carrying through innovation in a most pragmatic manner. The present has to be cloaked in the past in order to be acceptable.[7]

Domitian's "obsessive concern with administrative detail"[8] included strict adherence to the traditional religion of the city of Rome. Already as Caesar, Domitian was invested with several priestly offices: *augur, frater arvalis, pontifex* and *sacerdos collegiorum omnium*. On acceding to the imperial throne after the death of Titus he became *pontifex maximus*. This is nothing out of the ordinary – but it gave him considerable power over the religious life of Rome.[9] And, apparently to some surprise, he made use of that power. Religious laws were now strictly maintained, as can be seen from his crackdown on the Vestals virgins: the virgins who were not virginal, were executed. Everyone had to stick to the rules and regulations. Indeed, Domitian may have seen this as a specific mission that he had to fulfil: he was said to have called himself the *ultor deorum*, the "avenger of the gods".[10]

Lapsed ritual was re-instated. For instance, after the great fire of Rome Nero promised the erection of altars to ward of future fires, but this vow had been *diu neglectum nec redditum*, "neglected for a long time and not fulfilled". But no longer![11] In the black legend, Domitian's moralism and religious strictness were presented as nothing but the hypocrisy of an immoral ruler. In fact, we have reason to consider Domitian a pious man, possibly a man quite fearful of the gods – certainly no hypocrite.

Specific for Domitian was his great personal preference for specific gods: Jupiter Optimus Maximus, the Capitoline Jupiter, patron deity of Rome par excellence, and Minerva, another Capitoline deity. Because Jupiter had saved Domitian's life in 69, when an *aedituus*, sacristan, of the Capitoline Temple hid him from the Vitellian forces, he

---

2   Naerebout 2014. Cf. Woolf 2018.

3   'Heresy' or 'idolatry' are hardly possible in a polytheistic context: "Polytheism is an open system," in the classical formulation by Walter Burkert (1985, 176).

4   Charles 2002.

5   Galimberti 2016, 96, lists several indicators of Domitian's autocratic tendencies.

6   *Res Gestae (Monumentum Ancyranum)* 6.1. As Rutledge 2001, 83 reminds us, this moralistic streak was present in Roman society from well before Augustus.

7   Lind 1979.

8   Jones 1992, 107.

9   Considerable power, not absolute power; therefore, each *princeps* also joined all of the major priestly colleges, thereby claiming a monopoly over all the religious bodies that advised the Senate: R.M. Polk, *Circa deos ac religiones: Religion and the Emperor from Augustus to Constantine*, Dissertation Harvard University 2008, quoted by Suess 2011, 5.

10   Stat. *Silv.* 5.3.195-204.

11   *ILS* 4914.

built a shrine dedicated to Jupiter Conservator, later replaced by a temple to Jupiter Custos;[12] he restored the Capitoline temple after damage by fire in 80; he reorganized the *sodales Flaviales* who now focused on the cult of Jupiter;[13] in 86 he instituted the Capitolia (Capitoline Games – which survived until the fourth century[14]); and he preferred to stay at his Alban villa at the site of the ancient sanctuary of Jupiter Latiaris.[15]

His personal preference for Minerva was strong enough for him to have a *sacrarium*, shrine, to Minerva in his bedroom;[16] a new legion raised for the war against the Chatti was called Legio I Minervia; Minerva figured on coinage;[17] a new temple was built for Minerva Chalcidicia;[18] the *templum Castoris et Minervae* was restored;[19] a shrine for Minerva was erected in or near the temple of Divus Augustus;[20] the new Forum Transitorium included a temple to Minerva; [21] a yearly festival, the Quinquatria, for Minerva was instituted at Domitian's Alban villa;[22] and the huge equestrian statue put up in the Forum showed Domitian wearing his *paludamentum*, cuirass and sword, extending his right hand in a gesture of clemency, while holding a statue of his patron goddess Minerva in his left.[23]

But Domitian also paid special homage to the Egyptian gods; he may have felt compelled to do so, as the Flavian emperors before him had also supported Egyptian religion. Vespasian had cultivated a personal relationship with Serapis, Vespasian and Titus with Isis. But apart from family tradition, Domitian had his own reasons not to neglect the Egyptian gods: he had escaped from his opponents in 69 by mingling in disguise in an Isiac procession. Domitian had the Isis temple restored and obelisks erected.[24] Possibly Domitian considered Serapis

to be Jupiter in Egyptian guise, and Isis Minerva – which would make good sense from his point of view.[25]

Already several temples have been mentioned as built or restored by Domitian. He was a great builder who left a large architectural heritage in the city of Rome – not just temples, but also the Odeum and Stadium in the Campus Martius, as the infrastructure for the games he instituted.[26] He also inherited building projects of his father and brother: he finished the Colosseum, the Temple of Pax,[27] the Baths of Titus,[28] a new palace on the Palatine, the Arch of Titus *in sacra via*, the Temple of Vespasian[29] and the Temple of the Gens Flavia.[30] And one should add his benefactions abroad: amongst the sanctuaries that benefitted from his largesse are the Asklepieion at Pergamon,[31] the temple of Demeter at Ephesus, the temple of Artemis at the same place and the Apollo temple at Delphi.[32]

The work on the Temple of Vespasian and the Temple of the Gens Flavia shows the dynastic dimension. In the Campus Martius Domitian instigated a new temple in honour of his father and brother, the Templum Divorum.[33] Which brings us to the 'imperial cult' – which can sometimes be a misnomer, and sometimes not, depending on time, place, and person. Undoubtedly, most inhabitants of the Empire considered their ruler as not an ordinary human being, they knew that gods wander the earth and that deification of the deceased is an option, but they also sensed that the emperor, alive or dead, is in a different league compared to Zeus or Jupiter.[34] Need we choose between cult and mere reverence? One can pray to the emperor (or his *genius* or whatever: does that make much of a difference for the man in the street?) to save

12 Tac. *Hist.* 3.74, Suet. *Dom.* 5.1. The exact location is disputed.

13 Suet. *Dom.* 4.4, Escamez de Vera 2016, with the review by John Jacobs, *Bryn Mawr Classical Review* 2017.03.56.

14 Heinemann 2014, 224: "[Die Phänomene] dokumentieren nicht eine plötzliche, von idiosynkratischen Launen diktierte Hinwendung zu griechischen Wettkämpfen, sondern die politische Instrumentalisierung eines umfassenden gesellschaftlichen Prozesses." See Onno van Nijf, Robin van Vliet & Caroline van Toor in this volume.

15 Plin. *HN* 3.69.

16 Suet. *Dom.* 15.2.

17 Morawiecki 1977, Bülow-Clausen 2012, Girard 1981.

18 Nash 1968, II. 66-68, Richardson 1992, 256.

19 *Chronographus anni 354* (= *MGH* 9.143-148), 146. Or Castorum. Work must have been limited as the building is essentially Augustan (Richardson 1992, 75). Or a *sacellum* for Minerva was built against the back of the podium, see Richardson 1992, 255 s.v. Minerva, Templum. A completely new temple is not likely.

20 Mart. 5.53.1-2, *ILS* 1998.

21 *CIL* 6.953. The Forum: Richardson 1992, 167-169 s.v. Forum Nervae: "a triumph of ingenuity and imagination" (167).

22 Suet. *Dom.* 4.4.

23 Stat. *Silv.* 1.1.

24 See Miguel John Versluys in this volume.

25 Jones 1992, 101.

26 Even this could be used against the emperor: "You are not pious or ambitious in a noble way, you are out of your mind: you have a building mania; like the famous Midas, you want that everything you touch turns into gold and stone": Plut. *Publ.* 15.

27 Or replaced the cult statue? Stat. *Silv.* 4.3.17.

28 Thermae Titi (Titianae): Richardson 1992, 396-397.

29 Templum Vespasiani et Titi: *CIL* 6.938 = *ILS* 255 (only Vespasian is mentioned in the inscription, but the building was completed by Domitian).

30 Temple built on the site where Domitian was born; intended as a mausoleum for the Flavii Pasqualini, cf. the appendix in Southern 1997.

31 Habicht 1969, 6-8.

32 *ILS* 8905 = *CIL* 3.14203 = *Syll.*3.821a = *FD* 3.4,120.

33 In the oldest testimonia it is called Templum Divorum (*CIL* 6.10234 = *ILS* 7213), Richardson. 1992, 111, Nash 1968, I, 304. Cf. Richardson 1992, 110, fig. 26.

34 As Hannestad 1988, 130-135 puts it: "in the course of the first century AD it had become a firmly rooted tradition to conceptualize virtues and qualities of the emperor in minor deities ... in order to visualize how he has elevated above normal persons." Cf. Hölscher 2004, 88-90. On the Cancelleria Reliefs: Baumer 2008 and Paolo Liverani in this volume. The emperors are imagined on the reliefs meeting divine personified concepts at eye level.

us simple creatures, and also pray to the gods to protect the emperor. It is the emperor who makes things happen and guarantees the status quo because he is godlike or some kind of god – which is why (or/and which is helped by the fact that) his ancestors are gods, or a kind of gods. The emperor is also mortal – he might even be removed from office, murdered, struck out of collective memory. Imperial cult has ambiguity 'built in', so to say.[35]

And Domitian himself? By his time, not to enthusiastically embrace imperial cult or whatever it should be called, was no longer an option: we have seen the emperor propagating temples dedicated to his predecessors – and he himself would join in.[36] Also, the Flavian use of dynastic themes on coinage was put on a new footing by the appearance on reverses of members of the imperial family who were posthumously deified: Domitian's brother Titus;[37] his son, who died an infant;[38] his niece Julia, daughter of Titus;[39] and Flavia Domitilla, more likely his mother, Domitilla the Elder, than his sister. Domitilla also figures on the reverses of *aurei* that honour her deified husband.[40] Domitian is also said to have suggested, or decreed according to later authors, that he should be addressed henceforth as *dominus et deus*, which would mean that he entertained extreme ideas about his own divinity, but it is unlikely to be true.[41]

We have seen Domitian supporting religion; how about Domitian repressing it? His suspicions and prejudices can clearly be seen from the expulsion or expulsions of so-called philosophers (i.e., those publicly criticizing him; or, disconcertingly, those trying *not* to be involved in politics – heads, tails, you lose) and astrologers (not diviners: divination was part of traditional Roman religion). Domitian consulted astrologers – as did a great many people for many centuries – and thought highly of their predictions; all the more reason to be disconcerted when other members of the elite did the same and might ask dangerous questions, for instance about the length of their monarch's reign. Such people were conspirators trying to get otherworldly support and one could never know how persuasive they might be: trickery, magical practices, fickle fate, one had better be safe than sorry.

Other groups that modern commentators have supposed to have fallen foul of Domitian are Jews and Christians. Domitian might very well have been suspicious of the Jews in the Empire: his dynasty is after all very much rooted in the military successes of Vespasian and Titus in the Jewish War. But in fact, the only thing we hear of is the rigorous collection of the *fiscus Iudaicus* – the tax all Jews had to pay, now also collected from converts and from Jews not practicing their religion. That does not, however, add up to persecuting Jews or forbidding them to practice their religion: it seems to be mainly about income and holding up the law, in this instance a 'family tradition' as well, the *fiscus* having been instituted after the Jewish War.

Domitian has gone down as the second persecutor of the Christians, Nero being the first. In fact, there is no shred of evidence.[42] The *Apocalypse of John* has been read as referring to Domitian, but its dating is uncertain, and even when we accept a date towards the end of Domitian's reign, as stated by Irenaeus,[43] it is highly unlikely that the text refers to Domitian.[44] Pliny the Younger remarks that he had never attended a trial of Christians, which implies that such trials did take place during Domitian's reign.[45] But a couple of trials because of *impietas* and *maiestas* (atheism and treason/disloyalty) do not make a persecution. It was Eusebius who in his *Church History*, over two centuries later, stated that Domitian persecuted the Christians and from then onwards the legend of a Domitianic persecution gained ever more traction. Being a bad emperor, Domitian *must* have been an enemy of true believers: *iniusti imperatores*, unjust emperors, are *insecutores Christi*, persecutors of Christ, as Melito of Sardes put it.[46] But without any evidence that Christians were targeted empire-wide, the only thing we can say is that it may have been dangerous to be both a member of an important family and to be seen to sympathize with Jews or Christians, because in that way one would provide *delatores*, informers, with an opportunity to charge one with treason. Rather more important than chasing after a persecution that most likely never happened, is to be aware of the fact that the reign of the Flavians was a most important formative period for early Christianity, when it was likely that the Gospels took shape. There was religious fervour all around, and it included the emperor.

---

35   This is largely the position already taken by Price 1984, 94.

36   Adamo Muscettola 2000. In the *sacellum* of the Augustales at Misenum there are preserved marble over life-size, nude statues of Vespasian and Titus, and a bronze of Domitian, reworked as Nerva (after his *damnatio memoriae*), here Fejfer, fig. 6.

37   *RIC* 2 Domitian, 126-131.

38   *RIC* 2 Domitian, 132-136, where the deceased son is associated with his mother Domitia, *Divi Caesaris mater*, "Mother of the Deified Caesar"; Domitia Longina, Augusta, probably served as priestess of her own child's cult: an issue of *dupondii* shows Domitia pouring a libation over an altar inscribed *Divi Caesaris Mater* (*RIC*2 Domitian, 136). See also *RIC*2 Domitian, 152-155.

39   Julia Titi, *RIC* 2 Domitian, 147 (during her lifetime!), 683-684, 717-718, 760, 848-849 (posthumously).

40   Wood 2016, 135, cf. Wood 2010.

41   Dominik 1994, 158-159, Witulski 2010, 71. On all aspects of deification under Domitian: Chabrečková, 2017.

42   Speigl 1970.

43   *Adversus haeresos* 5.30,3.

44   Riemer 1998, and the summary in Riemer 2000, 75-76.

45   Plin. *Ep.* 10.96.1.

46   Melitho is supposed to be the source of Tertullianus, *Liber Apologeticus* 5.1-5. See on Christian responses to Domitian Maria Paola Del Moro in this volume.

"To protect the gods from being dishonoured with impunity by any sacrilege, he caused a tomb which one of his freedmen had built for his son from stones intended for the temple of Jupiter of the Capitol to be destroyed by the soldiers and the bones and ashes contained in it thrown into the sea."[47] Is there any reason to trust these words of Suetonius who has contributed more than any other author to the black legend about Domitian? Yes, there is: Suetonius is here speaking about the years *before* the emperor supposedly turned tyrant, and wants us to see the good, and godly, emperor. The tyrant of legend is contrasted with the pious *cultor deorum* – with an eye for detail and a severe disposition: for all we know, that is the real Domitian.

---

47   Suet. *Dom.* 8.5. Translated by J. C. Rolfe (Loeb Classical Library, 1914).

Master and God: Domitian's Art and Architecture in Rome

Diane Atnally Conlin

In late October 51, the *gens Flavia* welcomed a baby boy at their ancestral home on the Quirinal hill in Rome. Located on 'Pomegranate Street' (*ad Malum Punicum*), and now lost due in large part to the later construction of the Temple of the Flavian family in roughly the same location, the house had been the property of the newborn's grandfather, Titus Flavius Sabinus, a wealthy tax collector of equestrian rank and client of several powerful Roman families (see for Flavian Rome, Moormann, fig. 1).[1] The infant named Domitian (Titus Flavius Domitianus) entered the world as the second son of a seasoned and respected military legate of senatorial rank, Titus Flavius Vespasianus. Shortly after Domitian's birth, Vespasian took on the distinguished political mantle of consul elect, while Domitian's twelve-year-old brother, Titus (also Titus Flavius Vespasianus), continued his studies alongside Emperor Claudius' son, Britannicus, at the imperial court. Despite the military and political accomplishments of Domitian's relatives, there must have been little anticipation that the child of Sabine heritage born that autumn day would inherit the imperial scepter of Rome, and even less expectation that young Domitian would become the first emperor to suffer an official damnation by the Senate following his assassination in 96.

Nineteen years later, after the bloody civil wars following Nero's death in 68 that ended once Vespasian's allies' had defeated Vitellius and his supporters in late 69, Domitian was first introduced to Rome's inhabitants as a potential but decidedly junior heir to the throne through coins, the most expedient avenue for political messaging in Rome. Prior to Vespasian's triumphant arrival in the capital towards the end of 70 as the new ruler of the Roman Empire, the mint issued silver coins (*denarii*) with the unabbreviated names of Domitian and his older brother, Titus, accompanied by small-scale depictions. The imperial princes, designated as such by the honorific title, *Caesar*, were shown in traditional and easily recognizable compositions, including astride rearing horses as well as seated side by side in magistrates' chairs (fig. 1). Later that same year, facing busts of Titus and Domitian appear on the reverses of gold coins (fig. 2), a conventional numismatic design for dynastic succession already exploited by previous emperors, including Augustus and the ignoble Vitellius. Given the small size of the picture field on these gold issues, the coin portraits are little more than generic, youthful male heads, but the message was clear and direct. Vespasian's court advisors had directed

---

1   Suet. *Dom.* 1. For a summary of Domitian's early years and family connections, see Jones 1993, 1-3.

Fig. 1. *Aureus* minted in Lugdunum under Vespasian showing Titus and Domitian seated on curule chairs, 71. London, British Museum, inv. 1933,0414.1 (courtesy The Trustees of the British Museum).

Fig. 2. Aureus minted in Rome under Vespasian showing facing busts of Titus and Domitian on reverse, 70. Amsterdam, National Numismatic Collection, inv. RO-02920 (courtesy of De Nederlandsche Bank).

Fig. 3. *Aureus* minted in Rome under Vespasian; Domitian on a horse with a raised scepter, 73. London, British Museum, inv. R1874,0715.26 (courtesy The Trustees of the British Museum).

the moneyers at Rome responsible for engraving the coin dies (*signatores*) to craft types that would emphatically advertise the stability and blatant masculinity of the new Flavian dynasty.[2] Despite the preeminent position of his older and more battle-hardened brother, Domitian continued to appear regularly on his father's coins as a Caesar throughout Vespasian's decade-long reign, either beside his victorious brother or alone on a horse (fig. 3). Domitian's portrait bust did not appear on the obverse of a coin without his brother until 72, when his twenty-one year old, idealized profile was selected to adorn a limited series of bronze asses, and again in 73 for gold and silver issues minted during Domitian's second consulship as the junior crown prince-in-waiting.

His earliest sculpted portrait types appeared in 75, and are associated with contemporary coin images and marble portraits such as the full-length, heroically nude statue of young Domitian from Labicum, its bland portrait head re-carved from an earlier portrait of Nero (fig. 4).[3] Not surprising, Domitian's early portraits stress his physical resemblance to his father and older brother by emphasizing his similarly broad Flavian cranial structure, his small deep-set eyes, and his thin lips. Physiognomic congruity between the portraits of the Emperor and his Caesar sons was a critical component for reinforcing a cohesive dynastic image for the new ruling family. Possibly the nude Labicum statue, moreover, had been chosen to underscore Domitian's vitality and worthiness as the second heir to the throne.

When his older brother, Emperor Titus, died unexpectedly from an illness in 81, Domitian was almost thirty years old. He inherited without resistance or controversy not only the throne but also a capital city relatively little changed from the influential, citywide construction projects of Augustus.[4] The placement of the earlier Flavian structures commissioned by Domitian's father and his brother had been confined to the area previously occupied by Nero's audacious residential estate (the *Domus Aurea*), as well as the nearby zone of the imperial fora of Julius Caesar and Augustus, the founders of the previous Julio-Claudian dynasty. In 70/71, Vespasian had rebuilt out of necessity the Temple of Jupiter Optimus Maximus on the Capitoline hill after the sacred shrine's destruction in 69 as a result of the political violence during

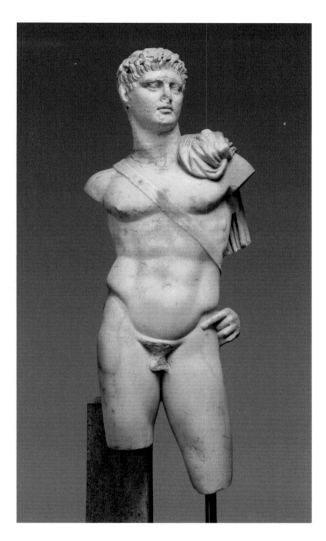

Fig. 4. Portrait of Domitian from Labicum in heroic nudity, c. 75. Munich, Glyptothek, inv. GL 394 (State Collections of Antiquties and Glyptothek Munich, photo Renate Kühling).

the last days of Vitellius' short reign. In addition to this important temple refurbishment and his completion of Nero's neglected and partially dismantled temple to the Divine Claudius on the Caelian hill, Domitian's father also constructed or initiated the erection of two significant victory monuments financed with the spoils of his successes in the Jewish Wars: the Flavian amphitheater (the Colosseum), begun in 70/71 on what had once been the artificial lake of Nero's Golden House; and the innovative, museum-like portico complex known as the Temple of Peace (*Templum Pacis*) constructed close by Augustus' grand public forum and dedicated in 75 in conjunction with Vespasian's extension of the sacred boundary of the city (*pomerium*).

Unlike long-lived Vespasian, Titus enjoyed little time to make an impact on the topographical narratives of

---

2   For a discussion of *signatores*, see most recently Bond 2016, 126-132.

3   Portraits of Domitian are few in number due to the destructive consequences of his damnation in 96. Likewise, no posthumous images were commissioned. All of the surviving portraits of Domitian were made during his lifetime; many were subsequently re-carved with the aged, gaunt features of his successor, Nerva. See Jane Fejfer in this volume.

4   On Flavian interventions in Rome, see Eric M. Moomann in this volume.

Fig. 5. Portrait of Domitian, c. 88. Rome, Musei Capitolini, Museo del Palazzo dei Conservatori, inv. MC 1156 (photo Musei in Comune – Roma).

Rome given his truncated, two-year reign. Nevertheless, Domitian's older brother managed to complete his bath complex adjacent to the Colosseum in 80, erect a triple-bay triumphal arch at the eastern end of the Circus Maximus, dedicate the enormous entertainment amphitheater begun by their father, and begin construction on a stately temple at the west end of the Forum Romanum for the worship of Divus Vespasianus.[5] However, disaster struck the capital again in 80 when a devastating fire destroyed significant parts of the city, including the recently rededicated Temple of Jupiter Optimus Maximus.[6] Much of Rome, including a large area of the Campus Martius, was in need of repair when Domitian ascended the imperial throne on September 14, 81.

During the early years of his reign, Domitian focused on speedy projects that would quickly bolster his legitimacy and enhance his as yet untested military reputation by underlining his familial relationships with both Vespasian and Titus. Over a century earlier, Augustus had overtly celebrated his unique status as the son and heir of a god, the Divine Julius Caesar; Domitian, on the other hand, could claim two gods as his predecessors and direct ancestors: his triumphant and respected father, and his illustrious and popular older brother. Domitian's early architectural activities and additions to the landscape of the city were surprisingly modest and, in retrospect, restrained despite the new construction opportunities afforded by the recent conflagration. In addition to completing Titus' unfinished rebuilding of the once again destroyed Temple of Jupiter Optimus Maximus, he commissioned the ingenious maze of underground corridors (*hypogeum*) under the arena of the Flavian amphitheater as well as at least one structure for gladiatorial training (Ludus Magnus) adjacent to the amphitheater. Domitian also constructed a facility for mock sea battles (*naumachia*) somewhere in Rome, completed and rededicated the Corinthian temple of the Divine Vespasian in the Forum Romanum to include his divinized brother, Divus Titus, and erected a single-bay triumphal arch to commemorate Titus' decade old Judean victories across the open area of the Forum Romanum opposite the *Templum Divi Vespasiani et Titi*. On either side of the interior surfaces of the arched passageway, large relief panels sculpted from Greek Attic marble artfully depict the crowded triumphal procession celebrated by his dead and divinized brother, with particular visual emphasis given to the captured religious paraphernalia, especially the great seven-branched, golden menorah looted by Roman troops from the Second Temple at Jerusalem (Levick, figs. 1-3).[7]

The placements of Domitian's early construction efforts in the heart of the old Roman forum may betray his evolving topographical strategy; the Arch of Titus (with the colossal Flavian amphitheater rising high in the sky behind it) and the rededicated Temple of Divine Vespasian and Titus effectively enclosed and thereby spatially controlled the earlier buildings of Augustus and the Julio-Claudians within new Domitianic monumental brackets. At the outset of his fifteen-year reign, Domitian appears to have consciously and overtly celebrated the glorious reputations of his immediate kin through changes to the urban topography of Rome; simultaneously, he began to deliberately elevate his own imperial authority by commissioning projects to emulate and ultimately surpass the pre-existing structures of Rome's first and now legendary emperor, Augustus. Later in 91, Domitian would complete this narrative with his bronze equestrian statue (*Equus Domitiani*), a now lost but once colossal monument extravagantly praised in poetry by Statius that was erected in the open area of the Forum Romanum facing

5   On the baths, see Suet. *Tit.* 7.3 and Dio Cass. 66.25.1.
6   Dio Cass. 66.24.

7   On this and other reliefs, see Paolo Liverani in this volume.

east towards the Arch of Titus and the Colosseum off in the distance.[8] No doubt Domitian expected that, like Augustus, he too would rise to the heavens in apotheosis and be forever worshipped as a deity alongside his divine father.

Reflection and innovation were also combined in the design of Domitian's mature portraits. Created around 88, his official imperial portrait was a curious blend of familiar Flavian facial similarities reborn with inventive details that curiously correspond to unusual physical traits of earlier emperors (fig. 5). In sculpture, Domitian continued to resemble his father and brother, but his adult portraits were also distinct and individualized. For most images based on Domitian's officially sanctioned third portrait type – an official image which appears to have remained relatively unchanged for the rest of his reign – the artists retained a realistic rendering of his facial features while also adding idiosyncratic attributes, such as the protruding upper lip (similar to Gaius Caligula) and an artfully coifed hairstyle of thick curls (similar to Nero's Helios-inspired tiara hairdo), this despite Domitian's notorious baldness. In portraiture, Domitian's likeness had evolved into a visual amalgamation of both the Julio-Claudian and Flavian dynasties. His public visage represented the venerated past and the superior present simultaneously.[9]

During his fourteenth consulship and soon after completing his second campaign on the Danube against the Dacians in 89, Domitian embraced the responsibilities of his role as sole *imperator* and master (*dominus*) of Rome. He began to install new monuments into the topography of the city, many of which no longer directly aggrandized the memories of his divinized immediate predecessors. For example, in conjunction with his newly established Greek-style festival in honor of Jupiter, the Capitoline Games (*Ludi Capitolini*) first held in 86, Domitian commissioned an impressive footracing track (*stadium*) as well as a recital auditorium (*odeum*) in the central Campus Martius, an area recently damaged by fire in 80.[10] Together, Domitian's new entertainment facilities flanked the western sides of the earlier Baths of Nero and the public pool (*stagnum*) of Augustus' colleague, Agrippa. East of these prominent Julio-Claudian monuments, Domitian also heavily restored the unique, hybrid Egyptian-Roman temple precinct of Isis and Serapis,[11] as well as the curious complex dedicated to the divine Vespasian and Titus known as the Porticus Divorum, a structure similar in design to Vespasian's *Templum Pacis* and one that possibly replaced the early imperial civic building known as the Villa Publica. The famous but still controversial marble Cancelleria reliefs

Fig. 6. Aureus with Minerva holding spear on reverse, minted at Rome under Domitian, 83 (March-Sept), RIC II (revised second edition), 168.

Fig. 7. Relief fragment from the *Templum Gentis Flaviae* representing a soldier. Rome, Museo Nazionale Romano, Palazzo Massimo alle Terme, inv. 310257 (courtesy of Ministero per i Beni e le Attività Culturali e per il Turismo – Museo Nazionale Romano).

depicting Vespasian's *adventus* and Domitian's *profectio* may have originally adorned an arch attached to or located with the Divorum complex (Liverani, figs. 2-3). Again, Domitian's monuments in the central Campus Martius were designed to frame and thereby constrain the pre-existing Augustan and Neronian urban narratives. In 89, he also finished construction of a final monument in the Colosseum zone, a structure possibly begun by his

---

8   Stat. *Silv.* 1.1. See Muth 2010.
9   See on portraits, Jane Fejfer and Caroline Vout in this volume.
10   See Onno van Nijf, Robin van Vliet & Caroline van Toor in this volume.
11   See Miguel John Versluys in this volume.

older brother. Known as the Meta Sudans, the massive conical shaped fountain served as the final declaration of Flavian domination over the razed palace of Nero. The enormous fountain also marked the junction of four of Augustus' regions of the city and the eastern terminus of the Via Sacra. Like Augustus, Domitian exploited the visibility and symbolism of heavily trafficked areas of the capital.

At around the same time as these constructions in the central Campus Martius and the area of the Colosseum, Domitian likely began his grand residence on the Palatine Hill (finished in 92) with its multiple levels, winding corridors, staircases, fountains, statues, ornate gardens, private quarters, and posh staterooms. The complex known as the Domus Augustana and the Domus Flavia, completely altered the topography of the Palatine, and no other monument of Domitianic Rome better represents Domitian's aspiration to be the new living god (deus) of the capital and the Empire.[12] Silver Age poets, such as Statius, praised in effusive verse the palace's location, scale, and decorative program. By constructing a massive residence on the Palatine within viewing distance of Jove's shrine on the Capitoline and close by the older Temple of Apollo Palatinus, Domitian not only challenged the legacy of pious Augustus but also the omnipotent power of Domitian's favorite male Olympian, Jupiter. Another favorite and most honored deity of Domitian was Minerva. Struck as early as the first year of his reign, images of the martial goddess dominated the reverses of Domitianic gold and silver coins (fig. 6). Minerva, goddess of war, wisdom, and craft, remained Domitian's beloved and ever-present patron deity until the end of his fifteen-year reign.[13] He constructed at least two temples to her in Rome: a small round temple to Minerva Chalcidica near the Divorum in the Campus Martius; and the much larger Temple of Minerva with its long, narrow portico referred to as the Forum Transitorium (later rededicated as the Forum of Nerva) located between the fora of Caesar and Augustus and Vespasian's Temple of Peace.

One of the last structures built by Domitian in Rome was his bold, innovative temple to the Flavian Family (Templum Gentis Flaviae) on the Quirinal Hill on the spot of his uncle's house in which Domitian had been born roughly four decades earlier. Nothing substantial remains of the tomb-temple structure except for sculptural and architectural fragments that may have decorated an arch or altar built somewhere within or nearby the hilltop temple temenos (fig. 7). The Temple of the Flavian family not only served as a funerary monument celebrating yet again the Judean conquests of Domitian's divine father and brother, but the scale and preeminent location of the building also challenged the dominance of the Mausoleum of Augustus in the northern Campus Martius. Moreover, Domitian's project elevated the status of Quirinal hill to a topographical keystone equal to both the Capitoline and Palatine hills. Domitian's projects, be they reconstructions (the temple of Jupiter Optimus Maximus) or new edifices (the imperial palace and the temple-tomb to the Flavian family), now towered over the city below on three of Rome's most venerated hills and thereby created a sacred triangle of Domitianic architectural projects. After Domitian's assassination in 96 and subsequent damnation by the Senate, his ashes were secretly interred by his nursemaid, Phyllis, within the walls of the now lost temple of the Flavian family on the Quirinal.[14] The exact date of the destruction of the Templum Gentis Flaviae is unknown, but it seems likely the structure did not exist for long after the rise to power of Rome's next great imperial builder, Trajan.

---

12   See Aurora Raimondi Cominesi & Claire Stocks and Natascha Sojc in this volume.
13   See Frederick G. Naerebout in this volume.
14   Suet. Dom. 23.

Man and God: Literature

Antony Augoustakis & Emma Buckley

Thanks to authors such as Tacitus and Pliny, our common understanding is that Domitian was a monster whose reign of terror left an indelible mark on Roman history, rectified only by the deceased Emperor's *damnatio memoriae*. According to these and other post-Domitianic writers, there is a clear distinction between the reign of that bad Emperor and Domitian's successors, Nerva and Trajan, who put all their efforts into restoring what their predecessor had destroyed. Moreover, what was most distinctive about the age of Domitian was a silencing suppression of free speech: the people of Rome, who endured the tyrannical rule of this perverted Emperor, could not voice their opposition without facing dire consequences. According to Tacitus, though it was *possible* to be a good citizen even under such a bad Emperor, life under Domitian amounted to *seruitus* (slavery), since informers made it difficult, even impossible, for people to interact in conversation.[1]

And yet Tacitus and Pliny flourished under Domitian, and from the inception of the Flavian dynasty, many authors celebrated the virtues and accomplishments of its last Emperor. Furthermore we have unusually rich literary resources surviving in this period: four epics (Valerius Flaccus' *Argonautica*; Statius' *Thebaid* and *Achilleid*; and the historical epic *Punica* by Silius Italicus);[2] occasional and lyric poetry from the prolific writers Statius and Martial; technical literature of various kinds, including military tactics (Frontinus' *Stratagemata*), education and rhetoric (Quintilian's *Institutio Oratoria*), and that ambitious encyclopedia of the natural world and 'inventory' of empire (Pliny the Elder's *Natural History*).[3] The historian Flavius Josephus, who fought against Vespasian in the First Jewish-Roman War (66-73) but ended up serving within the imperial household, provides a unique perspective on both Rome's recent history with Judaea (*Bellum Iudaicum*) and the larger sweep of human history from a Jewish perspective (*Antiquitates Iudaicae*). Other writers in Greek 'adjacent' to Domitian were Plutarch – who visited Rome throughout the Flavian period and may have spoken before Domitian himself – and Dio Chrysostom, the orator, historian, and philosopher who was actually banished by the Emperor in 82.[4] And this is before we remark upon the tantalizing traces of lost work, or

---

1. Tac. *Agr.* 2.3. Cf. also esp. *Agr.* 42.4-5. On the portraits of Domitian by Tacitus and Pliny, see Schulz 2019 and Szoke 2019.
2. Statius' *Achilleid* is unfinished and only one and half books long; Valerius' epic, which breaks off suddenly in its eighth book, has also been long regarded as incomplete, though Penwill 2010 suggests the abrupt ending is deliberate. See on epic Claire Stocks in this volume.
3. Hurlet 2016, 21 provides larger overview of Flavian sources.
4. On Plutarch, see Stadter 2013, esp. 19-21 who notes, however, that Plutarch did not publish the *Parallel Lives* until after Domitian's death, and was critical of Domitian's 'mania for building' (*Publ.* 15.6). On Plutarch, Dio, and other figures in Greek literature, see Kemezis 2016.

those who lived under the Flavians but chose to comment on the regime only after the death of its last *princeps* Domitian – Juvenal, Tacitus, Pliny the Younger, and even Suetonius – the very names that then shape the looming, tyrannical and savage Domitian for posterity.

Given this abundance of sources and perspectives, in the sections below we can only sketch a few dominant strands in the depiction of the Emperor, seeking to show how literary artists respond to Domitian in 'real time'; we then consider, in the aftermath of his death, how they, together with later historians and biographers, reconfigure their presentation of the Emperor, his life and achievements. In broad terms, during Domitian's rule (81-96), they laud the Emperor as a capable military leader, a talented literary artist in his own right, a benefactor (re)building city and empire, a corrector of morals, and an awe-inspiring semi-divine presence. One can speculate whether the literary figures who praise the Emperor are sincere in their laudatory references to the last of the Flavians, or whether hidden criticism can be detected in their otherwise apparent glorification of the regime.[5] What is not in question is the complexity of literary evocation of and response to Domitian, the symbiotic relationship of Emperor and writer, and the interaction of literary and imperial authority in a distinctly new evolution of the role of emperor under Domitian.[6] These writers do not just 'describe' Domitian: they make him, forming his representation and negotiating his relationship with the audience in ways analogous to the epigraphic, numismatic, and other material representations of the Emperor.[7]

Approaching the Emperor

Roman epic's concern with national identity and the projection of imperial power make it a natural place to find 'Domitian' in literature, but while the Flavian epicists tend to begin their texts with encomium of the Emperor, they make use of another common feature of the genre – the *recusatio* (or 'refusal') – to avoid writing a whole epic on the martial achievements of Domitian.[8] Statius claims in the proem to his mythological epics that he is not yet ready to tackle Domitian's victories over the

Fig. 1. Bronze portrait bust of a young boy, ca. 50-68. New York, Metropolitan Museum of Art, inv. 66.11.5.

Dacians and Germans, or his exploits as a young man in the civil war, when he fought on the Capitol of Rome.[9] Valerius Flaccus' *Argonautica*, whose mythological theme is the quest of Jason for the Golden Fleece, 'sets' itself in the reign of Vespasian, and salutes the young Domitian as a talented poet able to render his brother Titus' destruction of Jerusalem in 71.[10]

Silius Italicus, author of the seventeen-book *Punica*, does not even directly address the Emperor in the proem, but – via the prophetic voice of Jupiter – also praises Domitian as distinguished poet and warrior, as part of larger praise of the Flavian dynasty.[11] This extract gives a flavour of the encomium:[12]

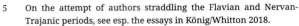

---

5   On the attempt of authors straddling the Flavian and Nervan-Trajanic periods, see esp. the essays in König/Whitton 2018.

6   See, for instance, Nauta 2002, Ley 2016, 140, Augoustakis/Buckley/Stocks 2019.

7   For Juvenal, we follow Braund's (2004) translation; for Statius Shackleton Bailey/Parrot 2015; and for Martial, Shackleton Bailey 1993. The rest of the translations are our own.

8   Virgil's *Georgics* offers the model for proemial praise of Caesar Octavian, but also the precedent for the decision in verse to defer an epic on the leader's martial exploits.

9   *Theb.* 1.17-33, cf. *Ach.* 1.14-19. A poem Statius *did* write on Domitian's German wars, performed at Domitian's Alban palace, does not survive but is the subject of the poet's recollection in his *Silvae* (4.2.66-67). On Statius' *Silvae* and Domitian, see below.

10 *Arg.*1.12-14.

11 *Pun.* 3.607-629, cf. 14.686-688. Domitian's literary talents are also praised by Quintilian (*Inst. Or.* 4 *praef.*, 10.1.91: his excellence in oratory), while Frontinus' *Stratagemata* offer a positive portrayal of Domitian as leader (1.1.8, 1.3.10, 2.3.23, 2.11.7) and merciful victor, sparing the Lingones from Roman plunder (4.3.14, cf. *Pun.* 14.684-688).

12 *Pun.* 3.612-629.

huic laxos arcus olim Gangetica pubes
summittet uacuasque ostendent Bactra pharetras.
hic et ab Arctoo currus aget axe per urbem,
ducet et Eoos, Baccho cedente, triumphos.
idem indignantem tramittere Dardana signa
Sarmaticis uictor compescet sedibus Histrum.
quin et Romuleos superabit uoce nepotes
quis erit eloquio partum decus. huic sua Musae
sacra ferent, meliorque lyra, cui substitit Hebrus
et uenit Rhodope, Phoebo miranda loquetur.
ille etiam, qua prisca, uides, stat regia nobis,
aurea Tarpeia ponet Capitolia rupe
et iunget nostro templorum culmina caelo.
tunc, o nate deum diuosque dature, beatas
imperio terras patrio rege. tarda senectam
hospitia excipient caeli, solioque Quirinus
concedet, mediumque parens fraterque locabunt;
siderei iuxta radiabunt tempora nati.

To him the youths of Ganges will at some point surrender their unstrung bows, and the Bactrians will show him their empty quivers. He will lead from the north his chariot through the city and will celebrate a triumph for his victory in the east, with Bacchus yielding his place to him. The same man will restrain the Danube to its seat among the Sarmatians as a conqueror, a river who denied to bear Roman standards. In addition, he will surpass with his voice all descendants of Romulus talented in eloquence. To him the Muses will bring their sacred gifts: he will be better in music than him who made the River Hebrus stop and Mount Rhodope come to him; he will sing more wonderfully than Phoebus. He will build a golden Capitol on the Tarpeian rock, where, you see, our old plane stands, and he will join the top of my temple to the sky. Then, son of gods and father of gods to be, rule the lands blessed with paternal sway. The house of heaven will receive you in old age and Quirinus will yield his throne to you, as your father and brother place you in their midst: and the temple of your starry son will gleam next to you.

Voiced by the king of the gods and arbiter of fate, who maps Rome's rise to greatness from its point of greatest danger – the threat of Hannibal and Carthage – to Domitian's eventual apotheosis, these words are not just embedded panegyric of an emperor, impressive though he is in eloquence and ability to bring peace. Rather, Silius makes Domitian's accomplishments, future military victories, and eventual apotheosis the climax and *telos* of all Roman history – an up-to-date iteration on an ideology of epic first programmed by Virgil for Augustus.[13]

When epic praises Domitian, it does it in proem and prophecy, and in Silius' case from the rather distant vantage point of the history of the Roman Republic. But we gain a much closer view of the Emperor in the humbler genres of lyric and epigram. Perhaps the two authors who claim to come closest to Domitian are Martial and Statius, who both boast Domitian as patron, and whose different depictions of the life of Rome and its society often interact with the Emperor both directly and indirectly.[14] In Statius' *Silvae*, five books of apparently 'occasional' but of course highly crafted poetry in a variety of verse-forms and idealized landscapes, the poet presents us with Domitian as an overwhelming presence, whose personal impact on Rome and Italy is cosmic in its resonance. The first poem does not gaze at Domitian directly, offering instead an awe-inspiring recreation of the atmosphere at Rome during his great building projects, and focusing in particular on a colossal equestrian statue of the Emperor erected in the Forum Romanum to celebrate Domitian's military victories over the Dacians and Chatti.[15] Evoking the sheer size of the statue via comparison to the Trojan horse and Mars' Bistonian steed, Statius blurs statuary with human form to describe a godlike Domitian whose peace-demanding posture quells further war but retains clear martial menace:[16]

dextra uetat pugnas, laeuam Tritonia uirgo
non grauat et sectae praetendit colla Medusae,
ceu stimulis accendit equum; nec dulcior usquam
lecta deae sedes, nec si pater ipse teneres.
pectora, quae mundi ualeant euoluere curas
et quis se totis Temese dedit hausta metallis.
it tergo demissa chlamys, latus ense quieto
securum ...

Your right hand bans battles. The Tritonian maiden (sc. Minerva) is no burden to your left as she holds out severed Medusa's neck as though to spur the horse forward. Nowhere did the goddess choose a sweeter place to rest, not even, Father, if yourself held her. Your breast is such as may suffice to unwind the cares of the world; to make it, Temese has given her all, exhausting her mines. A cloak hangs down your back. A quiet sword protects your side ...

13   For a reading of Scipio Africanus 'as' Domitian, see esp. Marks 2005, esp. 283-288 on Silius and Domitian.

14   On Statius and Martial, see Nauta 2002; on Statius, e.g. Newlands 2012; on Martial, e.g. Lorenz 2002 and Spisak 2007.

15   The statue was destroyed after Domitian's death. For more on its location, see Thomas 2004 and Muth 2010. See in this volume Jane Fejfer and Diane Atnally Conlin. On this poem, see Geyssen 1996.

16   *Silvae* 1.1.37-44.

This gigantic statue does not just impose itself on the landscape of Rome, cannibalizing space and dominating both land and sky; it also seems, in Statius' eyes, to overwrite Roman history. Statius performs a similar blending of spatial and temporal domination when he regards Domitian through the prism of the Via Domitiana, a great infrastructure project between Sinuessa and Puteoli that drastically shortened the journey-time between Rome and Naples, in *Silvae* 4.3. As Statius frames the Emperor as a civilizing force, his presence imprinted upon not just Rome but all Campania, he once again (as in *Silvae* 1.1) stresses the intense noise and activity of the road-building process, and the awe-inspiring scale of clamour and domination of nature. Indeed, the river-god Vulturnus thanks him as 'kind orderer of my plains' and ' ... supreme arbiter and conqueror of my bank,'[17] while the Sibyl of Cumae, celebrated prophet of Rome's destiny, offers her own eulogy, predicting for Domitian perpetual youth and future world-conquest on the model of Bacchus and Hercules. Indeed, the Sibyl begins her prophecy by greeting Domitian as *already* a god, and Jupiter on earth: 'See! He is a god, him Jupiter commands to rule the happy earth in his stead.'[18]

Given the overwhelming scope of Domitian's power, it is no wonder, then, that when Statius recounts time spent in the actual presence of Domitian, in a poem of thanksgiving celebrating his invitation to dine at Domitian's palace on the Palatine in *Silvae* 4.2, what we find is no intimate gathering or celebration of Domitian's more 'human' side.[19] Instead, Statius casts the palace itself, its materials of construction and decoration, as an expression of Domitian's worldly domination, and deems the feast comparable only to the banquets held by Jupiter himself. Statius even makes this banquet the occasion of his own rebirth, in the presence of this Jupiter on earth:[20]

medius uideor discumbere in astris
cum Ioue et Iliaca porrectum sumere dextra
immortale merum. steriles transmisimus annos;
haec aeui mihi prima dies, hic limina uitae.
tene ego, regnator terrarum orbisque subacti
magne parens, te, spes hominum, te, cura deorum,
cerno iacens?

It seems to me that I recline with Jupiter among the stars and take immortal wine offered by Trojan hand. Sterile are the years behind me. This is the first day of my span, here is the threshold of my life. Do I behold you as I recline, sovereign of the lands, great parent of a world subdued, you, hope of mankind, you, care of the gods?

Statius' awe-inspiring depiction of Domitian sets the Emperor within a highly mannered literary universe encompassing the elite society of Rome, its villas and leisure spaces, amounts to an aesthetic 'legitimation' of the new imperial model: the intimidating but benign autocracy of Domitian.[21] The epigrammatist Martial, however, forms his vision of Domitian amidst a literary world that wallows in the crowded, bustling daily life of Rome. The prose preface to Martial's first book of *Epigrams* warns the reader that he is writing in the accusatory and jesting tradition of Catullus, tells the ostentatiously prudish to stay away, and vaunts his own poetic fame. But even within the latitude afforded by the satirical perspective of epigram, Martial consistently visualizes Domitian's power as divine, the impact of his presence as awe-inspiring, and the effects of his presence as miraculous. The Emperor is featured as the most noble conqueror of Rome's enemies even from a young age (*Ep.* 2.2), a true god (*deum*, 5.3), and on occasion as 'master and god' (*dominus et deus*)[22] even within the grubby world that Martial depicts – one that relies on one up-man-ship, currying favour, and ceaseless striving for one's own advancement.

Epigram 9.66 offers a good example of tone sophisticated negotiation of Emperor within the epigrammatic register. Martial playfully addresses Fabullus (a repeat target of his biting pen), who has appealed to the Emperor, the *dominus et deus*, for a special privilege, the *ius trium liberorum* (a status for those who had given birth to three children, with financial and other benefits to the holder):

Vxor cum tibi sit formosa, pudica, puella,
*   quo tibi natorum iura, Fabulle, trium?*
quod petis a nostro supplex dominoque deoque
*   tu dabis ipse tibi, si potes arrigere.*

Since you have a wife, who is beautiful, chaste, and young, Fabullus, what do you want with the Rights of Three Children (*ius trium liberorum*)? What you seek as a petitioner from our lord and god, you will give yourself, if you can have an erection.

Now Domitian's power is refracted within a Rome where dupes, profiteers, the morally compromised and

---

17   *Silvae* 4.3.72, 83-84: *camporum bone conditor meorum* and *maximus arbiter meaeque/uictor perpetuus ... ripa.*

18   *Silvae* 4.3.128-129: *en hic est deus, hunc iubet beatis/pro se Iuppiter imperare terris.* On *Silvae* 4.3, see esp. Coleman 1988, 102-135, Newlands 2002, 284-325, Smolenaars 2006, Kreuz 2016, 276-304.

19   On *Silvae* 4.2, see esp. Coleman 1988, 82-101, Newlands 2002, 260-283, Malamud 2007.

20   *Silvae* 4.2.10-16.

21   On Statius' *Silvae* and Domitian, see esp. Rosati 2015.

22   E.g. 5.8.1, 7.34.8, 8.2.6.

the sexually dysfunctional are ridiculed by Martial's moralizing pen. The joke, of course, is that if only the impotent Fabullus could 'get it up', he could have three children himself, with no need of special privileges. But the larger context is also important. Fabullus' humiliation is assured when he advertises his impotence with the request, and such embarrassment is compounded when the Emperor with divine power over the whole world is ludicrously beset with such a pathetic petition.[23] And as part of a couplet of poems (cf. 9.64) aimed against petitioners of the Emperor, the epigram succeeds not just in humiliating Fabullus, but also in its indirect aggrandizement of Domitian and the extreme power differential laid bare. Finally, Martial's play on the *ius trium liberorum* does not simply remind us in turn of his own 'closeness' to the Emperor – for the epigrammatist boasts elsewhere that he *has* received this very honour from the *princeps* (2.92) – but it also hints at another major aspect of imperial self-projection – Domitian's self-stylization as *pudicus princeps*. Indeed, Martial dedicates the fifth book of the *Epigrams* to Domitian himself, warning that in place of the 'wanton' material of his first four books,[24] 'the fifth jokes with our Lord, for Germanicus to read without a blush in the presence of the Athenian maid (sc. Minerva).'[25] In other words, Martial will serve up the kind of poetry that Domitian can read with the virgin goddess Pallas, material befitting the Emperor who took up the post of *censor perpetuus* in 85 and who strenuously enacted moral reform at Rome.[26]

This power differential has in fact been modelled by Martial himself at the beginning of Book 1 with a cycle of poems on, for, and even 'by' Domitian:

> *Contigeris nostros, Caesar, si forte libellos,*
> *terrarum dominum pone supercilium.*
> *consueuere iocos uestri quoque ferre triumphi,*
> *materiam dictis nec pudet esse ducem.*
> *qua Thymelen spectas derisoremque Latinum,*
> *illa fronte precor carmina nostra legas.*
> *innocuos censura potest permittere lusus:*
> *lasciua est nobis pagina, uita proba.*
> (*Ep.* 1.4)

Caesar, if you happen to light upon my little books, put aside the frown that rules the world. Even the triumphs of Emperors usually tolerate jests, and a warlord is not ashamed to be matter for a quip. Read my verses, I beg, with the expression with which you watch Thymele and jesting Latinus. A censor can permit harmless fun. My page is wanton, but my life is virtuous.[27]

> *Do tibi naumachiam, tu das epigrammata nobis:*
> *uis, puto, cum libro, Marce, natare tuo.*

I give you a sea fight, you give me epigrams. I think you want to be in the water with your book, Marcus.

> *Aetherias aquila puerum portante per auras*
> *illaesum timidis unguibus haesit onus:*
> *nunc sua Caesareos exorat praeda leones*
> *tutus et ingenti ludit in ore lepus.*
> *quae maiora putas miracula? summus utrisque*
> *auctor adest: haec sunt Caesaris, illa Iouis.*[28]

As the eagle bore the boy (sc. Ganymede) through the airs of heaven, the timid talons did not harm their clinging freight. Now Caesar's lions are won over by their prey and the hare plays safely in the massive jaws. Which do you think to be the greater sensation? Behind both stands the highest man. The one is Caesar's, the other Jove's.

Right from the beginning, then, Martial 'enacts' the dominant themes of Domitianic imperial presentation: the intimidating power of the Emperor, via his depiction as military commander; his role as censor, in charge of societal morality, and responsible for enforcing standards of public behaviour; and his miraculous, suprahuman power, one that explicitly aligns Domitian with Jupiter, making him a 'god-on-earth'. But he also enacts his own role in this representation of Domitian, laying bare the negotiation of power between the Emperor with the power to drown the poet, and the poet who can speak for and even 'as' the Emperor, mediating and making comprehensible the overwhelming power he affords the last Flavian *princeps*.

---

23 As Henriksén 2012, 279 argues, "the fact (sc. that Fabullus is impotent) ... is humiliating, and his attempted solution – to bother the authority second only to Jupiter himself -naturally outrageous."

24 *lasciuos ... libellos*, 5.2.5.

25 5.2.6-8: *quintus cum domino liber iocatur;/ quem Germanicus ore non rubenti / coram Cecropia legat puella.* Martial also dedicates Book 8 to Domitian, praising his "celestial modesty" (*caelesti uerecundiae*, 8 *praef.* 9).

26 See Grelle 1980 and (for Martial) Lorenz 2002.

27 *Ep.* 1.5.

28 *Ep.* 1.6.

Rejecting the Emperor

In the tenth book of Martial's *Epigrams*, the poet evokes the title *dominus et deus* again – but now times have changed:[29]

Frustra, Blanditiae, uenitis ad me
attritis miserabiles labellis:
dicturus dominum deumque non sum ...
non est hic dominus, sed imperator,
sed iustissimus omnium senator,
per quem de Stygia domo reducta est
siccis rustica Veritas capillis.
hoc sub principe, si sapis, caueto
uerbis, Roma, prioribus loquaris.

Flatteries, you come to me in vain, you poor creatures with your shameless lips. I am not about to speak of 'lord and god' ... There is no lord here, but a commander-in-chief and the most just of all senators, through whom rustic, dry-haired Truth has been brought back from the house of Styx. Under this ruler, Rome, beware, if you are wise, of talking the language of earlier days.

With the assassination of Domitian in 96 and the accession of Nerva, who died in 98 and was swiftly succeeded by Trajan (the object of Martial's admiration here), we see a startling volte-face, within a 'revised edition' put out after the death and *damnatio* of Domitian. But even as Rome began the process of 'editing out' Domitian in statuary, inscriptions, and public spaces, Martial's revisionary re-writing of the Emperor was accompanied by a whole host of other voices who now began to speak up. In place of the epic encomium offered by Silius Italicus, for example, Domitian's military competence is savaged by Juvenal in his fourth satire, a 'mock epic' that recalls the time Rome was slave to a 'bald Nero'[30] who summoned his generals and advisors to a grand council. There they were asked to debate the best way to cook a fish! The satire revels in the absurdity of Domitian's advisors (a far from impressive bunch) hurrying as though to hear news of national importance and discussing gravely the appropriate fate of a turbot. But the satire carries a real sting in the tail. These advisors cannot conceal their terror: 'the pallor of that awful, mighty friendship.'[31] And Juvenal ends by wishing that Domitian had limited himself to such banality, if it also curtailed his reign of terror in Rome:[32]

Atque utinam his potius nugis tota illa dedisset
tempora saeuitiae, claras quibus abstulit Vrbi
inlustresque animas inpune et uindice nullo.

All the same, if only he had devoted the whole of those savage times to such frivolities, instead of depriving Rome of some noble and glorious souls, getting away with it, with no one to take revenge!

Domitian's other virtues and achievements come under equally sustained attack in the aftermath of his death. Two prominent figures of senatorial rank, Tacitus and Pliny, do as much as anyone to re-set the imperial narrative, casting the arrival of Nerva and Trajan as liberation from oppression, and enforcing a strict and overt dichotomy between the wicked Domitian and the good new emperors. Tacitus' *Agricola* from c. 98 sets the Roman subjugation of Britain against senatorial enslavement to Domitian, and pits a *true* example of Roman leadership – his father-in-law *Agricola*, the mastermind of Britain's conquest – in constant counterpoint with the inept and tyrannical Domitian, who conceals his fear, distrust, and secret hatred of the superior commander and man.[33] Pliny's *Panegyricus*, the written edition of a speech in thanksgiving of Trajan delivered in 100, expands this praise/blame polarization to vast proportions, constantly framing Trajan as *optimus princeps* against a tyrannical Domitian who fulfils all the categories of negative characterisation and rhetorical invective. Pliny's Domitian is a physically menacing figure, who lurks in his palace; he practises cruel violence against his own family, elite citizens and the people alike; he displays the classic faults of avarice, anger, and cowardice; and his demands of divine status serve as index of his tyranny.[34] In his *Epistles*, apparently written after Domitian's death, Pliny provides a more personal, though no less carefully crafted, record of the fraught and dangerous personal and political existence of Rome's elite citizens under Domitian, once again contrasting 'then' and 'now' and celebrating the return of *libertas*.

Twenty-five years later, Suetonius' damning biography of the Emperor (c. 120), which combined anecdote and vignettes of the Emperor's life with a typological account of the Emperor's virtues and vices, codified this deeply pessimistic picture. Suetonius now charts a dark beginning for Domitian in 'great poverty and infamy,'[35] the young Domitian's ambitious and malignant rivalry with his brother Titus, his *pretence* of modesty and *feigned* interest in poetry (*Dom.* 2). While offering an account of Domitian's private life and various public interactions in the amphitheatre, law-courts and senate, he explains Domitian's motivations within the context of an innate "savage cruelty, not only

---

29   10.72.1-3, 7-14.
30   4.32: *caluo ... Neroni.*
31   4.74-75: *miserae magnaeque sedebat/pallor amicitiae.*
32   4.151-154.

33   Esp. *Agr.* 39-43.
34   *Ep.* 2.3-4, 52.3, 54.4, 58.
35   *Dom.* 1.1: *inopia tantaque infamia.*

excessive, but also calculated and unexpected,"[36] and he often connects the Emperor's tyrannical character, his dissimulation, and his arrogance with his overweening desire for power, and his self-fashioning as *dominus et deus* not just in person but now also in the documentary record.[37] It was because of this arrogance, cruelty and overreach, Suetonius concludes, that Domitian became "an object of terror and hatred to all."[38] And after his paranoia extended to the senseless execution of his 'ineffectual' cousin Flavius Clemens, he was finally undone by a conspiracy that included his friends, his freedmen, and even his own wife, Domitia.

The sharp distinctions between 'Domitian' and 'after Domitian'; the construction of Domitianic silence and slavery, versus post-Domitianic *libertas*; the extent to which imperial policies, imperial panegyric and even imperial self-representation changed very much after Domitian, is still up for debate. Modern scholars, in particular, have cautioned us to remember that the denigration of Domitian in the voices of Martial, Pliny, and Tacitus is at the same time an 'unwriting' of their own previous selves, and a sophisticated self-fashioning for a new era. At the same time, it is clear that Domitian's distinctive personality, his comfort with autocracy and his desire to be divine does catalyse new modes of literature of and for the Emperor. Domitian's own father Vespasian had downplayed imperial associations with divinity, joking on his deathbed, so Suetonius tells us, "Oh dear, I think I'm becoming a god."[39] Augustus, the first Emperor and exemplary model for all who came after, claimed status only as 'first citizen' (*princeps*), and 'first among equals' (*primus inter pares*). Nero, the last Julio-Claudian Emperor and avowed 'anti-type' for the Flavian dynasty, at least set out (again, as Suetonius tells us) claiming to rule by the watchwords of generosity, mercy, and affability (*comitas*). Such efforts to level citizen and emperor are conspicuously lacking in evocations of Domitian in Martial, Statius and the Flavian epicists. A new vision of imperial power is embodied, one that aims to get close – but not too close – to a new conceptualization of the Emperor as god on earth.[40]

---

36   *Dom.*11: *non solum magnae, sed etiam callidae inopinataeque saeuitiae.*
37   Suet. *Dom.* 13. Cf. Dio Cass. 67.4.7: Ἤδη γὰρ καὶ θεὸς ἠξίου νομίζεσθαι, καὶ δεσπότης καλούμενος καὶ θεὸς ὑπερηγάλλετο. ταῦτα οὐ μόνον ἐλέγετο ἀλλὰ καὶ ἐγράφετο ("for he even insisted upon being regarded as a god and took the greatest pride in being called "master" and "god." These titles were used not merely in speech but also in written documents"). Later writers adopt this view (Aur.Vict. *De Caes.* 11.2, Eutr. 7.23, Oros. 7.10).
38   *Dom.* 14: *terribilis cunctis et inuisus.*
39   *Vesp.* 23.4: *uae, puto deus fio.*
40   For further reading, see Augoustakis/Buckly/Stocks 2019, Jones 1992, Leberl 2004, König/Whitton 2018, Ley 2016, Nauta 2002.

PART VI

Fall and Afterlife Regime Change/Reputation in Antiquity

Anchoring Egypt. The *Iseum Campense* and Flavian Rome

Miguel John Versluys

In 80 the *Campus Martius* was devastated by fire, along with many other parts of the centre of ancient Rome. This catastrophe allowed Domitian to rebuild the *Urbs* on his own terms. His *Neugestaltung* is therefore also an important source on cultural history, as it allows us to speculate how Domitian imagined his rule and his Empire. What important anchors from the past mattered to him and his self-presentation? How did he imagine the dynastical future to take shape?

The temple for the "Egyptian gods" on the *Campus Martius* was rebuilt on a grand scale by Domitian and, although this was part of a much larger building boom, it evidently mattered. We are certain that there already had been a temple for Isis and her consort in this area previously, as Cassius Dio, in his account of the Judean war, tells us that Vespasian and Titus spent the night before their triumph in Rome at or near the temple of Isis on the *Campus Martius*.[1] A Vespasian coin dated to 71 shows a temple with Egyptian (iconographical) characteristics and, as such, must refer to the *Iseum Campense* and this occasion (fig. 1).[2]

The exact chronology and topography of the sanctuary remain debated. It is, for instance, not always clear if the available sources relate to the sanctuary (re)built by Domitian or the later reconstruction under Hadrian. There also is a heated discussion on the earlier, pre-Flavian worship of the "Egyptian gods" on the *Campus Martius* and its relation to the *Iseum Campense* temple. Most scholars now assume that Domitian already constructed a large complex of about 70 x 200 metres. The (later) *Forma Urbis* shows that it might have consisted of three parts: a semi-circular water basin surrounded by niches to the south; a large courtyard flanked by two monumental arches in the centre, with to the north a vast space to be reconstructed as temple square or temple garden (fig. 2). The marble plan from the Severan period carries the inscription *SERAPAEU(M)*, which indicates that Serapis was also venerated in the sanctuary, at least at the beginning of the third century.

Almost nothing of this remarkable complex's architecture has been preserved. A lot of its (architectural) decorations, however, have been unearthed on and around the *Campus*

---

1 Dio Cass. 51.16.3-4.
2 For all information on the *Iseum Campense*, its bibliography, the various debates briefly mentioned here as well as the temple of Beneventum, see most recently Versluys 2017, Versluys/Bülow-Clausen/Capriotti Vittozzi 2018 and Nagel 2019. For its position within Domitian's Rome, see Moormann 2018 and Eric M. Moormann in this volume. For Domitian and Egypt, see Olaf Kaper in this volume.

Fig. 1. Bronze sesterce of Vespasian, Rome, 71, showing a temple with Egyptian (iconographical) characteristics, probably referring to the *Iseum Campense*. Berlin, Staatliche Museen zu Berlin, Münzkabinett (courtesy Staatliche Museen in Berlin, Antikensammlung).

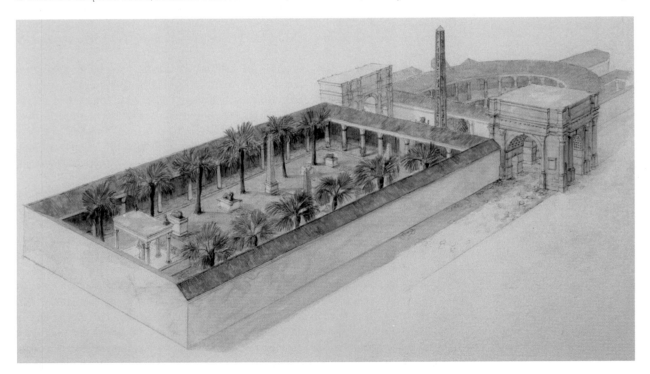

Fig. 2. Artistic impression of the *Iseum Campense*, pencil on paper, 2017, by Menno Balm (courtesy mennobalm.nl).

Martius from the Renaissance onwards. It is important to realise that many of the *Aegyptiaca Romana* that populate Rome's museums and cityscape today originally come from the *Iseum Campense*. It that respect, this enormous complex, the largest temple for the "Egyptian gods" in the western Mediterranean, can be characterised as one of ancient Rome's most notable absent presences.

The obelisk re-used by Gian Lorenzo Bernini as the centrepiece of his *Fontana dei Quattro Fiumi* on Piazza Navona comes from the *Iseum Campense* (fig. 3). It might

Fig. 3. *Fontana dei Quattro Fiumi* by Bernini on Piazza Navona, with the obelisk from the *Iseum Campense*. Rome (photo Katja Lembke).

Fig. 4. Diorite statue of Domitian as pharaoh from the temple of Beneventum. Benevento, Museo del Sannio, inv. 1903 (photo author).

well have decorated the central courtyard of the complex. On this obelisk, Domitian presented himself in hieroglyphs as divine pharaoh to the Roman people. The temple of Isis in Beneventum offers an important comparison to the *Iseum Campense* in terms of Flavian ideology and its relation to Egypt; from this sanctuary even a statue of Domitian as pharaoh has been preserved (fig. 4). The famous statue of the reclining Nile surrounded by putti, now in the Vatican Museums (fig. 5), comes from the *Iseum Campense* and was probably displayed in the water basin alongside its counterpart, a statue from the Tiber now in the Louvre. Also the large granite columns (so-called *columnae caelatae*), which show a remarkable display of priests of Isis carrying (Egyptian) objects, and which are now in the Capitoline Museums, were originally part of the complex. Objects from the *Iseum Campense* that currently still adorn the city of Rome itself include the so-called Dogali obelisk; the lions flanking Michelangelo's stairs to the Capitol; the large foot in the Via del piè di marmo (fig. 6) and *Madama*

Lucrezia, one of Rome's *pasquinade*-bearing statues and now at Piazza Venezia, amongst others.[3]

Through the finds of all these remarkable objects, the *Iseum Campense* soon developed into an important and much-debated subject for the contemplation of Egyptian history and its relation to European civilisation. In that respect, it can be characterised as an important *lieu de mémoire*, in the sense that defining parts of the mnemohistory of Egypt were shaped in Rome on the basis of the *Iseum Campense* and its finds. Athanasius Kircher is only one of many scholars that can be mentioned as an example in this respect. But what was the meaning of the complex in the Flavian period and, specifically, for Domitian?

The *Iseum Campense* was, first of all, an important place of worship in the city of Rome. It was a sanctuary for

---

3   For these objects and their functioning in Rome from the Renaissance to the twenty-first century see Part 3 of Versluys/ Bülow-Clausen/Capriotti Vittozzi 2018, with an essay by Arthur Weststeijn on the Dogali obelisk and the altar of the fallen fascists.

Fig. 5. The reclining Nile surrounded by putti, from the *Iseum Campense*. Vatican Museums, Museo Chiaramonti, inv. 2300 (courtesy Universität Freiburg, Fotothek Klassische Archäologie).

the "Egyptian gods", namely Isis, Serapis and related gods from the Isiac circle like Harpocrates. Originally these gods came from Egypt and had an Egyptian background. In the Hellenistic period, however, they had become thoroughly universalised and, as such, they became part and parcel of Roman religious practices, especially in the first century BC. Much later, in the Flavian period, we see that sometimes the original, Oriental background of such gods is emphasized again; apparently to make them stand out as something special in the vast polytheistic spectrum that characterised Roman religious practice.[4] It is possible, however, that the Flavian (re)building of the *Iseum Campense* marked the *official* entry of Isis in the Roman pantheon; namely, following Vespasian's victory in Judaea and the East, which served almost as foundation myth for the Flavian dynasty and their "new beginnings" of the Roman Empire.[5]

In the second place, the *Iseum Campense* thus became an important and distinctly Flavian monument. Egypt

seems to have mattered greatly to the *Flavii*; some scholars even argue that it is one of the main ingredients of their (novel) self-definition and self-presentation.[6] By making Isis and the Egyptian gods part of the imperial system in the way they did, the Flavians even seem to have created a tradition that would strongly influence later (Roman) history, for example, Hadrian and his reign. Clear examples of this are the depictions of Antinous and the paramount role of the concept of Egypt in the *Villa Hadriana*.[7]

The concept of anchoring is key to this Flavian choice in two respects. As Suetonius[8] mentions, Vespasian was of humble origins and in need of *auctoritas* and *maiestas*. When quite unexpectedly proclaimed emperor, Vespasian therefore rushed to Alexandria, capital of the eastern Mediterranean, in order to anchor himself into various important (Roman) traditions related to that

---

4   For this 'Orientalisation' of Roman gods in the Flavian era see
     Versluys 2013 and Nagel 2019. For Flavian religious policy more in
     general see Frderick G. Naerebout in this volume.
5   As suggested by Scheid 2004 and 2009.

6   For this debate see the various contributions to Part 2 of Versluys/
     Bülow-Clausen/Capriotti Vittozzi 2018, the critical evaluation by
     Stefan Pfeiffer in particular, as well as Capriotti Vittozzi 2014.
7   For which see in general Versluys 2012 and, with a presentation
     of the finds from the newly discovered Antinoeion at the Villa
     Hadriana, Mari/Sgalambro 2007.
8   Suet. *Vesp.* 7.2.

Fig. 6. Foot of a colossal statue, presumably Isis, from the *Iseum Campe*nse. Rome, Via del piè di marmo (photo Lidy Peters).

city in particular and to the East more in general. The idea of Egypt as an old standing civilisation that formed the basis of the Roman *oikoumene*, together with other cultures of the past such as ancient Greece, will certainly have played a role herein, as will the image of Alexander the Great. Secondly, and even more importantly, the image of Augustus will have played a role. The Roman Empire had, in fact, started from the moment that Augustus sailed back from Alexandria, after having defeated Mark Antony and Cleopatra, thus ending the civil war. By going to Alexandria, after a victory in the East, and sailing back to Rome from there to take control of the Empire after a period of turmoil, Vespasian now did exactly the same thing. The Flavian dynasty marked a distinctly new phase in the development of the Roman Empire. In this particular way, that new beginning was firmly anchored in both the imperial past of the Roman Empire as well as in the global past of the *oikoumene*.

Portraiture and Memory Sanctions

Caroline Vout

Memories are Made of This

Romans worked hard to ensure that they were remembered. For elite Romans, the quest for distinction, and for lasting commemoration of this distinction (through, for example, the award of an honorific statue complete with an inscription or "elogium" listing their achievements), began early in life in military and political service. It ideally ended in a public funerary procession that cemented their status in the community. In this procession, masks of the deceased's ancestors, which were normally kept in the atrium of the family home, were worn by relatives and paraded through the city in an awesome display of aristocratic agency. This was their city; they were the city's past, present and future. Memory's backward glance is always about looking to the future. The wealthier the family, the flashier the funeral, hence the need for sumptuary legislation to control funerary extravagance and associated feasts and monuments. In controlling consumption, this legislation militated against over-ambition by enforcing social hierarchies, and stressing that the individuals celebrated and integrated in Rome were as exemplary as they were exceptional. If those left behind were one day to join this group, they had to play within these limits.[1]

Unsurprisingly, given this premium on a publicly sanctioned, shared sense of social memory, and on exemplarity, elite Romans also invested heavily in stemming normal processes of commemoration, side-lining citizens deemed unworthy of community membership. Such 'memory sanctions' took many forms, exclusion of an effigy from the funerary procession being just one of them. Names and titles were erased from inscriptions and official documents, properties confiscated, wills annulled, and images pulled from their pedestals. In the process, the person in question was effectively ejected from the political landscape, and history, or at least the roll-call of role models, was airbrushed accordingly.[2] Not that they were forgotten. The shame afforded them resided in repeat performance of neglect, in creating gaps in the record as well as bringing closure, in making their elision from the annals visible. If Livy is right, and what chiefly makes the study of history "wholesome and profitable" is ... "that you behold the lessons of every kind of experience set forth as a conspicuous monument," and from these you "choose for yourself and for your own political system what to

---

1   An excellent overview is provided by Flower 1996.
2   See the works listed at the end of this essay (note 44), and, on late antiquity, Hedrick 2000.

imitate," and "from these mark for avoidance what is shameful in the conception and shameful in the result,"[3] then public enemies were as indispensable as paragons of virtue. Heroes, and the lessons they had to teach, were sustained by their antitheses.

Public Enemy Number One

After his assassination in 96, Domitian was public enemy number one. Only the second Emperor to suffer memory sanctions formally mandated by the Senate,[4] whose authority he had flouted when alive, he was not accorded a public funeral but put on a bier by those who bury the poor and speedily cremated by his nurse. His ashes were then secretly carried to their resting place, where they were mixed with those of his niece[5] – a move that militated against the kinds of corpse abuse often inflicted on criminals,[6] but also one that denied him his integrity. Rather it was his statues that got it in the neck, many of them, according to Pliny the Younger, not only dashed to the ground but hacked to pieces before being melted down into something practical and pleasurable.[7] Out of tyranny came economic gain, as the tyrant was removed and the city's fortunes were revived under his immediate successors, Nerva and Trajan. Writing, like Pliny, with the benefit of hindsight, Cassius Dio draws particular attention to the recycling of Domitian's gold and silver images, and to Nerva's prohibition of statues of these same materials.[8] Both of these materials pointed to divine pretension.[9] They must have reminded readers of Augustus's claims to have removed nigh on 80 silver statues of himself and used the money to dedicate golden offerings in the Temple of Apollo in his name and the name of those who had dedicated the originals.[10]

Domitian's erasure was imperative if the Principate was to survive in a form acceptable to the senate over and above the soldiers, who clamoured for his deification.[11] But it also, inevitably, threatened the Principate, the success of which depended on military as well as senatorial loyalty, and on a limited number of imperial statue types, offices and titles. As the individual whose image was most reproduced, the emperor was at the top of the exemplarity-apex. Topple his cuirassed, togate or equestrian statues, or attack his coins and inscriptions, and one risked toppling the system. Hence the emphasis on recyclability as much as destruction; and, with it, the possibility of a brighter future in debt to an august past. Many of Domitian's portraits had themselves been recut from images of Nero,[12] whose enforced suicide in 68 had opened the door to civil war and a change of dynasty from Julio-Claudian to Flavian. Just as Domitian's portraits had cannibalised these, so it was appropriate that, as the last of the Flavians, he should suffer a similar fate and join Nero as a negative exemplar. For him too to be a blip or blot on the landscape, rather than the apocalypse, the door had again to be left open. It was safer for Nerva to step into well-worn shoes than to present himself as a game-changing innovator.

Abusing Domitian's Portraits

For every one of Domitian's images and inscriptions that must have been subjected to hammer blows or thrown into the river,[13] another was warehoused as valuable marble stock or immediately recut. Such was the premium that the Romans put on the face (in part because of the premium that the Greeks put on the body) with all of the judgment about a person's character and potential for leadership that the ancient study of physiognomics brought with it, that attackers often went for the eyes, nose and mouth of a statue.[14] In an expansive empire, in which few people had seen the emperor in the flesh, an empire without film, the emperor *was* his image in a more urgent sense even than today, and his image imbued with the kind of charisma and authority that allowed it to take his place in a law court.[15] A quick look at a marble relief, likely to be from his villa at Castel Gandolfo, reveals that Domitian's features have been removed: no eyes as if to see, no nose as if to smell, no mouth as if to talk (fig. 1). This was not senseless violence, but the silencing of a ruler, robbing him of his capacity to meet the viewer's gaze. Only the ears remain. Perhaps the conceit was that Domitian should hear the taunts of his aggressors.[16]

Elsewhere, in Asia Minor, someone saw fit to scratch Domitian's face, name and title off a bronze coin, leaving his wife Domitia, who had been eyeball to eyeball with him, to stare into the abyss. On the reverse, a seated Zeus holding a sceptre and sacrificial dish reminds us of the power he used to wield: whether on coins or in the

3   Livy, 1. *praef.* 10. Helpful here is Bell/Hansen 2008.
4   Varner 2004, 111.
5   Suet. *Dom.* 17.3.
6   Varner 2001 and Hinard 1984.
7   Plin. *Pan.* 52.4-5. On this violence to statues, a phenomenon now known as '*damnatio memoriae*', see Varner 2004, Stewart 2003, 267-299 and Huet 2004.
8   Dio Cass., 68.1 and 2.
9   Fejfer 2008, 166-168.
10   *RG* 24.2 and Suet. *Aug.* 52.
11   Suet. *Dom.* 23.

12   See Jane Fejfer in this volume and Bergmann/Zanker 1981, 349-374.
13   For example, the bronze miniature of Domitian found in the Tiber (Ny Carlsberg Glyptotek, inv. no. 768; here Fejfer, fig. 4).
14   On the face, Nodelman 1993, and on the tendency, beyond Roman culture, to attack the face of an image, Freedberg 1989.
15   Severian of Gabala (writing in c. 400), *On the Creation of the World* 6.5 (*PG* 56. 489-490).
16   Varner 2004, cat. 5.2, fig. 108a-b.

Fig. 1. Relief showing Domitian's face damaged. Castel Gandolfo, Antiquarium Barberini, inv. 36392 (courtesy Governorato SCV – Direzione dei Musei, all rights reserved).

Fig. 2. Bronze sestertius from Asia Minor featuring Domitian (damaged) and Domitia. Amsterdam, Nationale Numismatische Collectie, De Nederlandsche Bank, inv. 30723 (courtesy Nationale Numismatische Collectie, De Nederlandsche Bank, Amsterdam).

works of the Flavian poets, he had been cast as Jupiter's earthly equivalent (fig. 2).[17]

Now he was obsolete, expunged as Nero had been expunged, so as to give his wife, the daughter of one of Nero's most popular generals in the East, her moment in the spotlight. Nero's shadow cannot be avoided: coins and gems from early in Nero's reign had also shown him face to face with a female, albeit this time, his mother; indeed one of them, an amethyst, on which both of their profiles were defaced, was still valuable enough in the third century to be included in the grave of an adult male in Germany.[18] See the similarity, and it is as though Domitian is doubly damned as Nero's complex afterlife is called into service. Nero too had been popular in the east, so much so that after his death, a number of imposters there had claimed to be him.[19] Equally unexpected is that 25 years after Domitian dies and is condemned as a tyrant, brick-stamps from the factory of Domitia, who at the time was implicated in his murder, still read "From the Sulpician brickyards of Domitia, *wife of Domitian*".[20]

"What is worse than Nero? What is better than his baths?"[21] No emperor's reputation was unequivocal, and Domitian was as accomplished as Nero when it came to his building. His forum, for example, was almost complete when he died, and was seamlessly dedicated by Nerva.[22] In fact, only about 40% of Domitian's extant inscriptions show signs of erasure: not all of the others were turned over and re-carved any more than his well-preserved portraits survive because all of them were warehoused.[23] At Aphrodisias, again in Asia Minor, a togate statue of Domitian's earliest portrait type was erected in 83 in the *scaenae frons* of the theatre, where it and its inscribed base remained intact until an earthquake uprooted them centuries later.[24] This does not mean that the Aphrodisians were off message, or followed the army in being peculiarly devoted to his memory, nor does it mean that senatorial sanctions had "failed". Much of what we now call "imperial imagery" was locally motivated and funded; to buck the trend in this way was to assert autonomy. And as the son of Vespasian and brother of Titus, Domitian, monster or no monster, was still related to gods. The unpredictability of memory sanctions, and the loss of control that this unpredictability underlines, was arguably their power,

---

17   Varner 1995, 203 and 2004, 115, and, on Domitian's affiliation with Jupiter, Jones 1992, 99-100.

18   Zwierlein-Diehl 2007, 324, plate 227, 980a-b, who notes that the damage might be connected to the memory sanctions suffered by Agrippina in 59.

19   Pappano 1937.

20   *CIL* XV 548a-549d (dating to 123) and Varner 1995, 205.

---

21   Mart. 7.34.4.

22   See e.g. Varner 2004, 133 and D'Ambra 1993.

23   Flower 2006, 240.

24   Varner 2004, 134 with bibliography. And, for a useful introduction to Domitian's statue-types, Zanker 2018.

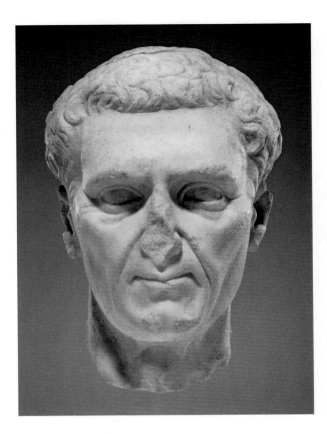

Fig. 3. Portrait of Domitian reworked as Nerva. Malibu, J. Paul Getty Museum, inv. 83.AA.43 (photo J. Paul Getty Museum).

Not that their features were at all similar. Domitian had been but 45 when assassinated, and had appeared in his statuary as smooth faced and youthful, his hair carefully coiffed. The 66-year-old Nerva was pinched and craggy in contrast, in line with his advanced years and with a style of portraiture that had defined the elite of the Republic, a style that emphasised the gravitas that came with age; that had pitched "real", serious-minded Romans against idealised, gym-loving Greeks.[27] 68 had witnessed a revival of this style to counter the images that had depicted Nero as a philhellenic dynast.[28] There was now an equivalent imperative. Adapting a portrait of Domitian so as to make it more wizened was to make the imperial image grow up, to ensure that empire learned from experience, to promise the senate it was back in control. Contemporary poet Martial imagines Brutus, Cato and other heroes of the past coming back from the dead to pay homage.[29]

A few of these Domitian-Nerva hybrids, such as the head now in the J. Paul Getty Museum in Malibu/Los Angeles (fig. 3), exaggerate these differences, making the crow's feet and naso-labial lines, and thus the substitution of one emperor for another, more marked than usual.[30] Look at the hair and the forehead which is now strangely un-furrowed, and they betray the head's previous identity. It is as though what the viewer is seeing is metamorphosis, and a metamorphosis which, like the famous poem, which itself ends with the apotheosis of Caesar, Augustus and Ovid, speaks explicitly of "forms changed into new entities",[31] of immortality and impermanence. Whatever Nerva's failings, he would not be emperor forever. There is also, as with Ovid's relationship with earlier epic, an air of belatedness about the Getty and similar sculptures, an awareness that this belatedness is no cause for regret, but "a source of power", and recognition that "imitation is the path to innovation and liberation".[32] In some examples, such as Frieze A of the Cancelleria reliefs, named after the palazzo in Rome where they were discovered, re-cutting has resulted in a hawkish profile or under-sized skull,[33] so that Domitian is visibly reduced and Nerva made to seem ill-suited to the role (Liverani, fig. 3). Perhaps this too is his saving grace. The pandering of Martial's Brutus, Cato and friends questions their exemplarity. Now that another dynasty is deposed, exemplary virtue is overrated: the

and the damage done to an image worse when put next to those that escaped. Perhaps Domitia's brickstamps are more predictable than we thought: by refusing to relinquish control, she galvanised Domitian's celebrity.

Domitian, Nerva and Beyond

Almost all of Nerva's surviving sculpted portraits were recut from images of Domitian.[25] Ruling for just over a year, the aged emperor barely had time to go it alone. Nor could he afford to. Unpopular with the military, his best chance was for change within continuity, even if this meant having his portrait put onto a Jupiter body of the kind that Domitian had so controversially coveted.[26] There was a sense in which the demand for Domitian's damnation excused this kind of imperial posturing – turning it from vain to imperative.

25   Varner 2004, 115. On re-cutting and image reuse (not always as a result of memory sanctions), see also Bergmann/Zanker 1981, esp. 380-403, and Blanck 1969, Jucker 1981, Galinsky 2008 and Prusac 2011.
26   Varner 2004, 115-117.

27   On this "veristic" style of portraiture, Pollini 2012, 13-68.
28   Zanker (2018, 223) is right to note that Nero's post 59 portraits were already far removed from Julio-Claudian idealism.
29   Mart. 11.5.
30   Varner 2004, 118 and cat. 5.12 with bibliography.
31   Ov. *Met.* 1.1-2.
32   Kilgour 2012, xiii. voeg toe in noot 32: For another example, see in this volume Fejfer fig. 1.
33   Varner 2004, 119. On these reliefs, see Paolo Liverani in this volume with fig. 3.

Fig. 4. Bronze cavalry face-mask. Leiden, Dutch National Museum of Antiquities, on loan from Erfgoed Leiden en Omstreken, inv. no. ELo 2001-500 (photo Dutch National Museum of Antiquities).

uncomfortable relationship of Nerva's statues to the past underwrites his modernity.[34]

The more obvious the adaptation, the more modern, or self-consciously, "post-modern" Nerva was made to seem. Take the equestrian bronze statue from a complex associated with the Augustales, an order of priests, many of them former slaves, with responsibility for the imperial cult, at Misenum on the Bay of Naples (Fejfer, fig. 6).[35] It reminds us that elites were not the only ones with a stake in the game; that all sectors of society were involved both in upholding the emperor's authority and in doing him down, that here too, emotions might have run so high that his image was deliberately knocked over. Instead of removing Domitian's head and replacing it with another, the restorer simply sliced off the front of the face and awkwardly added Nerva's features. Perhaps this was a matter of expediency. But the resulting join is all too obvious, the original lock-scheme on the rear portion of the head a glaring mismatch with the new fringe. If anything, the emperor looks as though he is riding into battle in a mask of the kind that was normally attached to cavalry face-mask helmets of the period, his identity not so much revised as obscured (fig. 4). A recut inscription confirms that this is now Nerva, but it is a "Nerva-ness"

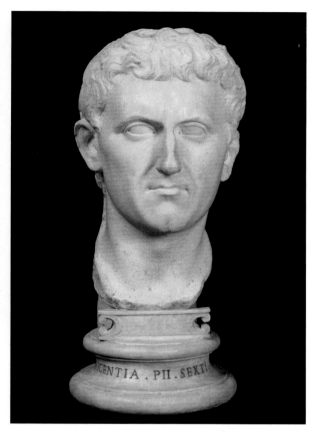

Fig. 5. Portrait of Domitian recut as Nerva. Vatican Museums, Sala dei Busti, 317, inv. 674 (courtesy Governorato SCV – Direzione dei Musei, all rights reserved).

that is paper thin, a veneer. Viewers might remember Nero's reputation on stage in masks bearing his own features, his dying words, or indeed Augustus on his deathbed, supposedly honing his image by combing his hair, setting his features, and asking for applause.[36] The "staginess of power"[37] was alive and well, a protection mechanism not only for the play-acting emperor, but for an increasingly knowing audience.

The dynamism of this statue reminds us too that not all Domitian-Nerva hybrids were designed to exaggerate Nerva's age. Some (*e.g.* fig. 5) are more youthful looking than Nerva's coin portraits, with only the very faintest of naso-labial lines.[38] Their impression is that Nerva has been rejuvenated by his accession, back to what he looked like in his prime when he had received substantial honours from Nero for his role in suppressing the Pisonian conspiracy.[39] Now all he had to do was secure an heir, and soon Trajan

---

34   I am indebted here to Morello 2018.

35   See Vout 2008, with bibliography. See Jane Fejfer in this volume.

36   On Nero, see Bartsch 1994 and on Augustus, Suet. *Aug.* 99.1.

37   Bartsch 1994, 193.

38   Varner 2004, 116.

39   Grainger 2003, 29.

Fig. 6. Marble portrait of Domitian recut as a Tetrarch or as Constantine around 300. Boston, Museum of Fine Arts, inv. 89.6 (photo Museum of Fine Arts).

Trajan's image-makers preferred to distance themselves from the Flavians by adopting a style reminiscent of Julio-Claudian portraiture with its brushed-forward fringe, the smooth-faced youthfulness of Domitian's images provided a bridge across, and a bridge that extended into late antiquity. A marble bust, today in the collection of the Museum of Fine Art in Boston (fig. 6), has been identified as a Domitian recut into a portrait of a Constantinian ruler, its eyes slightly enlarged and its pupils drilled to give it the uncompromising stare associated with the Tetrarchy out of which Constantine was created.[41] Again trace-elements of Domitian confer a reassuring classicism. By then, if not before, his portraits had become a raw material that was valuable for its imperial style over and above its Domitian-specific subject-matter. If his rule had turned him from private individual to quasi-god, his death had turned him back into modelling clay.

World without End, Amen

No icon is unassailable. When Domitian died in 96, the reaction was violent. Many of his images were attacked as though the flesh and blood emperor and/or immediately ejected from their bases. Ultimately, however, all that this did was to confirm the power of these images – as did the fact that no new portraits were made, and others were left unfinished. Even the completed ones were but works in progress, offering up material for new manifestations of imperium, a familiar outline of a role for his successors to inhabit. Nerva came to do this in different ways, sometimes looking even older than his years, sometimes turning back time to appear eerily well-preserved, sometimes, as was the case with the Jupiter-statues, with an eye to the future, and sometimes with a lack of conviction that made him seem insubstantial and transient. Whereas Domitian's name could be removed from an inscription, leaving the generic, yet still authoritative, *Imp. Caesar*,[42] any portrait statue had to be made whole again if it were to resume a public position that wasn't only about lack. To erase his having been there was to interrupt the continuity that took one right back to Augustus and his embrace of classicism.[43] It was also to underestimate the power of the past tense. Domitian, Nero, and with them, tyranny, were dead. Safeguarding the Principate depended on remembering that.[44]

was declared his successor, his military merits working to appease the soldiers. At the time that the imperial baton passed to him, he was the same age as Domitian had been when he died. It was no surprise that throughout the empire, more of Domitian's portraits were recut – this time into Trajan's smooth features, enabling the new emperor to slot straight in to the system.[40] In this process, it is Nerva's importance that is downplayed, he, almost, who is made to seem like the blip or interruption. For all that

---

40   Varner 2004, 122-123.

41   Varner 2004, 124 and cat. 5.30, and 2000, cat. no. 40.
42   Flower 2006, 237. Cf. the inscription on the modius from Carvoran (see Barbara Birley & Frances McIntosh in this volume, with fig. 6).
43   Still seminal on this is Zanker 1987.
44   Suggestions for further reading: Bergmann/Zanker 1981, Blanck 1969, Flower 2006, Varner 2004, Vout 2008.

Domitian and the Temples of Egypt

Olaf E. Kaper

Already before Rome took over the rule of Egypt after the suicide of Cleopatra VII, the country was home to two cultures: the ancient Egyptian heritage next to the Hellenistic Greek culture. The two traditions existed side by side. Whereas in other parts of the eastern Mediterranean, such as Syria, the local artistic and architectural traditions had largely become a hybrid of Hellenized and indigenous elements,[1] in Egypt the local art forms and architecture continued unaltered next to Hellenized art and architecture. The advent of Roman rule did not alter this situation.

In religious matters, the Roman emperors even actively continued the policy of the Ptolemaic kings, because they invested in the religious infrastructure of the country, and this was especially the domain where the traditional Egyptian art forms persisted. Especially during the first decades of Roman domination, the emperors generously financed building projects at the local temples.

At the same time, however, there was a major departure from Ptolemaic policies, in that the Roman administration took measures to curtail the economic and political power of the temples. All land holdings of the temples were confiscated and the priesthood was subjected to strict rules.[2] Augustus and Tiberius still had entirely new temples built, *e.g.* in Nubia with clear political motives,[3] but later emperors were generally satisfied with building additions to existing temple buildings.[4]

It is remarkable how the policy of temple building in Egypt did not bear any relation to the private opinions of the emperors involved. The Egyptian temples from the Roman period were covered in images showing the emperor in the role of Pharaoh, bringing offerings to animal-headed gods, and yet these images were apparently not considered offensive to the person or the office of the emperor.[5] Especially Augustus and Tiberius had a personal dislike for the oriental cults, and Tiberius had the temple of Isis in Rome closed.[6] Yet in Egypt, these two emperors had many temples built in which they are shown worshipping sacred bulls and other Egyptian animal-headed divinities.[7]

---

1   Cf. Segal 2013.
2   Stadler 2012, 457-458.
3   Hölbl 2004a, 15-21. The temple of Taffeh, now in Leiden, also dates from this time; ibid, 102-104.
4   Kákosy 1995, 894-912.
5   On the negative Roman attitude towards the Egyptian animal gods, cf. Smelik/Hemelrijk 1984.
6   Kaper 1998, 140, Pfeiffer 2010, 62-63.
7   Hölbl 2000, 25.

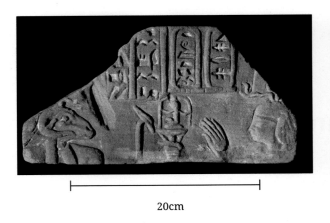

Fig. 1. Relief fragment of Domitian and Amun-Re. Cambridge, Fitzwilliam Museum, inv. E.1.2003 (photo Fitzwilliam Museum).

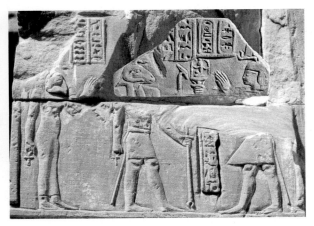

Fig. 2. Composite photo of the fragment of fig. 1 inserted into the remains of a doorjamb at Deir el-Hagar (image Jochen Hallof).

20cm

A Relief Fragment from Deir el-Hagar

Figure 1 shows a fragment of temple relief depicting the Emperor Domitian offering to the ram-headed Amun-Re.[8] The fragment derives from the jamb of an interior doorway of the temple of Deir el-Hagar in the oasis Dakhla, in the Western Desert of Egypt (figs. 2-3).[9] Domitian is depicted with a generically shaped face and crowned with a traditional type of crown composed of ram's horns and ostrich feathers. There is nothing in the image that relates to the emperor personally apart from his name that is written in hieroglyphs in the first (left) cartouche.[10] The second cartouche has the name Caesar written inside. The offering that Domitian is presenting to the god has as its central image a kneeling figure of the god Heh, a symbol of eternity, wearing a

Fig. 3. The temple of Deir el-Hagar in Dakhla Oasis (photo Anton Ivanov, adobestock.com).

---

8   Fitzwilliam Museum no. E.1.2003, Beinlich/Hallof 2003, Ashton 2004, 30-31.

9   Identification in Beinlich/Hallof 2003. On this temple, cf. Kaper 1997, 19-26, 36-40.

10   On the exceptional order of the names in the cartouches in the oases: Kaper 2012, 143-144, 159 [Table 6.8].

Fig. 4. Relief on the outer wall of the temple at Esna, depicting Domitian as Pharaoh smiting his enemies. This relief has symbolic and no historical significance, but it is illustrative of the major work of decoration undertaken at some temples under Domitian, which survived despite the *damnatio memoriae* (photo O.E. Kaper).

sun disc on his head and holding two palm branches.[11] It is a purely symbolic gift, for which the Pharaoh receives a long reign in return.

Under the Julio-Claudians, the mood in Rome was still largely against the oriental cults, but under the Flavians, Isis became a mainstream phenomenon.[12] As a sign of her wide acceptance, the goddess was depicted with a more noticeable Egyptian appearance and her mystery cult was spreading everywhere. The temple of Isis in Rome, the Iseum Campense, was destroyed by fire in 80, and Domitian restored the building and he also erected an obelisk there with hieroglyphic inscriptions.[13] An Egyptian sphinx with the features of Domitian may also be from here.[14] At the same time, there were two obelisks erected at the Isis temple of Benevento, inscribed in the name of Domitian, but these were gifted by a private donor, Rutilius Lupus.[15] In Benevento there was also a statue set up of Domitian as Pharaoh, in the Egyptian style, as well as statues of the baboon of Thoth and the Apis bull.[16] On the basis of these items it has been concluded that Domitian was exceptionally devoted to the

Fig. 5. Doorjamb with inscription at Deir el-Hagar. Domitian is named in two cartouches, in one of which the element Domitian has been plastered over. In between the cartouches is the title *divi filius* in its Egyptian translation (photo O.E. Kaper).

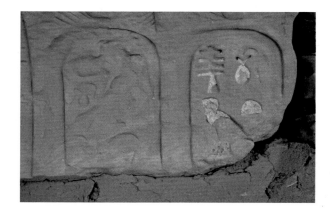

Fig. 6. Fragment of a cornice of Domitian from the top of the outerwalls of the Deir el-Hagar temple. The hieroglyphs spelling Domitian have been filled with gypsum plaster (photo O. E. Kaper).

11   Beinlich 2008, vol. 1, 189-191, vol. 2, 34-35, Cauville 2011, 200-201.
12   Rüpke 2018, 267.
13   Now in the Piazza Navona: Moormann 2018, 171-172, Nagel 2019, 1073-1077, Morenz/Sperveslage 2020, 13-43. It has been suggested that the obelisk was first erected in Egypt, but its texts and images, with their focus on Isis, speak against this. See Miguel John Versluys in this volume, with his fig. 3.
14   Rome, Musei Capitolini, Beck/Bol/Kaminski 2005, 712-713 [324].
15   Pfeiffer 2010, 129, Spier/Potts/Cole 2018, 262-264, Morenz/Sperverslage 2020, 37-39.
16   Benevento, Museo del Sannio 1893 and 1918, Müller 1969, 41-42, 86-87, Poole 2016, 102 [78], 103 [79]. Here Versluys, fig. 4.

Egyptian gods, and to Isis in particular.[17] However, Stefan Pfeiffer has argued convincingly against this, because of the biased nature of some of the source material, because of the Emperor's explicit adherence to Jupiter and because none of the evidence goes beyond what is expected of an emperor.[18] Also in the temples in Egypt itself, the reign of Domitian did not differ markedly from that of any other emperor.

Domitian's *Damnatio Memoriae* in Egypt

After Domitian's death his name and images were affected by a *damnatio memoriae* that was imposed by the Senate.[19] In contrast to other parts of the Roman world, many images of Domitian have survived in Egypt. The *damnatio* only rarely affected his name in Egyptian texts and in Greek inscriptions in Egypt and never his images as Pharaoh (fig. 4). Also the pharaonic statues in Rome and Benevento mentioned above survived without damage, because such Egyptian style images were not part of the emperor cult.[20] It is likely, however, that images of Domitian as Roman emperor were damaged also in Egypt, because none of these survive.[21]

The relief fragment from Deir el-Hagar (fig. 1) was probably also affected by the *damnatio memoriae*, because everywhere in the temple the name Domitian has been removed. The hieroglyphs were simply covered with plaster (fig. 5), and where the signs were incised these were entirely filled with plaster (fig. 6). A new name would have been written on the plaster, but no trace of this survives. In the relief in Fig. 1, the name of Domitian was probably once covered in plaster. The name Caesar in the second cartouche was never affected, which shows a respect for the office of the emperor, while denouncing the former holder of the office.[22] It is still not explained why Domitian was removed from this temple, but not from other temples of the same area, nor from any other temple in Egypt, as far as we know.[23] The name of Nero at Deir el-Hagar, also subject to a *damnatio memoriae*, was not removed.

Elsewhere in Egypt, the *damnatio memoriae* against Domitian is only known to have been carried out in the temple of Isis at the harbour town of Berenike on the Red Sea. Many Greek votive inscriptions were placed in the forecourt of this temple, two of which carried the name Domitian, and both were removed.[24] Also elsewhere in Berenike, in a temple in the harbour area, a Greek votive inscription was altered by erasing the name Domitian.[25] It is likely that there were Romans involved in these actions, even members of the imperial army, who carried out the instructions of the Senate, because Berenike was frequently visited by Romans.[26] But a similar zeal was not displayed in any other temple in Egypt.[27]

17   Hölbl 2004b, 531, Pollini 2018, 216.
18   Pfeiffer 2010, 124-135.
19   Varner 2004, 111-135, Bönisch-Meyer/Witschel 2014.
20   Pfeiffer 2010, 134-135, Brophy 2015, 35-36.
21   No statues of Domitian are included in Brophy 2015.
22   Devauchelle 2007 discusses some later emperors whose names were similarly removed from Egyptian temple walls.
23   Kaper 2012, 142.
24   Sidebotham et al 2019, 15.
25   Zych 2017, 114, 128, fig. 28 left.
26   On the *damnatio* of Domitian in inscriptions outside of Egypt: Martin 1987.
27   Further reading: Arnold 1999, Hölbl 2000, Lembke/Minas-Nerpel/Pfeiffer 2010, Minas-Nerpel 2012, Morenz/Sperveslage 2020.

Domitian's Damned Memory in the Fourth and Fifth Centuries

Maria Paola Del Moro

Domitian's *abolitio memoriae* is a particular case of disharmony among the three social powers that formed the Roman Empire: the Senate, the Army and the people. Suetonius records the reaction to the announcement of the Emperor's death in 96: the people remained indifferent, the soldiers were indignant and wanted to proclaim him god and avenge him. The Senate, however, welcomed the announcement and, during a meeting in the Curia, cursed his memory, throwing his shields and his images to the ground. Finally the Senate degreed that his name should be chiseled out of his inscriptions, to erase his memory completely.[1]

Among the various instances which shaped 'Domitian's fortune'. Domitian was violently stabbed to death in his bedroom as part of an organized conspiracy. Though subject to stabbing, Domitian's body was not further violated by being deprived of a burial ceremony. Domitian was not declared *hostis publicus*. However, the funeral was considered 'indecorous', and the body was carried away by *vespillones* in a simple wooden coffin. This was normally the way to bury people of a low social status. Domitian's faithful nurse, through an act of private *pietas* or mercy cremated the Emperor's body in the villa by the Via Latina. The ashes were later put in the *Templum Gentis Flaviae* and mixed with those of his beloved Julia.[2] That his burial was acknowledged at the time and remembered thereafter is indicative of a certain level of tolerance toward Domitian by some among the political elite, even after his death and despite the memory sanctions applied by the senate – a tolerance most likely resulting from the influence of the military who remained devoted to Domitian's memory. The Senate and the new Emperor himself, Nerva, left Domitian's perpetrators to the praetorians' bloody revenge.

The elimination of all that represented, and could have represented Domitian, was carried out solely by the Senate. This was possible through official acts, and in a more subtle way, through the composition of a hostile historiography. Contemporary historians such as Pliny and Tacitus followed by Suetonius and Dio Cassius, cleverly constructed the image of a tyrant by using propaganda that was extremely favorable to a regime of so-called 'adopted emperors'. Their gloomy portrait of the last of the Flavian dynasty as an unworthy and vicious individual functioned as a counter-point to the depiction

---

1   Suet. *Dom.* 23. See also Dio Cass. 68.1 and Plin. *Pan.* 52.4-5. Among the rich biography: Jones 1992, 193-196, Bianchi 2014, 48-51. To focus on the image of the *princeps*: Waters 1964. See here contributions by Barbara Levick, Jane Fejfer, Caroline Vout and Claire Stocks.
2   Suet. *Dom.* 17, Dio Cass. 67.18.

Fig. 1. Domenico Fetti, Emperor Domitian, oil on canvas, 1610s. Paris, Musée du Louvre.

Christians. The Christian sources between the first and the beginning of fourth century provide a list of persecutions brought about by the following emperors: Nero, Domitian,[5] Trajan, Marcus Aurelius, Septimius Severus, Maximinus Thrax, Decius, Valerian, Aurelian and Diocletian.[6]

Just like the non-Christian authors who precede them, these Christian writers emphasize the extreme cruelty of some of the Roman emperors. Nero condemned Roman Christians to such atrocious tortures that they aroused a sense of compassion in non-Christians since it was "not for the public good, but to glut one man's cruelty, that they were destroyed" Domitian was "not less perverse".[7]

In his *De mortibus persecutorum*, written between 313 and 316, Lactantius observes that Domitian "while exercising hateful power" and only because he was inspired by demons, persecuted the righteous people. He was punished for his crimes

and for [God's] vengeance the fact that he was killed in his palace was not enough: even the memory of his name was erased... the Senate pursued his name in such a way that it did not leave any traces of his images and of his titles, and having decreed the heaviest punishments, even in death it branded him solemnly with everlasting infamy. Annulled, therefore, the acts of a tyrant...[8]

Lactantius followed pro-senatorial sources[9] using, however, quite explicit language, with evident references to demons and divine revenge. As an upholder of Romanness, Lactantius underlined that the crime of killing the *princeps* had taken place in "his own palace" and he also highlighted the importance of the legislative authority of the Senate. To Lactantius' Christian perspective, the Senate was God's instrument and the annulment of the Tyrant's acts corresponded to the triumph of the Church.[10]

In the first part of *Historia Ecclesiastica* , written after 313 by Eusebius of Caesarea,[11] the bleak beginning describes Domitian's great cruelty: "Heir to Nero's hatred and of his struggle against God."[12] In one passage, Eusebius

of Trajan as the "new man" and the "virtuous one". The grim interpretation of an emperor who "surpassed his predecessors in cruelty, luxury and avarice",[3] has been transmitted over time through texts. These descriptions are more comparable to those of Nero, rather than to other members of Domitian's family. The manipulation of Domitian's memory was heavily influenced by the political directives of the time.[4]

We see this type of depiction repeated by writers throughout history, time and time again. A significant example is provided by the historical literature of the fourth and fifth centuries. Its writers were both pagan and Christian. Both categories of writers came from a classical background and tradition. They, in fact, represented different ways of analyzing and interpreting history.

The Church implemented its personal *abolitio memoriae* against the Roman emperors who were considered guilty of the worst crime: persecution of the

---

3   Zos. 1.8. About the cruelty of the *princeps*: Suet. *Dom.* 10-13.

4   Among the writers are included authors of all literary genres. For compositions by Juvenal and Martial: Santorelli 2011, Russotti 2017. Less known, but important as attributed to the poetess Sulpicia, who lived under Domitian – but maybe work of an author of the fourth-fifth century – is the co-called *Satura*: Massaro 2009. See Gregori/Spinelli 2019.

5   For the complexity of the question: Sordi 1984, 50-61, Cuesta Fernández 2012, 130-137.

6   Reduced to seven by Tertullian in the *Apologeticum* by omitting Trajan, Septimius Severus, Maximinus Thrax, and Aurelian In the *Apology of Christianity* presented to Marcus Aurelius by Melito of Sardes, however: "Unique among everyone only Nero and Domitian" (Euseb. *Hist. Eccl.* 4.26.9).

7   Tac. *Ann.* 15.44.5.

8   Lact. *Mort. Pers.* 3.1-4.

9   Lettieri 2013.

10   Among "many Christians ", who could come back from the exile (Euseb. *Hist Eccl.* 20.9) there was John the Evangelist. (18.20.8-9, Oros. 7.10).

11   Prinzivalli 2013.

12   Euseb. *Hist. Eccl.* 3.17-20.

Fig. 2. Agnolo Gaddi, Stories of St. John. Vision in Patmos, fresco, 1385. Florence, Santa Croce, Castellani Chapel.

also quotes Tertullian who called Domitian "half Nero" and described him as unable to fully imitate his predecessor's wickedness: "He immediately gave up, calling back those who were in exile."[13] Irrespective of whether or not this was true, the quote seems to confirm the tradition of a diminishing comparison between the two emperors. Another proof of this comparison is the nickname given to Domitian which was "bald-headed Nero".[14]

The works of these two Constantinian-age writers set the foundation and therefore the spread of Christian historiography. Nonetheless, in the fourth and fifth centuries it was still important to produce historiography free from references to Christianity. This literature was addressed to a pagan public with quite a rich, classical, cultural background. Examples of such, are readings of Eutropius and Aurelius Victor.

In his *Brevarium ab Urbe Condita*, composed after 369, Eutropius summarized Domitian's figure as *exitiabilis tyrannus*. [15] In the moral confrontation between himself and the Flavian, Eutropius compared Domitian to his more infamous predecessors:

> More similar to Nero, Caligula, or to Tiberius than to his father and brother...Dragged to the extremes of lust, anger, cruelty and avarice he inspired hatred towards himself, to such an extent to extinguish the merit of both his father and brother. His pride was also execrable so that in turn he became unpopular for

his heinous and most outrageous crimes. For this very reason, some conspirators killed him in the Palace. His body was carried away, with great ignominy, by some *vespillones* and was buried without honour.[16]

According to ancient sources on Domitian's death, Eutropius also presented the killing in the palace and the dishonourable funeral as the punishment for an emperor who was notorious for his vices. The ignominious treatment reserved for Domitian's body was against the principles of the Romans. This is the reason why this fact was narrated, not only by the Christian authors Orosius and Jerome in the fifth century,[17] but was also repeated by Aurelius Victor, one of the writers connected to the pagan cultural background. In the scarce biography of the *Epitome de Caesaribus*, written at the beginning of the fifth century, he compares Domitian to Caligula, dominated by lust. Domitian perished in a conspiracy and "the Senate decided to bury him *more gladiatorio* [in the manner of a gladiator] and that his memory had to be eliminated."[18]

Analyzing some of the fourth and fifth century sources, we obtain the image of continuity that was "constructed" after the Emperor's death. His memory can be considered damned in all ways. This damnation was unavoidable as a result of the betrayal and death that he suffered. His funeral was of no better. His memory dissipated in time and space. Domitian was damned as an evocation of grandiose evilness, in the end he was damned for all of eternity.

---

13   Tert. *Apolog.* 5.4.
14   Juv. 4.38. See Charles 2002.
15   Eutr. 8.1. See Bordone 2010.

16   Eutr. 7.23.
17   Oros. 7.10.7, Jer. *Chron.* Helm, 192g.
18   Aur. Vict. *Caes.* 11.1-13. See Ayashi 2017, in particular 68-83.

When we analyse the sources on Domitian from the fourth and fifth century, we see that there is continuity between these accounts and those that immediately followed the assassination of Domitian. This continuity suggests that rather than being a slow and evolving process of damnation, Domitian was condemned from the outset: betrayed, murdered, ignominiously buried – damnation was unavoidable. Any memory of the positive aspects of his rule dissipated into time and space, leaving Domitian a legacy of grandiose evilness. The perpetuation of *this* image is illustrated in the chronicles of the emperors, written by the Greek pagan historian Zosimus in around 507:[19]

Domitian surpassed all his predecessors in cruelty, luxury and avarice." For this reason he was killed by someone of his entourage "receiving the punishment his actions deserved."

---

19   Conca 2007.

'An Enemy of God' on the Imperial Throne? The Reception of Domitian during the Middle Ages

Nine Miedema

Medieval *Damnatio Memoriae* of Domitian

The twelfth-century German *Kaiserchronik* leaves no doubt about the qualities of Domitian as an emperor: *daz riche besaz sin brůder Domitianus. / der was ain gotes widerwarte, / di cristen můt er harte, / er was ain ahtær der cristenhaite* – Domitian, his [Titus's] brother, gained power over the Empire. He was an enemy of God; he brought the Christians into difficulties, he was a persecutor of Christianity.[1] Henry of Munich even states in his fourteenth-century chronicle, *der selb dient dem valant*, he served the devil.[2]

Not only in vernacular discourses, but also in many learned Latin chronicles which followed the writings of Eusebius of Caesarea (early fourth century) in Sophronius Eusebius Hieronymus's Latin translation (late fourth century), medieval authors have often agreed in their depiction of Domitian as a ruthless tyrant, remorselessly decimating the number of Christians.[3] Medieval chronicles, particularly those which describe both clerical and secular rulers in parallel listings and which have been very influential since Hugo of St. Victor and Otto of Freising (both twelfth century), and especially since Martin of Troppau's version (thirteenth century),[4] hardly ever leave out Domitian as one of the most obdurate persecutors of Christians.[5] According to these texts, which used the numerous versions of homilies and of the lives of saints as sources,[6] Domitian's most

---

1. See the new digital edition of the *Kaiserchronik*, manuscript A1, fol. 23vb-24ra (cf. *Kaiserchronik* 5.558-561).
2. Heinrich von München, ch. 22, v. 6.
3. Eusebius, 189-192. For a detailed description of the association of Domitian with apocalyptic writings, especially with St. John's Apocalypse, during the the first and early second century AD, see Mucha 2015.
4. Mierau 2016, 110.
5. E.g. *Secundus post Neronem Domitianus XPianos persequitur* (Eusebius, 192, fourth century); in similar wordings Frutolf von Michelsberg, 103 (eleventh century); Otto von Freising, 252; Martinus Polonus, ch. LXXXV (digital edition: http://www.mgh.de/ext/epub/mt/mvt002v003r.htm [6 March 2020]). Honorius Augustodunensis does not directly link the second persecution of the Christians to Domitian (*De imagine mundi libri tres*, 180-181). Reitz 2016 adds Orosius, *Historia adversum paganos* (fifth century), 7.10, and Sidonius Apollinaris, *Epistolae*, 5.7.6 (fifth century). – A systematic persecution of Christians, as many of the medieval texts insinuate, during the reign of Domitian is unlikely (Gross 1959, Reitz 2016).
6. Influential examples are: Jacobus a Voragine, 56 (thirteenth century), Beda, 44-49 (eighth century). Reitz 2016 adds Paulus Diaconus, *Historia Romana* 7.23 and 8.1 (eighth century).

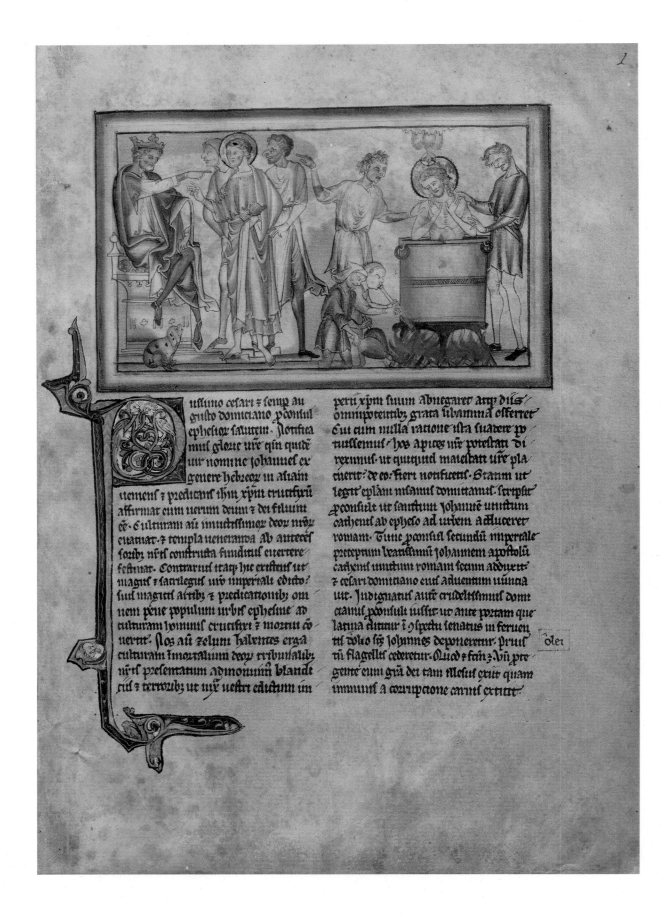

uistino cesari ꝫ semp au
gusto domiciano ꝓconsul
ephesioꝛ salutem. Glorifica
mus gloꝛie uꝛe ꝙin quide
uꝛ nomine iohannes ex
genere hebꝛeoꝛ in asiam
ueniens ꝫ pꝛedicans ihm xpm crucifixi
affirmat eum uerum deum ꝫ dei filium
ee. Sulturam aut inuictissimoꝛ deoꝛ moꝛ
eriatur ꝫ templa ueneranda ab antecef
soꝛibꝩ nꝛis constructa funditus euertere
festinat. Contrarius itaꝙ hic existens ut
magus ꝫ sacrilegus uꝛo imperialt edicto
suis magicis artibꝩ ꝫ pꝛedicattonibꝩ om
nem pene populum urbis ephesine ad
culturam hominis crucifixi ꝫ moꝛtui co
uertit. Illos aut zelum habentes erga
culturam immoꝛtalium deoꝛ tribunalibꝩ
nꝛis pꝛesentatum admonuimꝩ blande
cius ꝫ terroꝛibꝩ ut nisi uestri edictum in

perii xpm suum abnegaret atꝙ dits
omnipotentibꝩ grata libamina offerret
sic eum nulla rattone ista suadere po
tuissemus. hos apices uꝛe potestatt di
reximus. ut quicquid maiestatt uꝛe pla
cuerit. de eo fieri notificetis. Statim ut
legit eplam misimus domittanus. scripsit
ꝓconsul ut sanctum iohanne uinctum
cathenis ab epheso ad urbem Alluceret
romam. Tunc ꝓconsul secundū imperiale
pꝛeceptum leuiscimꝩ iohannem apostolū
cathenis uinctum romam secum adduxit
ꝫ cesari domittano eius aduentum nūcia
uit. Indignatus aute crudelissimus dom
eianus ꝓconsuli iussit ut ante poꝛtam que
latina dicitur ꝫ conspectu senatus in feruen
tt dolio sꝫ iohannes deponerettur. prius
ꝙ flagellis cederettur. Quod ꝫ factū ꝫ ipo pꝛe
sente cum grā dei tam illesus exiit quam
immunis a coꝛruptione carnis extitit.

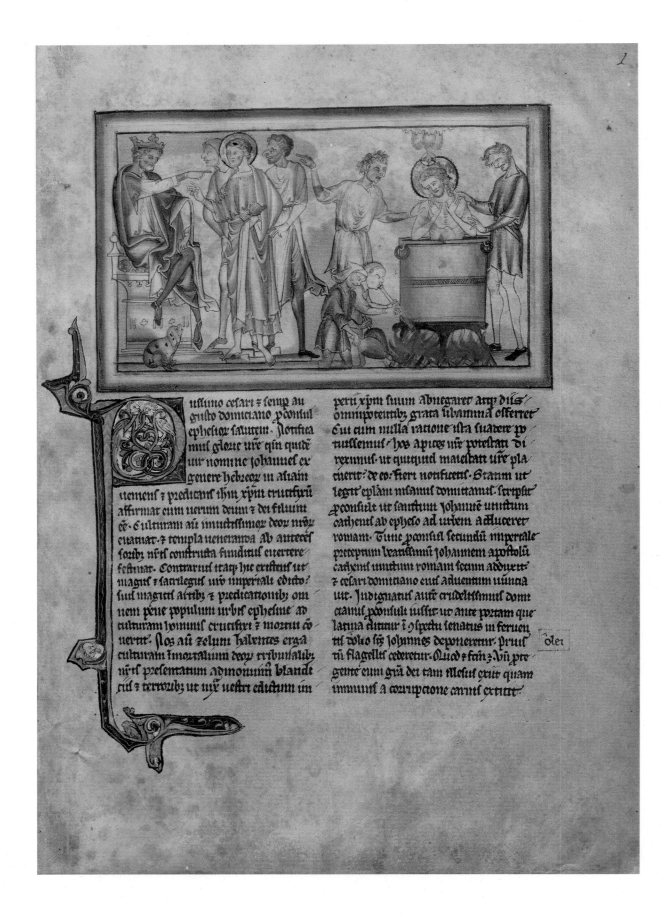

olei

Fig. 2. Stefan Lochner, Domitian ordering St. John the Evangelist to be boiled in oil; painting on wood, after 1435. Frankfurt am Main, Städel Museum, inv.-nr. 824 (photo Städel Museum).

scandalizing deed was his supposed attempt at murdering John the Evangelist: according to these stories, the Emperor was culpable of having exiled the Evangelist to Patmos after unsuccesfully trying to boil him in oil (cf. figs. 1-3).[7] During the late Middle Ages, Domitian was obviously thought to have been such a menace to Christendom that the widespread fourteenth- to sixteenth-century pilgrims' guide *Mirabilia Romae vel potius Historia et descriptio urbis Romae*, in its German version, also attributed the death of the famous martyr Laurentius of Rome to him, who died long after Domitian († 258).[8]

Beyond these negative portrayals of Domitian, Eusebius's dissemination of the information that Domitian used the title *Dominus et Deus*, interpreted in a Christian

Fig. 1 (left). Emperor Domitian speaking to St. John the Evangelist and St. John in a vat of boiling oil; miniature in 'Getty Apocalypse', ca. 1255-1260. Malibu, The J. Paul Getty Museum, Ms. Ludwig III.1 (83.MC.72), fol. 293r (photo J. Paul Getty Museum).

7   Reitz 2016 sees the first examples of this tradition in Tertullian and Origen (third century). See also for example Eusebius, 192, Regino von Prüm, 6 (tenth century), Otto von Freising, 255, Martinus Polonus, ch. LXXXV, *Kaiserchronik*, A1, fol. 24ra-b (*Kaiserchronik*, 5.567-644), Heinrich von München, ch. 22, v. 115-156. In Jacob van Maerlant's famous, but incomplete *Spiegel historiael* (thirteenth century) a description of Domitian's life is missing. Late medieval Roman pilgrims' guides also mention this event in their description of a church of which the patrocinium still recalls the attempted martyrdom: San Giovanni a Porta Latina with the oratory of San Giovanni in Oleo (cf. Miedema 2001, 562-565).

8   Miedema 2003, 277-278 (for further references to Domitian as a persecutor of Christians, especially of St. John, see 93, 160, 180, 230-231, and Miedema 2001, 186-188, 485, 584). The Latin version of the text does not mention Domitian here (Miedema 2001, 584). Reitz 2016 shows that the death of Dionysius of Paris († ca. 250) was also attributed to Domitian.

GOD ON EARTH: EMPEROR DOMITIAN

context as a sure sign of *superbia*, did not help to create sympathy for the Flavian emperor.[9] Thus, it does not come as a surprise that some of the medieval chronicles elaborate on the way he was said to have died. The conspiracy against Domitian, as described by the ancient writers Suetonius and Dio Cassius, becomes in these chronicles a plot that results from the emperor having contracted leprosy; while trying to flee from the conspirators, Domitian is tossed into the Tiber by his shying horse – thus leaving his soul to the devil[10] with no bodily remains to be commemorated.[11]

Instead of banning the memory of Domitian altogether (or as a countereffect caused by the attempt to ban his memory),[12] many medieval religious and historical discourses thus maintain a vivid remembrance of the last Flavian emperor as one of the worst tyrants of the Roman empire.[13] The humanist tradition did not necessarily correct this image: Giovanni Boccaccio briefly mentions Domitian in a chapter called *Imperatores miseri plures*,[14] stating:

> *Veru*[m] *alios Domitian*[us] *anteibat insolens, queritans, du*[m] *a*[m]*pliari p*[ri]*ncipat*[us] *sui videret*[ur] *gloria, se a cubicularijs int*[er]*emptu*[m] [et] *populari sandapil*[a] *deportatu*[m], [et] *cu*[m] *dedecore tumulatu*[m].

> The insolent Domitian preceded others, who, when the glory of his reign was seen to grow, deserved to be killed by his servants, to be removed on a simple litter and to be buried without solemnity.

This may have influenced even perceptions of Domitian in modern scholarship.[15]

Medieval Appreciation of Domitian

Yet, not all medieval texts project a negative image of Domitian; it did not need the new humanist tradition[16] to emphasize the positive elements already present in antique writings (it should be kept in mind that Suetonius, for example, in his description of Domitian's life "differentiat[ed] an initially moderate regime from a later degeneracy").[17] Eusebius reminds his readers that Domitian's name was connected to many famous buildings in Rome, such as the Pantheon (cf. fig. 4), the Meta Sudans, and the Stadium that

Fig. 3. Albrecht Dürer, Domitian ordering St. John the Evangelist to be boiled in oil (woodcut from the German Apocalypse Series), ca. 1496-1498. Frankfurt am Main, Städel Museum, inv.-nr. 31501 D (photo Städel Museum).

---

9   Not all medieval chronicles refer to this fact, which was taken from Suetonius. Suetonius, however, does not seem to have interpreted Domitian using the title *Dominus et Deus* as a sign of pride as a sin. See, for example: *Primus Domitianus dominum se et deum appellari iussit* (Eusebius, 190); *Hic dominum ac deum se appellari scribique iussit, nullamque nisi auream vel argenteam statuam sibi in palatio statui permisit* (Frutolf von Michelsberg, 103); *Hic etiam in tantam prorupit vesaniam, ut se deum et dominum appellari ac coli fecerit* (Otto von Freising, 252); *Dominum et Deum primum appellari se iussit, nullam sibi nisi argenteam vel auream in Capitolio statuam passus est poni* (Martinus Polonus, ch. LXXXV); not in the *Kaiserchronik* and in Heinrich von München's *Weltchronik*.
10 *Kaiserchronik*, A1, fol. 24rb-va, 24ra (*Kaiserchronik*, 5.674, 5.677-678).
11 *Kaiserchronik*, A1, fol. 24rb (*Kaiserchronik*, 5.647-674). That Domitian, though having been described as a successful (albeit merciless) military commander (fol. 23vb-24ra; v. 5.562-563), was thrown from his bolting horse seems to emphasize the fact he had lost control not only over his subjects, but even over his animals. Henry of Munich rewrites the story as a suicide: Domitian dresses with all regalia and then forces his horse to jump off the bridge (Heinrich von München, ch. 22, v. 168-191).
12 Cf. Gizewski/Mlasowsky 2020.
13 Reitz 2016 points to the fact that Domitian was also used as a deterrent example in some of the princes' mirrors, e.g. the *Speculum regum* of Godfrey of Viterbo (twelfth century).
14 Quoted here from the first early print of *De viris illustribus* (https://digital.staatsbibliothek-berlin.de/werkansicht?PPN=PPN739807617&PHYSID=PHYS_0001, [1474]; originally written ca. 1355-1374), book 8, ch. 2, p. 230.
15 For a revision of Domitian's negative image see for example Gering 2011, Urner 1993.
16 Cf. Reitz 2016.
17 Reitz 2016.

Fig. 4. Domitian ordering the Pantheon to be built; miniature from *Les fait des Romains*; first quarter of the fifteenth century. London, British Library, Ms. Royal 20 C I, fol. 293r

still shapes Piazza Navona.[18] Henry of Munich may have had Eusebius in mind when he informed his readers that *ze pawen het er gůten sit* (Domitian was succesful at building projects).[19] From the fifth century onwards, a dozen saints bore the name 'Domitian',[20] which must mean that this name did not only evoke negative emotions, and that a trace

---

18   Eusebius, 190: *Multa opera Romae facta, in quis Capitolium, forum transitorium, diuorum porticus, Isium ac Sarapium, stadium, horrea piperataria, Uespasiani templum, Minerua Chalcidica, Odium, forum Traiani, thermae Traianae et Titianae, senatus[,] ludus matutinus, mica aurea, meta sudans et Pantheum.*

19   Heinrich von München, ch. 22, v. 25.

20   *Bibliotheca Sanctorum* 1964, 757-762.

of Domitian's good deeds may have survived.[21] Frutolf of Michelsberg (eleventh century) mentions the public baths Domitian allegedly built in Rome,[22] the twelfth-century *Mirabilia Romae* add Domitian's works on the buildings of the Forum,[23] the twelfth-century *Graphia aureae urbis Romae* and most fourteenth- and fifteenth-century versions of the *Mirabilia* refer to Domitian's palace,[24] without using the opportunity to mention any of the negative characteristics described above.

Henry of Munich states, Domitian *waz [...] gern den ratgeben mit*, he appreciated his counsellors.[25] A further decidedly positive reception of Domitian in the same spirit can be found in the fourteenth-century *Gesta Romanorum*, where he is called *prudens valde et per omnia justus, quoniam nulli parcebat, quin per viam justicie transiret*.[26] After wisely spending a large amount of money on three pieces of advice, all three turn out to save Domitian's life against conspirations; rewriting the emperor's biography once more, his end is described as follows: *vitam beatam finivit* – he ended his blessed life.[27]

Conclusion

The image of Domitian during the Middle Ages, that is from the fourth until the early sixteenth century, is diverse. Other than the religious discourses as found in homilies and the lives of saints (and partly in chronicles) might suggest, the last Flavian emperor was by no means seen in exclusively negative ways; different literary genres transmit varied interpretations of the ancient sources, showing that it may be worthwhile to initiate further research on the medieval reception of Domitian, which remains to date a rather neglected topic. It should be kept in mind that all medieval texts mentioned above were passed down in innumerable manuscripts and early prints. These indisputably show that during the Middle Ages Domitian's reign was by no means forgotten – neither the negative, nor the positive aspects of it.[28]

---

21   Reitz 2016 recalls that the sixth-century *Oracula Sibyllina* also praise Domitian.
22   *Mirabilia*, 58. The baths cannot be identified.
23   Frutolf von Michelsberg, 103; cf. Heinrich von München, ch. 22, v. 20.
24   This reference can be found in the twelfth-century *Graphia aureae urbis Romae* and was widespread in the *Mirabilia Romae* since the fourteenth century: *Palacium Domicianj in Transtiberyn / das palast Domiciani genseit der Tiber* (Miedema 1996, 345, cf. 406). Medieval authors probably placed the palace in Trastevere because the Mica Aurea, said to be in the neighbourhood of the palace, was located near Santi Cosma e Damiano in Mica Aurea in Trastevere.
25   Heinrich von München, ch. 22, v. 26.
26   *Gesta Romanorum*, ch. 103, 431-434, 431.
27   *Gesta Romanorum*, 433.
28   Further reading: Maßmann 1854, Gross 1959, Riemer 1998, Mucha 2015, Reitz 2016.

Bibliography

The abbreviations of periodicals, corpora, and reference works are those of the *Richtlinien* of the German Archaeological Institute (see https://www.dainst.org/documents/10180/70593/03_Liste+abzuk%C3%BCrzender+Zeitschriften_quer pdf/2646d351-8e5d-4e8b-8acd-54f3c272d3ff).

Aarts, A.A.C. (2012), "Scherven, schepen en schoeiingen. LR62: Archeologisch onderzoek in een fossiele rivierbedding bij het castellum van De Meern", *Basisrapportage Archeologie* 43, 31-48.

Acton, Karen (2011), "Vespasian and the social world of the Roman court", *AJP* 132, 103-124.

Adamo Muscettola, Stefania (2000), "Miseno: culto imperiale e politica nel complesso degli Augustali", *RM* 107, 79-108.

Alcock, Susan E. (1994), "Nero at Play? The Emperor's Grecian Odyssey", in: Jaś Elsner / Jamie Masters (eds.), *Reflections of Nero. Culture, History and Representation*, London, 98-111.

Aldrete, Gregory S. (2007), *Floods of the Tiber in Ancient Rome*, Baltimore, MD.

Alföldy, Geza (1995), "Eine Bauinschrift aus dem Colosseum", *ZPE* 109, 195-226.

Aliquot, Julien (2019), "Heliopolitan Capitolia: From Greek games to Christian pilgrimage", *Religion in the Roman Empire* 5, 145-169.

Amoenissimis ... aedificiis (2017), *Lo scavo di Piazza Marconi a Cremona*, I, *Lo scavo*, Mantova.

Amoenissimis ... aedificiis (2018), *Lo scavo di Piazza Marconi a Cremona*, II, *I materiali*, Mantova.

Andreau, Jean (2001), "Rome capitale de l'Empire, la vie économique", *Pallas* 55, 303-317.

Arata, Francesco Paolo (1997), "Un 'sacellum' d'età imperiale all'interno del Museo Capitolino: una proposta di identificazione", *BCom* 98, 129-162.

Arco (2017), various authors, "Arco di Tito. Scavo, anastilosi e ricostruzione virtuale dell'Arco di Tito al Circo Massimo", *BCom* 118, 161-250.

Arnold, Dieter (1999), *Temples of the Last Pharaohs*, New York/Oxford.

Ashton, Sally-Ann (2004), *Roman Egyptomania: A special exhibition at the Fitzwilliam Museum, Cambridge, 24 September 2004 – 8 May 2005*, London.

Augustakis, Antony / Buckley, Emma / Stocks, Claire (2019), "Un-damning Domitian. Reassessing the Last Flavian *princeps*", *IllClSt* 42, 233-452.

Augustus, *Kaiser Augustus und die verlorene Republik*, Berlin, 1988.

Ayahshi, Toshiaki (2017), *Sources et signification du 'Liber de Caesaribus' d'Aurélius Victor*, Archéologie et Préhistoire, HAL archives-ouvertes.fr., https://tel.archives-ouvertes.fr/tel-02055575/document.

Bablitz, Leanne E. (2007), *Actors and Audience in the Roman Courtroom*, London/New York.

Banti, A. (1983), *I grandi bronzi imperiali. Nerva, Traianus, Plotina, Marciana, Matidia. Selezione di sesterzi e medaglioni classificati secondo il sistema Cohen*, Florence.

Banti, A. (1986), *I grandi bronzi imperiali. Septimius Severus, Iulia Domna, Caracalla, Plautilla, Geta, Macrinus, Diadumenianus*, Florence.

Bartman, Elisabeth (1999), *Portraits of Livia*, Cambridge.

Bartoli, Alfonso (1929), "Scavi del Palatino (DomusAugustana) 1926-1928", *NSc* 5, 3-29.

Bartoli, Alfonso (1938), *Domus Augustana*, Rome.

Bartsch, Shadi (1994), *Actors in the Audience: Theatricality and Doublespeak from Nero to Hadrian*, Cambridge, MA.

Baumer, Lorenz (2008), "L'iconographie politique de Domitien: essai d'interprétation des reliefs dits 'de la Cancelleria'", *RA*, 189-192.

Beard, Mary / Hopkins, Keith (2005), *The Colosseum*, London.

Beck, Herbert / Bol, Peter C. / Kaminski, Gabriele (eds.) (2005), *Ägypten Griechenland Rom. Abwehr und Berührung*, Kat. Städelsches Kunstinstitut und Städtische Galerie 26. November 2005 – 26. *Februar 2006*, Frankfurt am Main.

Beda, *Venerabilis Bedae, anglo-saxonis presbyteri, opera omnia*, ed. Jacques-Paul Migne, vol. 5 (Patrologia Latina 94), Paris, 1862.

Beinlich, Horst (2008), *Handbuch der Szenentitel in den Tempeln der griechisch-römischen Zeit Ägyptens. Die Titel der Ritualszenen, ihre korrespondierenden Szenen und ihre Darstelllungen*, Dettelbach.

Beinlich, Horst / Hallof, Jochen (2003), "Found and lost: ein Block aus Deir el-Hagar unterm Hammer", *GöttMisz* 195, 7-11.

Bell, Sinclair / Hansen, Ingle Lyse (eds.) (2008), *Role Models in the Roman World: Identity and Assimilation*, Ann Arbor, MI.

Belli Pasqua, Roberta (1995), *Sculture di età romana in "basalto"*, Rome.

Benoist, Stéphane (2005), *Rome, le prince et la Cité*, Paris.

Bergmann, Marianne (2000), "Representation", in: Adolf H. Borbein / Tonio Hölscher / Paul Zanker (eds.), *Klassische Archäologie. Eine Einführung*, Berlin, 166-188.

Bergmann, Marianne / Zanker, Paul (1981), "'Damnatio Memoriae' Umgearbeitete Nero- und Domitianporträts Zur Ikonographie der flavischen Kaiser und des Nerva", *JdI* 96, 317-412.

Bernard, Jean-François (2014), "*Piazza Navona, ou Place Navone, la plus belle & la plus grande" : du stade de Domitien à la place moderne, histoire d'une évolution urbaine*, Rome.

Bertrand, Estelle / Chillet, Clément (2016), "Le *macellum Liviae* à Rome: vrai ou faux monument augustéen?", *MEFRA* 128, 469-485.

Bianchi, Edoardo (2014), "Il senato e la '*damnatio memoriae*' da Caligola a Domiziano", *Politica Antica* 1, 33-54.

Bianchini, Francesco (1738), *Del Palazzo de' Cesari*, Rome.

Bibliotheca Sanctorum, vol. 4, Rome, 1964.

Blake, Marion Elizabeth (1959), *Roman Construction in Italy from Tiberius through the Flavians*, Washington, DC.

Blanck, Horst (1969), *Wiederverwendung alter Statuen als Ehrendenkmäler bei Griechen und Römern*, Rome.

Boccaccio, Giovanni (1474), *De viris illustribus*, https://digital.staatsbibliothek-berlin.de/werkansicht?PPN=PPN739807617&PHYSID=PHYS_0001.

Bocciarelli, Dorian / Bizet, Maryvonne (2013), "Le *Macellum Magnum* et les dupondii de Néron", *RNum* 173, 271-281.

Bodel, John (2000), "Dealing with the Dead. Undertakers, executioners and potter's fields in Ancient Rome", in: Valerie M. Hope / Eireann Marshall (eds.), *Death and Disease in the Ancient City*, London/New York, 128-149.

Bol, Peter C. (1994), *Forschungen zur Villa Albani: Katalog der antiken Bildwerke* IV. *Bildwerke im Kaffeehaus*, Berlin.

Bond, Sarah E. (2016), *Trade and Taboo: Disreputable Professions in the Roman Mediterranean*, Ann Arbor, MI.

Bönisch-Meyer, Sophia (ed.) (2014), *Nero und Domitian. Mediale Diskurse der Herrscherrepräsentation im Vergleich*, Tübingen.

Bönisch-Meyer, Sophia / Witschel, Christian (2014), "Das epigraphische Image des Herrschers. Entwicklung, Ausgestaltung und Rezeption der Ansprache des Kaisers in den Inschriften Neros und Domitians", in: Sophia Bönisch-Meyer (ed.), *Nero und Domitian. Mediale Diskurse der Herrscherrepräsentation im Vergleich*, Tübingen, 81-179.

Bonnefond, Mireille (1987), "Transferts de fonctions et mutation idéologique: le Capitole et le forum d'Auguste", in: *L'Urbs. Espace urbain et histoire. Ier siècle avant J.-C. – IIIe siècle après J.-C.*, Rome, 251-278.

Bonomelli, E. (1953), *I Papi in campagna*, Rome.

Bordone, Fabrizio (2010), "La lingua e lo stile del *Breviarium* di Eutropio", *Annali Online di Lettere – Ferrara* 2, 143-162.

Borg, Barbara E. (2019), *Roman Tombs and the Art of Commemoration*, Cambridge.

Boschung, Dieter (2002), *Gens Augusta. Untersuchungen zu Aufstellung, Wirkung und Bedeutung der Statuengruppen des julisch-claudischen Kaiserhauses*, Mainz am Rhein.

Boyle, Antony J. / Dominik, William J. (eds.) (2003), *Flavian Rome. Culture, Image, Text*, Leiden.

Bradley, Keith R. (1973), "Imperial virtues in Suetonius' *Caesares*", *Journal of Indo-European Studies* 4, 245-253.

Bradley, Keith R. (1991), "The imperial ideal in Suetonius' 'Caesares'", *ANRW* 2.33.5, 3701-3732.

Bradley, Mark (2009), *Colour and the Meaning in Ancient Rome*, Cambridge.

Braund, Susanna (2004), *Juvenal and Persius*, Cambridge, MA.

Brienza, Emanuele (2016), *Valle del Colosseo e pendici nord orientali del Palatino. La via tra valle e foro: dal dato stratigrafico alla narrazione virtuale (64 d.C.-138 d.C.)*, Rome.

Brophy, Elizabeth (2015), *Royal Statues in Egypt 300 BC – AD 220: Context and Function*, Oxford.

Broucek, James (2015), "Thinking About Religion Before 'Religion': A Review of Brent Nongbri's Before Religion. A History of a Modern Concept", *Soundings. An Interdisciplinary Journal* 98.1, 98-125.

Brunsting, Hendrik / Steures, Dé C. (1995), "De baksteenstempels van Romeins Nijmegen I. Opgravingen castra 1950-1967, opgravingen Kops Plateau ca. 1986-1994", *OudhMeded* 75, 85-117.

Bruun, Christopher (1997), "Acquedotti e condizioni sociali di Roma imperiale: immagini e realtà", in: *La Rome impériale. Démographie et logistique*, Rome, 121-155.

Bruun, Christopher (2013), "Warum verfasste Frontin sein Werk über die Wasserversorgung Roms?", in: *Die Wasserversorgung im antiken Rom*, Bonn, 151-158.

Bukowiecki, Eva (2008), *La brique dans l'architecture impériale à Rome. Étude de quelques grandes chantiers du Palatin*, PhD Dissertation, Aix-Marseille I.

Bülow-Clausen, Kristine (2012), "Domitian between Isis and Minerva: the dialogue between the 'Egyptian' and 'Graeco-Roman' aspects of the sanctuary of Isis at Beneventum", in: *Mythos Supplemento* n.s. 3, 93-122.

Burkert, Walter (1985), *Greek religion*, Cambridge, Mass.

Burnett, A. (2011), "The Augustan Revolution Seen from the Mints of the Provinces", *JRS* 101, 1-30.

Busch, Alexandra W. (2001), *Militär in Rom. Militärische und paramilitärische Einheiten im kaiserzeitlichen Stadtbild*, Wiesbaden.

Buttrey, Theodore Vernon (2007), "Domitian, the Rhinoceros, and the date of Martial's Liber de Spectaculis", *JRS* 97, 101-112.

Cain, Petra (1993), *Männerbildnisse neronisch-flavischer Zeit*, Munich.

Caldelli, Maria Letizia (1993), *L'agon Capitolinus: storia e protagonisti dall'istituzione domizianea al IV secolo* (Studi pubblicati dall'Istituto italiano per la storia antica 54), Rome.

Caldelli, Maria Letizia (1997), "Gli agoni alla greca nelle regioni occidentali dell'Impero: la Gallia Narbonensis", *MemLinc* 9.4, 389-481.

Campbell, J.B. (1984), *The Emperor and the Roman Army. 31 BC-AD 235*, Oxford.

Candilio, Daniela (1990-1991), "Roma. Indagini archeologiche nell'aula ottagona delle Terme di Diocleziano", *NSc*, 165-183.

Capriotti Vittozzi, Gabriella (2014), "The Flavians: Pharaonic kingship between Egypt and Rome", in: Laurent Bricault / Miguel John Versluys (eds.), *Power, politics and the cults of Isis* (Religions in the Graeco-Roman World 180), Leiden/Boston, 237-259.

Carettoni, Gianfilippo et al. (1960), *La pianta marmorea di Roma antica. Forma Urbis Romae* I, Rome.

Carnabuci, Elisabetta (1996), *I luoghi dell'amministrazione della giustizia nel Foro di Augusto*, Naples.

Carradice, Ian (1982), "Coins, monuments and literature: some important sestertii of Domitian", in: Tony Hackens / Raymond Weiller (eds.), *Actes du 9ème congrès international de numismatique (Berne, septembre 1979)* I, Louvain-La-Neuve/Luxembourg, 371-383.

Cauville, Sylvie (2011), *L'offrande aux dieux dans le temple égyptien*, Leuven/Paris/Walpole.

Cavalieri, Marco (2005), "'Referre, revocare, restituire'. Forme e significati dell'urbanistica nella Roma di fine I sec. d.C.", *Res Antiquae* 2, 103-168.

Chabrečková, Barbora (2017), *The Imperial Cult During the Reign of Domitian*, Master Thesis, Masaryk University, Brno, https://www.academia.edu/34570051/The_Imperial_Cult_During_the_Reign_of_Domitian.

Champlin, Eric (2005), *Nerone*, tradizione italiana, Rome/Bari.

Charles, Michael B. (2002), "'Calvus Nero': Domitian and the mechanics of predecessor denigration", *ActaCl* 45, 19-49.

Chaudhuri, Pramit (2014), *The War with God: Theomachy in Roman Imperial Poetry*, Oxford.

Chausson, François (2003), "Domitia Longina: reconsidération d'un destin imperial", *JSav*, 101-129.

Ciancio Rossetto, Paola / Pisani Sartorio, Giuseppina (eds.) (2017), *Theatrum Marcelli*, Rome.

Cizek, Eugen (1984), *Nerone*, traduzione italiana, Milan.

Coarelli, Filippo (2008-2009), "Il circo di Caligola in Vaticano", *RendPontAcc* 81, 3-13.

Coarelli, Filippo (ed.) (2009a), *Divus Vespasianus. Il bimillennario dei Flavi*, Milan.

Coarelli, Filippo (2009b), "I Flavi e Roma", in: Filippo Coarelli (ed.), *Divus Vespasianus. Il bimillennario dei Flavi*, Milan, 68-97.

Coarelli, Filippo (2014), *Collis. Il Quirinale e il Viminale nell'antichità*, Rome.

Coarelli, Filippo (2018), "Isis Capitolina e Isis Campensis. Il culto ufficiale delle divinità egiziane a Roma", in: Miguel John Versluys / Kristine Bülow-Clausen / Giuseppina Capriotti Vittozzi (eds.), *The Iseum Campense from the Roman Empire to the Modern Age. Temple – monument – lieu de mémoire*, Rome, 61-77.

Coarelli, Filippo (2019), *Statio. I luoghi dell'amministrazione nell'antica Roma*, Rome.

Coarelli, Filippo (2020), *Il Foro Romano da Augusto al tardo impero*, Rome.

Cohen, Sarah T. (2008), "Augustus, Julia and the Development of Exile *Ad Insulam*", *CQ* 58, 206-217.

Coleman, Kathleen M. (1988), *Statius Silvae IV*, Oxford.

Coleman, Kathleen M. (1993), "Launching into history: aquatic displays in the Early Empire", *JRS* 83, 48-74.

Conca, Fabrizio (ed.) (2007), *Zosimo. Storia nuova*, Milan.

Cooley, Alison E. (2009), *Res Gestae Divi Augusti. Text, Translation, and Commentary*, Cambridge.

Corbier, Mireille (2006), *Donner à voir, donner à lire. Mémoire et communication dans la Rome ancienne*, Paris.

Cordes, Lisa (2014), "Preferred Readings: von Seneca zu Statius", in: Sophia Bönisch-Meyer (ed.), *Nero und Domitian. Mediale Diskurse der Herrscherrepräsentation im Vergleich*, Tübingen, 341-378.

Cordes, Lisa (2017), *Kaiser und Tyrann. Die Kodierung und Umkodierung der Herrscherrepräsentation Neros und Domitians*, Berlin/Boston.

Cordes, Lisa (2019), "Megalomanie und hohle Bronze. Die Kolossalstatue als Vehikel von Herrscherkritik", in: Karina Kellermann / Alheydis Plassmann / Christian Schwermann (eds.), *Criticising the Ruler in Pre-Modern Societies – Possibilities, Changes and Methods*, Bonn, 143-170.

Cosme, Pierre (2012), *L'année des quatre empereurs*, Paris.

Cowan, E. (2019), "Hopes and Aspirations/ Res Publica, Leges et Iura, and Alternatives at Rome", in: Josiah Osgood / Kit Morrell / Kathryn Welch (eds.), *The Alternative Augustan Age*, Oxford, 27-45.

Crisà, Antonino/Palmieri, Lilia (forthcoming), "The 'Calvatone Hoard 2018' (Cremona-Italy): archaeology and hoarding trends during the reign of Gallienus (AD 253-268)", *Revue Numismatique*.

Croisille, Jean-Marie / Perrin, Yves (eds.) (2002), *Neronia VI. Rome à l'époque néronienne* (Collection Latomus 268), Brussels.

Cuesta Fernández, Jorge (2012), "El cristianismo primitivo ante la civilización romana. Sobre la Imagen como "*Persecutores Christianorum*" de Nerón y Domiciano a través de las primitivas fuentes cristianas", *Antesteria* 1, 127-141.

D'Ambra, Eve (1993), *Private Live, Imperial Virtues: The Frieze of the Forum Transitorium in Rome*, Princeton, NJ.

Daehner, Jens / Lapatin, Kenneth (2015) (eds.), *Potere e pathos. Bronzi del mondo ellenistico*, Florence.

Daguet-Gagey, Anne (2000), "I grandi servizi pubblici di Roma", in: Elio Lo Cascio (ed.), *Roma imperiale. Una metropoli antica*, Rome, 71-102.

Daguet-Gagey, Anne (2007), "La *damnatio memoriae* dans l'espace urbain: les avatars de quelques monuments romains", in: Stéphane Benoist (ed.), *Mémoire et histoire. Les procédures de condamnation dans l'Antiquite romaine*, Metz, 113-129.

Daltrop, Georg (1966), *Die Flavier* (Das römische Herrscherbild), Berlin.

Damsky, Ben L. (1990), "The stadium Aureus of Septimus Severus", *AJNum* 2, 77-105.

Darwall-Smith, Robin H. (1994), "Albanum and the villas of Domitian", *Pallas* 40, 145-165.

Darwall-Smith, Robin H. (1996), *Emperors and Architecture: A Study of Flavian Rome* (Collection Latomus 231), Brussels.

De Angelis, Francesco (ed.) (2010), *Spaces of justice in the Roman Empire*, Leiden.

De Bruin, Jasper (2019), *Border communities at the Edge of the Roman Empire. Processes of Change in the Civitas Cananefatium* (Amsterdam Archaeological Studies 28), Amsterdam.

De Fine Licht, Kjeld (1974), "*Antrum Albanum*", *AnalRom* 7, 37-66.

De Haan, Nathalie (2013), "Inleiding", in: Vincent Hunink / Nathalie de Haan, *Aquaducten van Rome. De aquis urbis Romae. Geschreven door Frontinus, vertaald door Vincent Hunink en ingeleid door Nathalie de Haan*, Almere.

De Haan, Nathalie (2016), "Roman domestic building", in: Georgia L. Irby (ed.), *A Companion to Science, Technology, and Medicine in Ancient Greece and Rome*, Malden, MA, II, 711-729.

De Kleijn, Gerda (2001), *The Water Supply of Ancient Rome. City Area, Water and Population*, Amsterdam.

De Kort, Jan-Willem / Raczynski-Henk, Yannick (2014), "The Fossa Corbulonis between the Rhine and Meuse estuaries in the Western Netherlands", *Water History* 6.1, 51-71.

De Souza, Manuel / Devillers, Olivier (eds.) (2019), *Le Palatin, émergence de la colline du pouvoir à Rome* (Neronia X), Bordeaux.

Del Moro, Maria Paola (2007), "Il Foro di Nerva", in: Lucrezia Ungaro (ed.), *Il Museo dei Fori Imperiali nei Mercati di Traiano*, Milan, 178-191.

Deppmeyer, Korana (2008), *Kaisergruppen von Vespasian bis Konstantin. Eine Untersuchung zu Aufstellungskontexten und Intentionen der statuarischen Präsentation kaiserlicher Familien*, Hamburg.

Derks, Ton (2017), "Ein Bronzeblech mit Punzinschrift der 10. Legion aus Kessel (Niederlande)", *ZPE* 201, 270-272.

Devauchelle, Didier (2007), "Effacement des noms de personnes et martelages dans les textes égyptiens d'époque romaine", in: Stéphane Benoist / Anne Daguet-Gagey (eds.), *Mémoire et histoire: les procédures de condamnation dans l'antiquité romaine*, Metz, 3-20.

Di Giacomo, Giovanna (2020), "Geografia patrimoniale e tessuto sociale dell'ager Albanus e del restante territorio aricino dall'età augustea fino alle soglie dell'età severiana", in: Silvia Aglietti / Alexandra Busch (eds.), *Albanum I. Ager Albanus. Von republikanischer Zeit zur Kaiservilla / Dall'età repubblicana alla villa imperiale*, Harrassowitz, 57-123.

Dio Cassius, *Roman History* VII. *Books 56-60*, Translated by Earnest Cary, Herbert B. Foster (Loeb Classical Library 175), Cambridge, MA, 1924.

Dominik, William J. (1994), *The Mythic Voice of Statius: Power and Politics in the Thebaid*, Leiden.

Döpp, Siegmar (1996), "Das Stegreifgedicht des Q. Sulpicius Maximus", *ZPE* 114, 99-114.

Draycott, Jane (2018), "Hair Loss as Facial Disfigurement in Ancient Rome", in: Patricia Skinner / Emily Cock (eds.), *Approaching Facial Difference Past and Present*, London, 65-83.

Edelmann-Singer, Babette (2014), "Neros Vision von Rom – die urbanistische Utopie als politische Dystopie", in: Albert Dietl / Wolfgang Schöller / Dirk Steuernagel (eds.), *Utopie, Fiktion, Planung. Stadtentwürfe zwischen Antike und Früher Neuzeit*, Regensburg, 69-91.

Edmondson, Jonathan / Mason, Steve / Rives, Jason (eds.) (2005), *Flavius Josephus and Flavian Rome*, Oxford.

Elkins, Nathan T. (2019), *A Monument to Dynasty and Death. The story of Rome's Colosseum and the Emperors who built it*, Baltimore, MD.

Elsner, Jaś (1994), "Constructing Decadence: The Representation of Nero as Imperial Builder", in: Jaś Elsner / Jamie Masters (eds.), *Reflections of Nero*, London, 112-127.

Erdkamp, Paul (2013), "The food supply of the capital", in: Paul Erdkamp (ed.), *The Cambridge Companion to Ancient Rome*, Cambridge/New York, 262-277.

Escamez de Vera, Diego M. (2016), *Sodales Flaviales Titiales. Culto imperial y legitimación en época Flavia*, Louvain.

Eusebius, *Eusebius Werke* 7. *Die Chronik des Hieronymus / Hieronymi Chronicon*, ed. Rudolf Helm, Berlin, 1956.

Fagan, Garrett G. (1999), *Bathing in Public in the Roman World*, Ann Arbor, MI.

Fagan, Garrett G. (2011), *The Lure of the Arena. Social Psychology and the Crowd at the Roman Games*, Cambridge.

Favro, Diana (1996), *The Urban Image of Augustan Rome*, Cambridge.

Fejfer, Jane (2008), *Roman Portraits in Context*, Berlin/New York.

Fejfer, Jane / Bøggild Johannsen, Kristine (eds.) (2020), *Face to Face. Thorvaldsen and Portraiture*, Copenhagen.

Fejfer, Jane / Schneider, Rolf Michael (2020), "Faces in 3D. Thorvaldsen and Ancient Romans in Dialogue", in: Jane Fejfer / Kristine Bøggild Johannsen (eds.), *Face to Face. Thorvaldsen and Portraiture*, Copenhagen, 49-57.

Filippi, Fedora (2010), "Le indagini in Campo Marzio Occidentale. Nuovi dati sulla topografia antica: il Ginnasio di Nerone (?) e l''Euripus'", in: *Archeologia e infrastrutture. Il tracciato fondamentale delle Linea C della Metropolitana di Roma: prime indagini archeologiche* (*BdA* volume speciale), Rome, 39-92.

Fittschen, Klaus (1977), *Katalog der antiken Skulpturen in Schloss Erbach*, Berlin.

Fittschen, Klaus (2010), "The Portraits of Roman Emperors and their Families: controversial positions and unsolved problems", in: Björn C. Ewald / Carlos F. Noreña (eds.), *The Emperor and Rome Space, Representation and Ritual*, Cambridge, 221-246.

Fittschen, Klaus (2015), "Methodological Approaches to the Dating and Identification of Roman Portraits", in: Barbara E. Borg (ed.), *A Companion to Roman Art*, Chicester, 52-70.

Fittschen, Klaus / Zanker, Paul (1985), *Katalog der römischen Porträts in den Capitolinischen Museen und den anderen kommunalen Sammlungen der Stadt Rom 1. Kaiser-und Prinzenbildnisse*, Mainz am Rhein.

Flaig, Egon (1992), *Den Kaiser herausfordern: die Usurpation im römischen Reich*, Frankfurt am Main.

Flaig, Egon (2003), "Wie Kaiser Nero die Akzeptanz bei der Plebs urbana verlor. Eine Fallstudie zum politischen Gerücht im Prinzipat", *Historia* 52, 351-372.

Flory, Marleen B. (1998), "The meaning of *Augusta* in the Julio-Claudian period", *AmJAncHist* 13, 113-138.

Flower, Harriet (1996), *Ancestral Masks and Aristocratic Power in Roman Culture*, Oxford.

Flower, Harriet (2006), *The Art of Forgetting: Disgrace and Oblivion in Roman Political Culture*, Chapel Hill, NC.

Fraschetti, Augusto (1990), *Roma e il Principe*, Rome/Bari.

Frederick, David (2003), "Architecture and Surveillance in Flavian Rome", in: Boyle / Dominik 2003, 199-227.

Freedberg, David (1989), *The Power of Images: Studies in the History and Theory of Response*, Chicago.

Frutolf von Michelsberg, *Ekkehardi Chronicon universale*, ed. Georg Waitz (Monumenta Germaniae Historica, Series Scriptorum in Folio 6), Hanover, 1844.

Galimberti, Alessandro (2016), "The Emperor Domitian", in: Andrew Zissos (ed.), *A Companion to the Flavian Age of Imperial Rome*, Malden, 92-108.

Galinsky, Karl (2008), "Recarved Imperial Portraits: Nuances and Wider Contexts", *MemAmAc* 53, 1-25.

Garnesey, Peter (1988), *Famine and Food Supply in the Graeco-Roman World. Responses to Risk and Crisis*, Cambridge.

Garulli, Valentina (2018), "A Portrait of a Poet as a Young Man. The Tomb of Quintus Sulpicius Maximus on the Via Salaria", in: Nora Goldsmith / Barbara Graziosi (eds.), *Tombs of the Ancient Poets. Between Literary Rexception and Material Culture*, Oxford, 83-100.

Gasparini, Valentino / Veymiers, Richard (eds.) (2018), *Individuals and Materials in the Greco-Roman Cults of Isis*, Leiden/Boston.

Gasparri, Carlo (2009), *Le Sculture Farnese* II.1. *I Ritratti*, Naples.

Gee, Regina (2011-2012), "Cult and Circus *in Vaticanum*", *MemAmAc* 56-57, 63-83.

Gering, Jens (2012), *Domitian, dominus et deus ? Herrschafts – und Machtstrukturen in römischen Reich zur Zeit des letzten Flaviers*, Rahden/Westf.

Gesta Romanorum: *Gesta Romanorum*, ed. Hermann Oesterley, Berlin 1872, reprint Hildesheim 1963.

Geyssen, John W. (1996), *Imperial Panegyric in Statius: A Literary commentary on Silvae 1.1*, New York.

Ghini, Giuseppina (ed.) (2015), *Caligola. La trasgressione al potere*, Rome.

Giardina, Andrea / Balassarre, Ida (2004), "La *fossa Neronis* di Baia: tra Lucrino e Fusaro", in: *Viabilità e insediamenti nell'Itala antica* (ATTA 13), Rome, 331-334.

Gibson, Sheila / DeLaine, Janet / Claridge, Amanda (1994), "The triclinium of the Domus Flavia. A new reconstruction", *BSR* 62, 67-100.

Girard, Jean-Louis (1981), "Domitien et Minerve: une prédilection impériale", *ANRW* 2.17.1, 233-245.

Giuliani, Cairoli Fulvio / Verduchi, Patrizia (1987), *L'area centrale del Foro Romano*, Florence.

Gizewski, Christian / Mlasowsky, Alexander (2020), *"Damnatio memoriae"*, in: *Brill's New Pauly*, http://dx.doi.org.ru.idm.oclc.org/10.1163/1574-9347_bnp_e310400.

Gliwitzky, Christian (2017), "Zwischen Mode und Programm – Von Nero zu den Flaviern", in: Andreas Pangerl (ed.), *Portraits: 500 Years of Roman Coin Portraits*, Munich, 287-297.

Gliwitzky, Christian / Knauss, Florian S. (eds.) (2017), *Charakterköpfe. Griechen und Römer im Porträt*, Munich.

Goffman, Erwin (1981), "Footing", in: Erwin Goffman (ed.), *Forms of Talk*, Philadelphia, PA, 124-157.

González, Julian / Crawford, Michael H. (1986), "The Lex Irnitana: A New Copy of the Flavian Municipal Law", *JRS* 76, 147-243.

Graafstal, Erik P. (2002), "Logistiek, communicatie en watermanagement. Over de uitrusting van de Romeinse rijksgrens in Nederland", *Westerheem* 51, 2-27.

Gradel, Ittay (2002), *Emperor Worship and Roman Religion*, Oxford.

Grahame, Mark (2000), *Reading space. Social interaction and identity in the houses of Roman Pompeii. A syntactical approach to the analysis and interpretation of built space*, Oxford.

Grainger, John, D. (2003), *Nerva and the Roman Succession Crisis of AD 96-99*, London.

Grassi, Maria Teresa (ed.) (2013), *Calvatone-Bedriacum. I nuovi scavi nell'area della Domus del Labirinto* (Postumia 24/3), Mantova.

Grassi, Maria Teresa (2016), "Calvatone 2005-2014: le novità dell'ultimo decennio di scavi nel vicus padano di Bedriacum", in: Silvia Lusardi Siena / Claudia Peressi / Furio Sacchi / Marco Sannazaro, *Archeologia classica e post-classica tra Italia e Mediterraneo. Scritti in ricordo di Maria Pia Rossignani*, Milano, 183-188.

Gregori, Gian Luca / Spinelli, Tommaso (2019), "(Un)-damning Subplots: The Principate of Domitian between Literary Sources and Fresh Material Evidence", *IllClSt* 44, 242-267.

Grelle, Francesco (1980), "La *correctio morum* nella legislazione flavia", *ANRW* 2.13.2, 340-365.

Griffin, Miriam T. (1976), *Seneca, a Philosopher in Politics*, Oxford.

Griffin, Miriam T. (1984), *Nero. The end of a dynasty*, London.

Gross, Karl (1959), "Domitianus", *RAC* 4, 91-109.

Gsell, Stéphane (1894), *Essay sur le règne de l'empereur Domitien*, Paris.

Guilhembet, Jean-Pierre (2006), "Limites et entrées de la Rome antique: quelques rappels et quelques remarques", in: Françoise Michaud-Fréjaville / Noëlle Dauphin / Jean-Pierre Guilhembet (eds.), *Entrer en ville*, Rennes, 79-121.

Haalebos, Jan Kees (2000), "Traian und die Hilfstruppen am Niederrhein. Ein Militärdiplom des Jahres 98 n. Chr. aus Elst in der Over-Betuwe (Niederlande)", *SaalbJb* 50, 31-72.

Habicht, Christian (1969), *Die Inschriften des Asklepieions* (Altertümer von Pergamon VIII.3), Berlin.

Hannestad, Niels (1988), *Roman Art and Imperial Policy*, Aarhus.

Hardie, Alex (2003), "Poetry and Politics at the Games of Domitian", in: Antony J. Boyle / William J. Dominik (eds.), *Flavian Rome. Culture, Image, Text*, Leiden, 125-147.

Haselberger, Lothar (2007), *Urbem adornare. Die Stadt Rom und ihre Gestaltumwanderung unter Augustus / Rome's urban metamorphosis under Augustus* (*JRA* suppl. 64), Portsmouth, Rh.I.

Häuber, Chrystina (2021), *The Cancelleria Reliefs and Domitian's Obelisk in Rome in context of the legitimation of Domitian's reign. With studies on Domitian's building projects in Rome, his statue of Iuppiter Optimus Maximus Capitolinus, the colossal portrait of Hadrian (now Constantine the Great), and Hadrian's portrait from Hierapydna* (FORTVNA PAPERS 3), Munich.

Häuber, Chrystina (2020), *The Cancelleria Reliefs in the Vatican Museums, Domitian's Obelisk on the Piazza Navona in Rome and the legitimation of Domitian's reign. With a discussion of Domitian's other building projects in Rome* (FORTVNA PAPERS 3), Munich.

Hedrick, Charles, W. (2000), *History and Silence: Purge and Rehabilitation of Memory in Late Antiquity*, Austin, TX.

Heeren, Stijn (2014), "The Material Culture of Small Rural Settlements in the Batavian Area: a Case Study on Discrepant Experience, Creolisation, Romanisation or Globalisation?", in: Hannah Platts et al. (eds.), *TRAC 2013. Proceedings of the Twenty-Third Theoretical Roman Archaeology Conference King's College, London 2013*, Oxford, 159-173.

Heerink, Mark / Meijer, Esther (eds.) (in press), *Flavian Responses to Nero*, Amsterdam.

Heinemann, Alexander (2014), "Sportsfreunde: Nero und Domitian als Begründer griechischer Agone in Rom", in: Sophia Bönisch-Meyer (ed.), *Nero und Domitian. Mediale Diskurse der Herrscherrepräsentation im Vergleich*, Tübingen, 217-263.

Heinrich von München, *Die Weltchronik Heinrichs von München. Neue Ee*, eds. Frank Shaw / Johannes Fournier / Kurt Gärtner (Deutsche Texte des Mittelalters 88), Berlin, 2008.

Hekster, Olivier (2002), *Commodus An Emperor at the Crossroads*, Amsterdam.

Hekster, Olivier (2015), *Emperors and Ancestors: Roman Rulers and the Constraints of Tradition*, Oxford.

Hekster, Olivier / Manders, Erika / Slootjes, Daniëlle (2014), "Making History with Coins: Nero from a Numismatic Perspective", *The Journal of Interdisciplinary History* 45.1, 25-37, https://www.jstor.org/stable/43829562?seq=1#metadata_info_tab_contents.

Hekster, Olivier / Rich, John (2006), "Octavian and the Thunderbolt: The Temple of Apollo Palatinus and Roman Traditions of Temple Building", *CQ* 56, 149-168.

Henriksén, Christer (2012), *A Commentary on Martial, Epigrams Book 9*, Oxford.

Hesnard, Antoinette (2001), "L'approvisionnement alimentaire de Rome à la fin de la République et au Haut-Empire", *Pallas* 55, 285-302.

Hessing, Wilfried A.M. (1990), "Leidschendam: Rietvink", *Holland* 22, 342-343.

Hinard, François (1984), "La male mort: exécutions et statut du corps au moment de la première proscription", in: *Du châtiment dans la cité. Supplices corporels et peine de mort dans le monde antique*, Rome, 295-311.

Hoffmann, Adolf / Wulf-Rheidt, Ulrike (2000), "Vorbericht zur bauhistorischen Dokumentation der sogenannten Domus Severiana auf dem Palatin in Rom", *RM* 107, 279-298.

Hölbl, Günther (2000), *Altägypten im Römischen Reich. Der römische Pharao und seine Tempel I. Römische Politik und altägyptische Ideologie von Augustus bis Diocletian, Tempelbau in Oberägypten*, Mainz am Rhein.

Hölbl, Günther (2004a), *Altägypten im Römischen Reich. Der römische Pharao und seine Tempel II. Die Tempel des römischen Nubien*, Mainz am Rhein.

Hölbl, Günther (2004b), "Die römischen Kaiser und das ägyptische Königtum", in: Peter C. Bol / Gabriele Kaminski / Claudia Maderna (eds.), *Fremdheit – Eigenheit: Ägypten, Griechenland und Rom, Austausch und Verständnis* (Städel Jahrbuch 19), Stuttgart, 523-537.

Holleran, Claire (2011), "The Street Life of Ancient Rome", in: Ray Laurence / David J. Newsome (eds.), *Rome, Ostia, Pompeii. Movement and Space*, Oxford, 245-261.

Hölscher, Tonio (2004), *The Language of Images in Roman Art*, Cambridge.

Hölscher, Tonio (2009), "Rilievi provenienti da monumenti statali del tempo dei Flavi", in: Filippo Coarelli (ed.), *Divus Vespasianus. Il bimillennario dei Flavi*, Milan, 46-61.

Hölscher, Tonio (2015), "Roman Historical Representations", in: Barbara E. Borg (ed.), *A Companion to Roman Art*, Chichester, 34-51.

Honorius: Honorius Augustodunensis, *De imagine mundi libri tres*, ed. Jacques-Paul Migne (Patrologia Latina 172), Paris 1854.

Huet, Valérie (2004), "Images et *damnatio memoriae*", *CahGlotz* 15, 237-253.

Humphrey, John H. (1986), *Roman Circuses: arenas for chariot races*, London.

Hurlet, Frédéric (2016), "Sources and Evidence", in: Andrew Zissos (ed.), *A Companion to the Flavian Age of Imperial Rome*, Malden, 17-40.

Hurlet, Frédéric / Mineo, Bernard (2011), "Le pouvoir et ses représentations à Rome sous le principat d'Auguste", in: Frédéric Hurlet / Bernard Mineo (eds.), *Le Principat d'Auguste: Réalités et représentations du pouvoir. Autour de la Respublica restituta*, Rennes, 9-24.

Jacobus a Voragine: *Jacobi a Voragine Legenda aurea vulgo Historia Lombardica dicta*, ed. Theodor Graesse, Bratislava, 1890.

Jansen, Gemma (2011), "Toilets and Health", in: Gemma Jansen / Ann Koloski Ostrow / Eric M. Moormann (eds.), *Roman Toilets. Their Archaeology and Cultural History*, Leuven/Paris/Walpole, 157-164.

Johannowski, Werner (1994), "Canali e fiumi per il trasporto del grano", in: *Le ravitaillement en blé de Rome, Actes du colloque international organisé par le Centre Jean Bérard et l'URA 994 du CNRS, Napoli, 14-16 Février 1991*, Naples/Rome, 159-162.

Johansen, Flemming (1995), *Roman Portraits* II. *Ny Carlsberg Glyptotek*, Copenhagen.

Johnson, Allan C. / Coleman-Norton, Paul R. / Bourne, Frank C. (1961) *Ancient Roman Statutes. A Translation with Introduction, Commentary, Glossary, and Index*, Austin, TX.

Jones, Brian W. (1992), *The Emperor Domitian*, London.

Jones, Christopher P. (1998), "'Joint Sacrifice' at Iasus and Side", *JHS* 118, 183-186.

Jones, Christopher P. (2007), "Three new letters of the Emperor Hadrian", *ZPE* 161, 145-156.

Jucker, Hans (1981), "Kaiser- und Prinzenporträts als 'Palimpseste'", *JdI* 96, 236-316.

Kaderka, Karolina (2018), *Les décors tympanaux des temples de Rome*, Bordeux.

Kaiserchronik: *Die Kaiserchronik eines Regensburger Geistlichen*, ed. Edward Schröder (Monumenta Germaniae Historica, Scriptorum qui vernacula lingua usi sunt tomus 1), Hanover, 1895.

Kákosy, Laszlo (1995), "Probleme der Religion im römerzeitlichen Ägypten", *ANRW* 2.18.5, 2894-3049.

Kaper, Olaf E. (1997), *Temples and Gods in Roman Dakhleh: Studies in the Indigenous Cults of an Egyptian Oasis*, PhD Dissertation, Groningen.

Kaper, Olaf E. (1998), "Temple building in the Egyptian desert during the Roman period", in: Olaf E. Kaper (ed.), *Life on the Fringe: Living in the Southern Egyptian Deserts during the Roman and early-Byzantine Periods: Proceedings of a Colloquium... 1996*, Leiden, 139-158.

Kaper, Olaf E. (2012), "Departing from Protocol: Emperor Names in the Temples of Dakhleh Oasis", in: Jochen Hallof (ed.), *Auf den Spuren des Sobek: Festschrift für Horst Beinlich zum 28. Dezember 2012* (Studien zu den Ritualszenen altägyptischer Tempel 12), Dettelbach, 137-162.

Kemezis, Adam (2016), "Flavian Greek Literature", in: Andrew Zissos (ed.), *A Companion to the Flavian Age of Imperial Rome*, Malden, 450-468.

Kemmers, Fleur (2005), "Not at Random. Evidence for a Regionalised Coin Supply?", *Theoretical Roman Archaeology Journal*, 39-49.

Kienast, Dietmar / Eck, Werner / Heil, Matthäus (2017), *Römische Kaisertabelle. Grundzüge einer römischen Kaiserchronologie*, 6. überarbeitete Auflage, Darmstadt.

Kilgour, Maggie (2012), *Milton and the Metamorphosis of Ovid*, Oxford.

Koeppel, Gerhard M. (1984), "Die historischen Reliefs der römischen Kaiserzeit, 2. Stadtrömische Denkmäler unbekannter Bauzugehörigkeit aus flavischer Zeit", *BJb* 184, 1-65.

Köhne, Eckart / Ewigleben, Cornelia / Jackson, Ralph (2000), *Gladiators and Caesars: the Power of Spectacle in Ancient Rome*, Berkeley, CA.

Koloski-Ostrow, Ann Olga (2015a), *The Archaeology of Sanitation in Roman Italy. Toilets, Sewers, and Water Systems*, Chapel Hill, NC.

Koloski-Ostrow, Ann Olga (2015b), "Roman Urban Smells: the Archaeological Evidence", in: Mark Bradley (ed.), *Smell and the Ancient Senses*, London/New York, 90-109.

König, Alice / Whitton, Christopher (eds.) (2018), *Roman Literature under Nerva, Trajan and Hadrian: Literary Interactions, AD 96-138*, Cambridge.

Kramer, Norbert / Reitz, Christiane (eds.) (2010), *Tradition und Erneuerung Mediale Strategien in der Zeit der Flavier*, Berlin.

Kreuz, Gottfried (2016), *Besonderer Ort, poetischer Blick: Untersuchungen zu Räumen und Bildern in Statius' Silvae*, Göttingen.

Kyle, Donald G. (1998), *Spectacles of Death in Ancient Rome*, London.

La Rocca, Eugenio (1974), "Un frammento dell'Arco di Tito al Circo Massimo", *BMusRom* 21, 1-5.

La Rocca, Eugenio (2009), "Il Templum Gentis Flaviae", in: Filippo Coarelli (ed.), *Divus Vespasianus. Il bimillennario dei Flavi*, Milan, 224-233.

La Rocca, Eugenio (2014), *Augusto*, Milan.

La Rocca, Eugenio (2018), "L'urbanisme et les constructions claudiennes dans la ville de Rome", in: François Chausson / Geneviève Galliano (eds.), *Claude. Un empereur au destin singulier*, Paris, 141-153.

Langer, Susanne / Pfanner, Michael (2018), "Cancelleriareliefs A und B", in: *Vatikanische Museen, Museo Gregoriano Profano ex Lateranense, Katalog der Skulpturen 4. Historische Reliefs*, Wiesbaden, 18-90.

Lebek, Wolfgang Dieter (1989), "Die Mainzer Ehrungen für Germanicus, den älteren Drusus und Domitian (Tab. Siar. Frg. I 26-34; Suet. Claud. 1,3)", *ZPE* 78, 45-82.

Leberl, Jens (2004), *Domitian und die Dichter: Poesie als Medium der Herrschaftsdarstellung*, Göttingen.

Lee, Hugh M. (2014), "Greek Sports in Rome", in: Paul Christesen / Donald G. Kyle (eds.), *A Companion to Sport and Spectacle in Greek and Roman Antiquity*, Chichester, 533-542.

Leithoff, Johanna (2014), *Macht der Vergangenheit. Zur Erringung, Verstetigung und Ausgestaltung des Principats unter Vespasian, Titus und Domitian*, Göttingen.

Lembke, Katja / Minas-Nerpel, Martina / Pfeiffer, Stefan (eds.) (2010), *Tradition and Transformation: Egypt under Roman Rule. Proceedings of the International Conference, Hildesheim, Roemer- and Pelizaeus-Museum, 3-6 July 2008*, Leiden/Boston.

Lenski, Noel (2016), *Constantine and the Cities. Imperial Authority and Civic Politics*, Philadelphia, PA.

Lettieri, Gaetano (2013), "Lattanzio ideologo della svolta costantiniana", in: *Costantino I. Enciclopedia Costantiniana sulla figura e l'immagine dell'imperatore del cosiddetto Editto di Milano 313-2013*, Rome, II, 45-57.

Levick, Barbara (2002), "Corbulo's daughter", *GaR* 49, 199-211.

Levick, Barbara (2010), *Augustus. Image and Substance*, Harlow.

Levick, Barbara (2016), *Vespasian*, London/New York.

Ley, Jochen O. (2016), *Domitian: Auffassung und Ausübung der Herrscherrolle des letzten Flaviers*, Berlin.

Lind, Levi Robert (1979), "The tradition of Roman moral conservatism", in: Carl Deroux (ed.), *Studies in Latin literature and Roman history* 1, Brussels, 7-58.

Liverani, Paolo (1989), *L'antiquarium di Villa Barberini a Castel Gandolfo*, Vatican City.

Liverani, Paolo (1993), "Il Doriforo del Braccio Nuovo e l'Efebo tipo Westmacott di Castel Gandolfo. Nota sul restauro e sul contesto", in: Hans Beck/Peter C. Bol (eds.), *Polykletforschungen*, Berlin, 117-140.

Liverani, Paolo (1995), "'Nationes' e 'civitates' nella propaganda imperiale", *RM* 102, 219-249.

Liverani, Paolo (2000-2001), "Due note di topografia vaticana: il *theatrum Neronis* e i toponimi legati alla tomba di Pietro", *RendPontAcc* 73, 129-146.

Liverani, Paolo (2004), "Arco di Onorio – Arco di Portogallo", *BCom* 105, 351-370.

Liverani, Paolo (2005), "Porta Triumphalis, arcus Domitiani, templum Fortunae Reducis, arco di Portogallo", *ATTA* 14, 53-65.

Liverani, Paolo (2006-2007), "Templa duo nova Spei et Fortunae in Campo Marzio", *RendPontAc* 79, 291-314.

Liverani, Paolo (2008), "La villa di Domiziano a Castel Gandolfo", in: M. Valenti (ed.), *Residenze imperiali nel Lazio. Atti della Giornata di Studio – Monte Porzio Catone, 3 aprile 2004*, Monte Porzio Catone, 53-60.

Liverani, Paolo (2014), "Per una 'Storia del colore'. La scultura policroma romana, un bilancio e qualche prospettiva", in: Paolo Liverani / Ulderico Santamaria (eds.), *Diversamente bianco. La policromia della scultura romana*, Rome, 9-32.

Liverani, Paolo (2016), "Figurato e scritto: discorso delle immagini, discorso con le immagini", in: Caroline M. D'Annoville / Yann Rivière (eds.), *Faire parler et faire taire les statues. De l'invention de l'écriture à l'usage de l'explosif*, Rome, 353-371.

Lorenz, Sven (2002), *Erotik und Panegyrik: Martials epigrammatische Kaiser*, Tübingen.

Lugli, Giuseppe (1913). "Lo Scavo fatto nel 1841 nel ninfeo detto Bergantino sulla riva del lago di Albano", *BCom* 41, 89-148.

Lugli, Giuseppe (1914a), "Il Teatro della Villa Albana di Domiziano", *StRom* 2, 21-53.

Lugli, Giuseppe (1914b), "Le Antiche Ville dei Colli Albani prima della Occupazione Domizianea", *BCom* 42, 251-316.

Lugli, Giuseppe (1915), "Il teatro della Villa Albana di Domiziano", *StRom*, 21-53.

Lugli, Giuseppe (1917), "La Villa di Domiziano sui Colli Albani – Parte prima. Topografia Generale", *BCom* 45, 29-78.

Lugli, Giuseppe (1918), "La Villa di Domiziano sui colli Albani – Parte II. Le Costruzioni centrali", *BCom* 46, 3-68.

Lugli, Giuseppe (1919a), "La Villa di Domiziano sui colli Albani – Parte III. Le Costruzioni sparse", *BCAR* 47, 153-205.

Lugli, Giuseppe (1919b), "Castra Albana – un accampamento romano fortificato al XV miglio della Via Appia", *Ausonia* 9, 211-265.

Lugli, Giuseppe (1920), "La Villa di Domiziano sui Colli Albani – Parte IV. Monumenti figurati e decorativi", *BCom* 48, 3-69.

Luksen-IJtsma, A. (2010), *De limesweg in West-Nederland. Inventarisatie, analyse en synthese van archeologisch onderzoek naar de Romeinse weg tussen Vechten en Katwijk* (Basisrapportage Archeologie 40), Utrecht.

Mägele, Semra (2008), "A Colossal Portrait of Hadrian and the Imperial Group from the Roman Baths at Sagalassos", in: Thorsten Opper (ed.), *Hadrian. Empire and Conflict*, Harvard, 50-61.

Magi, Filippo (1945), *I Rilievi Flavi del Palazzo della Cancelleria*, Rome.

Magi, Filippo (1968-1969), "Il Polifemo di Castel Gandolfo", *RendPontAc* 41, 69-84.

Magi, Filippo (1973-1974), "I Marmi del Teatro di Domiziano a Castel Gandolfo", *RendPontAc* 46, 63-77.

Magi, Filippo (1976), "Omaggio a Venere (su Architravo domizianeo di Castel Gandolfo)", *RM* 83, 157-164.

Malamud, Martha A. (2007), "A Spectacular Feast: *Silvae* 4.2", *Arethusa* 40.2, 223-244.

Malmberg, Simon (2003), *Dazzling Dining. Banquets as an Expression of Imperial Legitimacy*, PhD Dissertation, Uppsala.

Mammel, Kathryn (2014), "Ancient Critics of Roman Spectacle and Sport", in: Paul Christesen / Donald G. Kyle (eds.), *A Companion to Sport and Spectacle in Greek and Roman Antiquity*, Chichester, 603-616.

Manderscheid, Hubertus (2000), "The Water Management of Greek and Roman Baths", in: Örjan Wikander (ed.), *Handbook of Ancient Water Technology*, Leiden/Boston/Cologne, 467-535.

Mann, Christian (2014), "Greek Sport and Roman Identity: The Certamina Athletarum at Rome", in: Thomas F. Scanlon (ed.), *Sport in the Greek and Roman Worlds: Greek Athletic Identities and Roman Sports and Spectacle*, New York, 151-189.

Marcattili, Francesco (2009), *Circo Massimo: architettura, funzioni, culti, ideologia*, Rome.

Manfrecola, Karolina (2020), "Aus zwei mach eins. Der Zusammenschluss zweier Villen zum Albanum des Domitian", in: Katja Piesker / Ulrike Wulf-Rheidt (eds.), *Umgebaut. Umbau-, Umnutzungs-und Umwertungsprozesse in der antiken Architektur*, Regensburg, 205-220.

Mari, Zaccario / Sgalambro, Sergio (2007), "The Antinoeion of Hadrian's villa: interpretation and architectural reconstruction", *AJA* 111, 83-104.

Marks, Raymond (2005), *From Republic to Empire: Scipio Africanus in the Punica of Silius Italicus*, Frankfurt am Main.

Martin, Alain (1987), *La titulature épigraphique de Domitien* (Beiträge zur klassischen Philologie 181), Frankfurt am Main.

Massaro, Emanuela (2009), "Sulpicia, una donna contro l'imperatore Domiziano", in: Angelo Favaro / Paolo Marpicati (eds.), *Domitianus dominus et deus. Atti del Convegno, Sabaudia, 23 Febbraio 2008*, n.pl., 93-100.

Maßmann, Hans Ferdinand (ed.) (1854), *Der keiser und der kunige buoch oder die sogenannte Kaiserchronik. Gedicht des zwölften Jahrhunderts* 3, Quedlinburg/Leipzig.

McCullough, Anna (2008), "Female gladiators in Imperial Rome: literary context and historical fact", *Classical World* 101, 197-209.

Medri, Maura (1996), "Suet. *Nero* 31.1: elementi e proposte per la ricostruzione del progetto della *domus Aurea*", in: Clementina Panella (ed.), *Meta sudans* I. *Un'area sacra* in Palatio *e la valle del Colosseo prima e dopo Nerone*, Rome, 165-188.

Mémoire (1998): *La mémoire perdue. Recherches sur l'administration romaine*, Rome.

Meneghini, Roberto / Rea, Rossella (eds.) (2014), *La biblioteca infinita*, Milan.

Miedema, Nine R. (1996), *Die "Mirabilia Romae". Untersuchungen zu ihrer Überlieferung mit Edition der deutschen und niederländischen Texte*, Tübingen.

Miedema, Nine R. (2001), *Die römischen Kirchen im Spätmittelalter nach den "Indulgentiae ecclesiarum urbis Romae"*, Tübingen.

Miedema, Nine R. (2003), *Rompilgerführer in Spätmittelalter und Früher Neuzeit: Die "Indulgentiae ecclesiarum urbis Romae" (deutsch / niederländisch). Edition und Kommentar*, Tübingen.

Mielsch, Harald (1999), *La villa romana*, Florence (original edition: *Die römische Villa. Architectur und Lebensform*, Munich 1987).

Mierau, Heike (2016), "Die lateinischen Papst-Kaiser-Chroniken des Spätmittelalters", in: Gerhard Wolf / Norbert H. Ott (eds.), *Handbuch Chroniken des Mittelalters*, Berlin, 105-127.

Migliorati, Luisa (2015), "Le Terme di Agrippa: considerazioni preliminari", in: Fedora Filippi (ed.), *Campo Marzio. Nuove ricerche*, Rome, 109-136.

Millar, Fergus (1984), "State and Subject: the impact of monarchy", in: Fergus Millar / Eric Segal (eds.), *Caesar Augustus. Seven Aspects*, Oxford, 37-60.

Minas-Nerpel, Martina (2012), "Egyptian Temples", in: Christina Riggs (ed.), *The Oxford Handbook of Roman Egypt*, Oxford, 362-382.

Mirabilia: Mirabilia Urbis Romae. Die Wunderwerke der Stadt Rom. Introduction, translation and commentary by Gerlinde Huber-Rebenich / Martin Wallraf / Katharina Heyden / Thomas Krönung, Freiburg i.Br./Basle/Vienna, 2014.

Miranda de Martino, Elena (2014), "Les sebasta de Naples à l'époque de Domitien. Témoignages épigraphiques", *CRAI* 158, 1165-1188.

Moormann, Eric M. (2003), "Some Observations on Nero and the City of Rome", in: Luuk de Blois et al. (eds.), *The Representation and Perception of Roman Imperial Power*, Amsterdam, 376-388.

Moormann, Eric M. (2018), "Domitian's remake of Augustan Rome and the Iseum Campense", in: Miguel John Versluys / Kristine Bülow-Clausen / Giuseppina Capriotti Vittozzi (eds.), *The Iseum Campense from the Roman Empire to the Modern Age. Temple – monument –* lieu de mémoire, Rome, 161-177.

Moormann, Eric M. in press, "Some Observations on the Templum Pacis – a Summa of Flavian Politics", in: Mark Heerink / Esther Meijer (eds.) (in press), *Flavian Responses to Nero*, Amsterdam.

Morandini, Francesca (ed.) in press, *La Vittora alata di Brescia. Non ho mai visto null di più bello*, Milan.

Morawiecki, Leslaw (1977), "The symbolism of Minerva on the coins of Domitianus", *Klio* 59, 185-193.

Morello, Ruth (2018), "Traditional *Exempla* and Nerva's New Modernity: Making Fabricius Take the Cash", in: Alice König / Chris Whitton (eds.), *Roman Literature Under Nerva, Trajan and Hadrian: Literary Interactions, AD 96-138*, Cambridge, 303-329.

Morenz, Ludwig D. / Sperveslage, Gunnar (2020), *Römisches Kaisertum in ägyptischem Gewand: Vom Pharao-fashioning der Imperatoren Augustus, Domitian und Hadrian*, Berlin.

Moretti, Jean-Charles (ed.) (2009), *Fronts de scène et lieux de culte dans le théâtre antique*, Lyon.

Moretti, Luigi (1953), *Iscrizioni agonistiche greche* (Studi pubblicati dall'Istituto Italiano per la Storia Antica 12), Rome.

Morley, Neville (2015), "Urban Smells and Roman Noses", in: Mark Bradley (ed.), *Smell and the Ancient Senses*, London / New York, 110-119.

Mourgues, Jean-Louis (1987), "The So-Called Letter of Domitian at the End of the *Lex Irnitana*", *JRS* 77, 78-87.

Mucha, Robert (2015), *Der apokalyptische Kaiser. Die Wahrnehmung Domitians in der apokalyptischen Literatur des Frühjudentums und Urchristentums*, Frankfurt am Main.

Müller, Hans W. (1969), *Der Isiskult im antiken Benevento und Katalog der Skulpturen aus den ägyptischen Heiligtümern im Museo del Sannio zu Benevento* (MÄS 16), Berlin.

Muth, Susanne (2010), "Auftritt auf einer bedeutungsschweren Bühne: Wie sich die Flavie im öffentlichen Zentrum der Stadt Rom inszenieren", in: Norbert Kramer / Christiane Reitz (eds.), *Tradition und Erneuerung. Mediale Strategien in der Zeit der Flavier*, Berlin, 485-496.

Naerebout, Frederick G. (2014), "Cuis regio, eius religio? Rulers and religious change in Greco-Roman Egypt", in: Laurent Bricault / Miguel John Versluys (eds.), *Power, politics and the cults of Isis*, Leiden, 36-61.

Nagel, Svenja (2019), *Isis im römischen Reich 2. Adaption(en) des Kultes im Westen*, Wiesbaden.

Nash, Ernest (1968), *Pictorial Dictionary of Ancient Rome*, London.

Nauta, Ruurd (2002), *Poetry for Patrons: Literary Communication in the Age of Domitian*, Leiden.

Nauta, Ruurd (2010), "Flauius ultimus, caluus Nero: Einige Betrachtungen zu Herrscherbild und Panegyrik unter Domitian", in: Norbert Kramer / Christiane Reitz (eds.), *Tradition und Erneuerung Mediale Strategien in der Zeit der Flavier*, Berlin, 239-270.

Nava, Stefano (forthcoming), "Gli affreschi delle domus", in: Maria Teresa Grassi (ed.), *Il Quartiere degli Artigiani a Calvatone*.

Neudecker, Richard (1988), *Die Skulpturenausstattung römischer Villen in Italien*, Mainz am Rhein.

Neudecker, Richard (2015), "Art in the Roman Villa", in Barbara E. Borg (ed.), *A Companion to Roman Art*, Oxford, 388-405.

Newlands, Carole (2002), *Statius' Silvae and the Poetics of Empire*, Cambridge.

Newlands, Carole (2012), *Statius, Poet between Rome and Naples*, Bristol.

Nicolet, Claude (2000), "De la ville à la 'mégapole'. L'inversion des signes: le cas de Rome", in: Claude Nicolet / Robert Ilbert / Jean-Charles Depaule (eds.), *Mégapoles méditerranéennes. Géographie urbaine rétrospective*, Rome, 888-895.

Nocita, Michela (2000), "L'ara di Sulpicio Massimo: nuove osservazioni in occasione del restauro", *BCom* 101, 81-100.

Nodelman, Sheldon (1993), "How to Read a Roman Portrait", in: Eve D'Ambra (ed.), *Roman Art in Context: An Anthology*, Englewood Cliffs, NJ, 10-26.

Nollé, Johannes (2009), "Beiträge zur kleinasiatischen Münzkunde und Geschichte 6-9", *Gephyra* 6, 7-99.

Nongbri, Brent (2013), *Before Religion. A history of a modern concept*, New Haven, CT.

Nutton, Vivian (2000), "Medical Thoughts on Urban Pollution", in: Valerie M. Hope / Eireann Marshall (eds.), *Death and Disease in the Ancient City*, London/New York, 65-73.

Opper, Thorsten (ed.) (2008), *Hadrian Empire and Conflict*, Harvard, MA.

Otto von Freising, *Ottonis episcopi Frisingensis Chronica sive Historia de duabus civitatibus*, translated by Adolf Schmidt, ed. Walther Lammers, Darmstadt, 2011.

Palmieri, Lilia (forthcoming), *Le terre sigillate di Calvatone-Bedriacum*.

Palombi, Domenico (2012a), "Da Traiano a Marco Aurelio. La *belle époque* di Roma imperiale", in: Eugenio La Rocca / Claudio Parisi Presicce (eds.), *I giorni di Roma. L'età dell'equilibrio (98-180 d.C.)*, Rome, 34-43.

Palombi, Domenico (2012b), "Roma. La città imperiale prima dei Severi", in: Natascha Sojc / Annette Winterling / Ulrike Wulf-Rheidt (eds.), *Palast und Stadt im severischen Rom*, Stuttgart, 23-61.

Palombi, Domenico (2013), "Roma, culto imperiale e paesaggio urbano", in: Federica Fontana (ed.), *Sacrum facere. Atti del primo seminario di archeologia del sacro*, Trieste, 119-164.

Palombi, Domenico (2016), *I Fori prima dei Fori. Storia urbana dei quartieri di Roma antica cancellati per la realizzazione dei Fori Imperiali*, Rome.

Palombi, Domenico (2017), "Antoninus Pius and Rome: *sobrius, parcus, parum largiens*", in: Christoph Michels / Peter Franz Mittag (eds.), *Jenseits des Narrativs. Antoninus Pius in den nicht-literarischen Quellen*, Stuttgart, 65-87.

Palombi, Domenico (2018), "*Urbs Roma – Urbs sacra*: forma e immagini della città", in: Alessandro D'Alessio / Clementina Panella / Rossella Rea (eds.), *Roma Universalis. L'impero e la dinastia venuta dall'Africa*, Milan, 130-141.

Panella, Clementina (ed.) (1996), *Meta sudans I. Un'area sacra* in Palatio *e la valle del Colosseo prima e dopo Nerone*, Rome.

Panella, Clementina et al. (2019), "Curiae veteres. Nuovi dati sulla frequentazione del santuario in età tardo-repubblicana", *ScAnt* 25, 41-71.

Pappano, Albert Earl (1937), "The False Neros", *CJ* 32, 385-392.

Paris, Rita (1994), "Proposta di interpretazione e ricostruzione", in: Rita Paris (ed.), *Dono Hartwig. Originali ricongiunti tra Roma e Ann Arbor. Ipotesi per il Templum Gentis Flaviae*, Rome, 75-83.

Parisi Presicce, Claudio (2008), "L'Arco di Tito al Circo Massimo: Frammenti inediti della decorazione scultorea", in: Eugenuio La Rocca et al. (eds.), *Le due patrie acquiste: studi di archeologia dedicati a Walter Trillmich*, Rome, 345-354.

Pavlogiannis, Onoufrios / Albanidis, Evaggelos / Dimitriou, Minos (2009), "The Aktia of Nikopolis: New Approaches", *Nikephoros* 22, 79-102.

Peachin, Michael (2004), *Frontinus and the* curae *of the* curator aquarum (Heidelberger Althistorische Beiträge und Epigraphische Studien), Stuttgart.

Penwill, John L. (2010), "Damn with great praise? The imperial encomia of Lucan and Silius", in: Andrew Turner et al. (eds.), *Private and public lies: the discourse of despotism and deceit in the Graeco-Roman world*, Boston/Leiden, 211-229.

Perassi, Claudia (2002), "Edifici e monumenti sulla monetazione di Nerone", in: Jean-Marie Croisille / Yves Perrin (eds.), *Neronia VI. Rome à l'époque néronienne* (Collection Latomus 268), Brussels, 11-34.

Pfanner, Michael (1983), *Der Titusbogen*, Mainz am Rhein.

Pfanner, Michael (1989), "Über das Herstellen von Porträts: Ein Beitrag zu Rationalisierungsmaßnahmen und Produktionsmechanismen von Massenware im späten Hellenismus und in der römischen Kaiserzeit", *JdI* 104, 157-257.

Pfanner, Michael (2020), "How long does an artist need for a portrait in marble?", in: Jane Fejfer / Kristine Bøggild Johannsen (eds.), *Face to Face. Thorvaldsen and Portraiture*, Copenhagen, 80-81.

Pfeiffer, Stefan (2010), *Der römische Kaiser und das Land am Nil: Kaiserverehrung und Kaiserkult in Alexandria und Ägypten von Augustus bis Caracalla (30 v. Chr. – 217 n. Chr.)*, Stuttgart.

Picozzi, Maria Grazia (1975-1976), "Una replica della testa dell'«Atleta Amelung» da Castel Gandolfo: problemi e ipotesi", *RendPontAc* 48, 95-125.

Pollini, John (2012), *From Republic to Empire: Rhetoric, Religion and Power in the Visual Culture of Ancient Rome*, Oklahoma City, OK.

Pollini, John (2017), "The 'lost' Nollekens Relief of an imperial sacrifice from Domitian's Palace on the Palatine: its history, iconography, and date", *JRA* 30, 97-126.

Pollini, John (2018), "Contact Points: The image and reception of Egypt and its Gods in Rome", in: Jeffrey Spier / Timothy Potts / Sara E. Cole (eds.), *Beyond the Nile: Egypt and the Classical World*, Los Angeles, CA, 211-217.

Poole, Federico (ed.) (2016), *Il Nilo a Pompei: Visioni d'Egitto nel mondo romano*, Turin/Modena.

Power, Tristan J. / Gibson, Roy K. (eds.) (2014), *Suetonius the Biographer. Studies in Roman Lives*, Oxford.

Price, Simon R.F. (1984), "Gods and Emperors: The Greek Language of the Roman Imperial Cult", *JHS* 104, 79-95.

Priester, Sascha (2002), Ad summas tegulas. *Untersuchungen zu vielgeschossigen Gebäudeblöcken mit Wohneinheiten und Insulae im kaiserzeitlichen Roms*, Rome.

Prinzivalli, Emanuela (2013), "Genere storico. La storiografia di Eusebio di Cesarea", in: *Costantino I. Enciclopedia costantiniana sulla figura e l'immagine dell'imperatore del cosiddetto Editto di Milano 313-2013*, Rome, II, 59-76.

Prusac, Marina (2011, 2016), *From Face to Face: Recarving of Roman Portraits and the Late-Antique Portrait*, Leiden.

Raimondi Cominesi, Aurora (2018), "Augustus in the Making: A Reappraisal of the Ideology behind Octavian's Palatine Residence through its Interior Decoration and Topographical Context", *Latomus* 77, 704-735.

Regino von Prüm, *Reginonis abbatis Prumiensis Chronicon cum continuatione Treverensi*, ed. Friedrich Kurze (Monumenta Germaniae Historica, Scriptores rerum Germanicarum in usum scholarum 50), Hanover, 1890.

Reitz, Christiane (2016), "Domitian", in: *Brill's New Pauly Supplements II*, vol. 7: *Figures of Antiquity and their Reception in Art, Literature and Music*, http://dx.doi.org/10.1163/2468-3418_bnps7_SIM_004625.

Reynolds, Joyce M. (1982), *Aphrodisias and Rome: Documents From the Excavation of the Theater at Aphrodisias* (JRS Monograph 1), London.

Richardson, Lawrence, Jr (1992), *A New Topographical Dictionary of Ancient Rome*, Baltimore, MD.

Rieger, Barbara (1999), "Die Capitolia des Kaisers Domitian", *Nikephoros* 12, 171-203.

Riemer, Ulrike (1998), *Das Tier auf dem Kaiserthron? Eine Untersuchung zur Offenbarung des Johannes als historischer Quelle*, Stuttgart/Leipzig.

Riemer, Ulrike (2000), "Domitian – (k)ein Christenverfolger?", *Zeitschrift für Religions- und Geistesgeschichte* 52.1, 75-76.

Robert, Louis / Lianou, M. / König, Jason (2010), "Two Greek Athletic Contests in Rome", in: Jason König (ed.), *Greek athletics*, Edinburgh, 120-140.

Rohrbacher, David (2010), "Physiognomics in Imperial Latin Biography", *ClAnt* 29, 92-116.

Rolfe, J.C. (1914), *Suetonius. Lives of the Caesars* I-II, Cambridge, MA (Loeb Classical Library).

Roman, Luke (2010), "Martial and the City of Rome", *JRS* 100, 88-117.

Rosati, Gianpiero (2015). "The *Silvae*: Poetics of Impromptu and Cultural Consumption", in: William J. Dominik / Carole E. Newlands / Kyle Gervais (eds.), *Brill's Companion to Statius*, Leiden, 54-72.

Rose, C. Brian (1997), *Dynastic Commemoration and Imperial Portraiture in the Julio-Claudian Period*, Cambridge.

Rose, Peter (2005), "Spectators and spectator comfort in Roman entertainment buildings: a study in functional design", *BSR* 73, 99-130.

Rosso, Emmanuelle (2008), "Les destins multiples de la *domus Aurea*. L'exploitation de la condemnation de Néron dans l'idéologie flavienne", in: Stéphane Benoist / Anne Daguet-Gagey (eds.), *Un discours en images de la condamnation de mémoire*, Metz, 43-78.

Roueché, Charlotte / de Chaisemartin, Nathalie (1993), *Performers and partisans at Aphrodisias in the Roman and late Roman periods: a study based on inscriptions from the current excavations at Aphrodisias in Caria* (JRS monographs 6), London.

Roymans, Nico / Derks, Ton (1994), "Het heiligdom te Empel. Algemene beschouwingen", in: Nico Roymans / Ton Derks (eds.), *De tempel van Empel. Een Hercules-heiligdom in het woongebied van de Bataven* (Graven naar het Brabantse verleden 2),'s-Hertogenbosch, 10-38.

Ruck, Brigitte (2007), *Die Großen dieser Welt. Kolossalporträts im antiken Rom*, Heidelberg.

Ruff, Christina (2012), *Ne quid popularitatis augendae praetermitteret. Studien zur Herrschaftsdarstellung der flavischen Kaiser*, Marburg.

Rüpke, Jörg (2018), *Pantheon: A New History of Roman Religion*, Princeton/Oxford.

Russotti, Ambra (2017), "Nunc est *(re)scribendum*: quando la morte di un tiranno cambia la vita di un poeta", *Camelunae* 18, 1-10.

Rutledge, Steven H. (2001), *Imperial Inquisitions. Prosecutors and informants from Tiberius to Domitian*, London.

Sablayrolles, Robert (2001), "La rue, le soldat et le pouvoir: la garnison de Rome de César à Pertinax", *Pallas* 55, 127-153.

Santangelo, Federico (2017), "Vespasiano: il rapporto con la città", in: *Amoenissimis ... aedificiis* (2017), 81-86.

Santorelli, Biagio (ed.) (2011), *Giovenale, Satire*, Classici Greci e Latini 167, Milan.

Scheid, John (2004), "Quand fut construit l'Iseum Campense ?", in: Ligia Ruscu et al. (eds.), *Orbis Antiquus. Studia in honorem Ioannis Pisonis* (Bibliotheca Musei Napocensis 21), Cluj/Napoca, 308-311.

Scheid, John (2009), "Le statut du culte d'Isis à Rome sous le Haut-Empire", in: Corinne Bonnet / Vinciane Pirenne-Delforge / Danny Praet (eds.), *Les religions orientales dans le monde grec et romain: cent ans après Cumont (1906-2006). Bilan historique et historiographique. Actes du Colloque (Rome, 16-18 Novembre 2006)* (Études de Philologie, d'Archéologie et d'Histoire Ancienne de l'IHBR 45), Brussels/Rome, 173-186.

Schmölder-Veit, Andrea (2016), "Brunnen und Nymphäen im Stadion und in der Domus Severiana auf dem Palatin", *RM* 112, 285-330.

Schneider, Rolf Michael (2004), "Gegenbilder im römischen Kaiserporträt; Die neuen Gesichter Neros und Vespasians", in: Martin Buchsel / Peter Schmidt (eds.), *Das Porträt vor der Erfindung des Porträts*. Frankfurt am Main, 59-76.

Schneider, Rolf Michael (2018), "Before the Empire: Egypt and Rome", in Jeffrey Spier / Timothy Potts / Sara E. Cole (eds.), *Beyond the Nile: Egypt and the Classical World*, Los Angeles, CA, 203-210.

Schnurbusch, Dirk (2011), "Rationalität und Irrationalität. Die Flavier in der biographischen Forschung", in: Alois Winterling (ed.), *Zwischen Strukturgeschichte und Biographie: Probleme und Perspektiven einer neuen Römischen Kaisergeschichte zur Zeit von Augustus bis Commodus*, Berlin, 277-294.

Schulz, Verena (2019), *Deconstructing Imperial Representation: Tacitus, Cassius Dio, and Suetonius on Nero and Domitian*, Leiden.

Scobie, Alex (1986), "Slums, Sanitation, and Mortality in the Roman World", *Klio* 68.2, 399-433.

Sear, Frank (2006), *Roman theatres. An architectural study*, Oxford.

Seelentag, Gunnar (2010), "Kinder statt Legionen: Die Vorbereitung der Nachfolge Vespasians. Der Befund der Münzen und methodische Bemerkungen zum Umgang mit den literarischen Quellen", in: Norbert Kramer / Christiane Reitz (eds.), *Tradition und Erneuerung Mediale Strategien in der Zeit der Flavier*, Berlin, 167-190.

Segal, Arthur (2013), *Temples and Sanctuaries in the Roman East: Religious Architecture in Syria, Iudaea/Palestina and Provincia Arabia*, Oxford/Oakville.

Shackleton Bailey, David Roy (1993), *Martial: Epigrams*, Cambridge, MA.

Shackleton Bailey, David Roy (2004). *Statius. Thebaid* I. *Thebaid: Books 1-7*, Cambridge, MA.

Shackleton Bailey, David Roy / Parrott, Christopher A. (2015), *Statius: Silvae*, Cambridge, MA.

Sidebotham Steven E. et al. (2019), "Results of the Winter 2018 Excavation Season at Berenike (Red Sea Coast), Egypt: The Belzoni Bicentennial Report", *Thetis* 24, 7-19.

Sluiter, Ineke (2017), "Anchoring Innovation: A Classical Research Agenda", *European Review* 25, 20-38.

Smelik, Klaas A.D. / Hemelrijk, Emily A. (1984), "'Who knows not what monsters demented Egypt worships?': Opinions on Egyptian animal worship in Antiquity as part of the ancient conception of Egypt", *ANRW* 2.17.4, 1852-2357.

Smith, R.R.R (1998), "Cultural Choice and Political Identity in Honorific Statues in the Greek East in the Second Century A.D.", *JRS* 88, 56-93.

Smith, R.R.R. (ed.) (2006), *Aphrodisias* II. *Roman Portrait Statuary from Aphrodisias*, Mainz am Rhein.

Smolenaars, Johannes J.L. (2006), "Ideology and Poetics along the Via Domitiana: Statius *Silv.* 4.3", in: Ruurd R. Nauta / Harmen Jan van Dam / Johannes J.L. Smolenaars (eds.), *Flavian Poetry*, Leiden, 223-244.

Sojc, Natascha (ed.) (2012), *Domus Augustana. Investigating the 'Sunken Peristyle' on the Palatine Hill*, Leiden.

Sommaini, Fabrizio (2019), "Il Complesso di Domiziano tra Foro Romano e Palatino. Storie, cronologie e strutture murarie dell'Aula Ovest", *RM* 125, 219-255.

Sordi, Marta (1984), *I Cristiani e l'Impero romano*, Milan.

Sordi, Marta (1999), "L'incendio di Nerone e la persecuzione dei Cristiani nella storiografia antica", in: Jean-Marie Croisille / Yves Perrin (eds.), *Neronia V. Néron: histoire et légende (*Collection Latomus 247), Brussels, 105-112.

Southern, Pat (1997), *Domitian Tragic Tyrant*, London/New York.

Speigl, Jakob (1970), *Der römische Staat und die Christen: Staat und Kirche von Domitian bis Commodus*, Amsterdam.

Spier, Jeffrey / Potts, Timothy / Cole, Sara E. (eds.) (2018), *Beyond the Nile: Egypt and the Classical World*, Los Angeles, CA.

Spisak, Art L. (2007), *Martial: A Social Guide*, London.

Stadler, Martin A. (2012), "Egyptian Cult: Evidence from Temple Scriptoria and Christian Hagiographies", in Christina Riggs (ed.), *The Oxford Handbook of Roman Egypt*, Oxford, 457-73.

Stadter, Philipp A. (2013), "Plutarch and Rome", in Mark Beck (ed.), *A Companion to Plutarch*, Chichester, 11-31.

Steinby, Eva Margarete (2018), "The Res Gestae of Q. Haterius Tychicus, Redemptor", in: Catherine M. Draycott et al. (eds.), *Visual Histories of the Classical World. Essays in Honour of R.R.R. Smith*, Turnhout, 309-316.

Stewart, Peter (2003), *Statues in Roman society: representation and response*, Oxford.

Stocks, Claire (2018), "Band of Brothers: Fraternal Instability and Civil Strife in Silius Italicus' *Punica*", in: Lauren Ginsberg / Darcy Krasne (eds), *After 69 CE – Writing Civil War in Flavian Literature* (Trends in Classics Supplementary Volumes 65), Berlin, 253-270.

Strasser, Jean-Yves (2001), "Études sur les concours d'Occident", *Nikephoros* 14, 109-155.

Strasser, Jean-Yves (2003), "La carrière du pancratiaste Markos Aurèlios Dèmostratos Damas", *BCH* 127, 251-299.

Strasser, Jean-Yves (2004), "Les Olympia d'Alexandrie et le Pancratiaste M. Aur. Asklèpiadès", *BCH* 128, 421-468.

Suess, Jessica (2011), *Divine Justification: Flavian Imperial Cult*, MA Thesis, Oxford, https://ora.ox.ac.uk/objects/uuid:d5963fbd-0a97-469a-bffa-1131a4083f86.

Szoke, Martin (2019), "Condemning Domitian or Und-damning Themselves? Tacitus and Pliny on the Domitianic 'Reign of Terror'", *IlClSt* 44.2, 430-452.

Tatarkiewicz, Anna (2014), "In search of auctoritas and maiestas. The Flavian dynasty and religions", *Electrum* 21, 117-131.

Tchernia, André (2000), "Subsistance à Rome: problèmes de quantification", in: Claude Nicolet / Robert Ilbert / Jean-Charles Depaule (eds.), *Mégapoles méditerranéennes. Géographie urbaine rétrospective*, Rome, 751-760.

Thériault, Gaétan (2012), "Culte des évergètes (magistrats) romains et agônes en Asie Mineure", in: Koray Konuk (ed.), *Stephanèphoros. De l'économie antique à l'Asie Mineure. Hommages à Raymond Descat*, Bordeaux, 377-388.

Thomas, Michael L. (2004), "(Re)locating Domitian's Horse of Glory: The *Equus Domitiani* and Flavian Urban Design", *MemAmAc* 49, 21-46.

Thornton, Mary Elisabeth Kelly / Thornton, Robert Lee (1989), *Julio-Claudian Building Programs: a Qualitative Study in Political Management*, Waucond, IL.

Todorov, Augustin (2017), *Face Value: the Irresistible Influence of First Impressions*, Princeton/Oxford.

Tomei, Maria Antonietta / Rea, Rossella (eds.) (2011), *Nerone*, Milan.

Tozzi, Pierluigi (ed.) (2003), *Storia di Cremona. L'età antica*, Cremona.

Tucci, Pier Luigi (2006), "L'Arx Capitolina tra mito e realtà", in: Lothar Haselberger / John Humphrey (eds.), *Imagining Ancient Rome. Documentation – Visualization – Imagination*, Portsmouth, Rh.I., 63-73.

Tucci, Pier Luigi (2017), *The Temple of Peace in Rome* I-II, Cambridge.

Ungaro, Lucrezia (2005), "Entry no. II.7.3", in: Francesco Paolo Fiore (ed.), *La Roma di Leon Battista Alberti. Umanisti, architetti e artisti alla scoperta dell'antico nella città del Quattrocento*, exhibition catalogue, Milan, 233-235.

Urner, Christiana (1993), *Kaiser Domitian im Urteil antiker literarischer Quellen und moderner Forschung*, PhD Dissertation, Augsburg.

Valentini, Giuseppe / Zucchetti, Roberto (1942), *Codice topografico della città di Roma* 2, Rome.

Van der Feijst, L.M.B. / Verniers, L.P. (2017), "Opmerkelijke graven", in: L.M.B. van der Feijst / L.P. Verniers / E. Blom (eds.), *De grafkamer van Huissen. Opgravingen in het kader van de aanleg van nieuwbouwlocatie Loovelden* (ADC Monografie 23), Amersfoort, 80-97.

Van Enckevort, Harry (2005), "The Significance of the Building Activities of Trajan and the Legio X Gemina for the Integration of the Batavians into the Roman Empire", in:

Zsolt Visy (ed.), *Limes XIX, Proceedings of the XIXth International Congress of Roman Frontier Studies Held in Pécs, Hungary, September 2003*, Pécs, 85-94.

Van Enckevort, Harry (2012), *Gebundelde sporen. Enkele kanttekeningen bij aardewerk en nederzettingen uit Romeins Nederland*, PhD Dissertation, Leiden.

Van Nijf, Onno / van Dijk, Sam (2020), "Experiencing Roman power at Greek contests: Romaia in the Greek festival network", in: Katell Berthelot (ed.), *Reconsidering Roman Power: Roman, Greek, Jewish and Christian perceptions and reactions*, Rome, 101-125.

Varner, Eric R. (1995), "Domitia Longina and the Politics of Portraiture", *AJA* 99, 187-206.

Varner, Eric R. (2000a), "Tyranny and the Transformation of the Roman Visual Landscape", in: Eric R. Varner (ed.), *From Caligula to Constantine: Tyranny and Transformation in Roman Portraiture*, Atlanta, GA, 9-26.

Varner, Eric R. (ed.) (2000b), *From Caligula to Constantine: Tyranny and Transformation in Roman Portraiture*, Atlanta, GA.

Varner, Eric R. (2001), "Punishment After Death: Mutilation of Images and Corpse Abuse in Ancient Rome", *Mortality* 6.1, 45-64.

Varner, Eric R. (2004), *Mutilation and Transformation: damnatio memoriae and Roman imperial portraiture*, Leiden/Boston.

Varner, Eric R. (2017), "Nero's Memory in Flavian Rome", in: Shadi Bartsch / Kirk Freudenburg / Cedric Littlewood (eds.), *The Cambridge Companion to the Age of Nero*, Cambridge, 237-258.

Versluys, Miguel John (2012), "Making meaning with Egypt: Hadrian, Antinous and Rome's cultural renaissance", in: Laurent Bricault / Miguel John Versluys (eds.), *Egyptian gods in the Hellenistic and Roman Mediterranean: Image and reality between local and global*, Caltanissetta, 25-39.

Versluys, Miguel John (2013), "Orientalising Roman gods", in: Corine Bonnet / Laurent Bricault (eds.), *Panthée. Religious transformations in the Graeco-Roman Empire* (Religions in the Graeco-Roman world), Leiden/Boston, 235-259.

Versluys, Miguel John (2017), "Egypt as part of the Roman *koine*: Mnemohistory and the Iseum Campense in Rome", in: Svenja Nagel / Joachim Friedrich Quack / Christian Witschel (eds.), *Entangled worlds. Religious confluences between East and West in the Roman Empire. The cults of Isis, Mithras, and Jupiter Dolichenus* (Orientalische Religionen in der Antike), Tübingen, 274-293.

Versluys, Miguel John / Bülow-Clausen, Kristine / Capriotti Vittozzi, Giuseppina (eds.) (2018), *The Iseum Campense from the Roman Empire to the Modern Age. Temple – monument – lieu de mémoire*, Rome.

Veyne, Paul (1976), *Le pain et le cirque*, Paris.

Veyne, Paul (2005), *L'empire gréco-romain* (Des travaux), Paris.

Vinson, Martha P. (1989), "Domitia Longina, Julia Titi and the Literary Tradition", *Historia* 38, 431-450.

Virlouvet, Cathérine (2000), "L'approvvigionamento di Roma imperiale: una sfida quotidiana", in: Elio Lo Cascio (ed.), *Roma imperiale. Una metropoli antica*, Rome, 103-135.

Volonté, Marina (2003), "Le domus: i pavimenti", in: Pierluigi Tozzi (ed.), *Storia di Cremona. L'età antica*, Cremona, 177-179.

Von den Hoff, Ralf (2009), "Caligula. Zur visuellen Repräsentation eines römischen Kaisers", *AA*, 239-263.

von Hesberg, Henner (1978-1980), "Zur Datierung des Theaters in der Domitiansvilla von Castel Gandolfo", *RendPontAcc* 51-52, 305-324.

von Hesberg, Henner (1981), "La *Scaenae Frons* del teatro nella villa di Domiziano a Castel Gandolfo", *Archeologia Laziale* 4, 176-180.

von Hesberg, Henner (2001), "*E cornu taurum*. Zu Fragmenten von Staatsreliefs im Albanum Domitiani", in: Cécile Evers / Athéna Tsingarida (eds.), *Rome et ses provinces. Genèse et diffusion d'une image du pouvoir. Hommage à Jean-Charles Balty*, Brussels, 237-257.

von Hesberg, Henner (2005), "Nutzung und Zurschaustellung von Wasser in der Domitiansvilla von Castel Gandolfo. Fragmente der Ausstattung von Brunnen und Wasserkünste", *JdI* 120, 373-421.

von Hesberg, Henner (2006), "Il potere dell'otium. La villa di Domiziano a Castel Gandolfo", *AC* 57, 221-244.

von Hesberg, Henner (2009), "Le ville imperiali dei Flavi: Albanum Domitiani", in: Filippo Coarelli (ed.), *Divus Vespasianus. Il bimillennario dei Flavi*, Milan, 326-333.

Vos, Peter C. et al. (2007), *Geo-landschappelijk onderzoek bij het waarderend archeologische onderzoeksproject met betrekking tot de Corbulo-grachtafzettingen aan de Veursestraatweg 118 te Leidschendam (opgegraven in mei 2004)* (TNO-rapport 2007-U-R0199/B), Utrecht.

Vout, Caroline (2008), "The Art of '*Damnatio Memoriae*'", in: Stéphane Benoist / Anne Daguet-Gagey (eds.), *Un Discours en images de la condamnation de mémoire*, Metz, 153-172.

Waelkens, Marc (2008) "The Antonine Dynastic Gallery at Sagalassos", *Archaeology online news*, http://archive.archaeology.org/news/articles/maurelius082708.html.

Wallace-Hadrill, Andrew (1983), *Suetonius: the Scholar and his Caesars*, London.

Wallace-Hadrill, Andrew (1993), *Augustan Rome*, London.

Wallat, Kurt (2004), Sequitur clades. *Die Vigiles im antiken Rom*, Frankfurt am Main.

Waters, Kenneth H. (1964*)*, "The Character of Domitian", *Phoenix* 18, 49-77.

Welch, Katherine E. (2007), *The Roman Amphitheatre. From its Origins to the Colosseum*, Cambridge.

Welch, Katherine E. (2018), "Neropolis", in: Catherine M. Draycott et al. (eds.), *Visual Histories of the Classical World. Essays in Honour of R.R.R. Smith*, Turnhout, 209-221.

Wiedemann, Thomas (1992), *Emperors and Gladiators*, London.

Wiedemann, Thomas (1996), "From Nero to Vespasian", *CAH*, 256-282.

Willems, Willem J.H. / van Enckevort, Harry (2009), *VLPIA NOVIOMAGUS – Roman Nijmegen. The Batavian capital at the imperial frontier* (JRA Supplement 73), Portsmouth, Rh.I.

Winterling, Alois (1999), *Aula Caesaris. Studien zur Institutionalisierung des römischen Kaiserhofes in der Zeit von Augustus bis Commodus (31 v. Chr. – 191 n. Chr.)*, Munich.

Winterling, Alois (2003), *Caligula. Eine Biografie*, Munich.

Winterling, Alois (ed.) (2011), *Zwischen Strukturgeschichte und Biographie: Probleme und Perspektiven einer neuen Römischen Kaisergeschichte zur Zeit von Augustus bis Commodus*, Berlin.

Witulski, Thomas (2010), *Kaiserkult in Kleinasien. Die Entwicklung der kultisch-religiösen Kaiserverehrung in der römischen Provinz Asia von Augustus bis Antoninus Pius*, Göttingen.

Wolsfeld, Anne (2014), "Der Kaiser im Panzer. Die bildliche Darstellung Neros und Domitians im Vergleich", in: Sophia Bönisch-Meyer (ed.), *Nero und Domitian. Mediale Diskurse der Herrscherrepräsentation im Vergleich*, Tübingen, 181-216.

Wolters Reinhard / Ziegert, Martin (2014), "Umbrüche – Die Reichsprägung Neros und Domitians im Vergleich", in: Sophia Bönisch-Meyer (ed.), *Nero und Domitian. Mediale Diskurse der Herrscherrepräsentation im Vergleich*, Tübingen, 43-80.

Wood, Susan (2010), "Who was Diva Domitilla? Some Thoughts on the Public Images of the Flavian Women", *AJA* 114, 45-57.

Wood, Susan (2016), "Public images of the Flavian dynasty: sculpture and coinage", in: Andrew Zissos (ed.), *A Companion to the Flavian Age of Imperial Rome*, Malden, 129-147.

Woolf, Greg (2018), "Fragments of an emperor's religious policy: The case of Hadrian", *Arys* 16, 47-61, https://doi.org/10.20318/arys.2018.4445.

Zachos, Konstantinos (2008), *ΑΚΤΙΑ. Αθλητικοί Αγώνες των αυτοκρατορικών χρόνων στη Νικόπολη της Ηπείρου*, Athens.

Zanker, Paul (1987), *Augustus und die Macht der Bilder*, Munich.

Zanker, Paul (2002), "Domitian's Palace on the Palatine and the Imperial Image", in: Alan K. Bowman et al. (eds.), *Representations of Empire. Rome and the Mediterranean World* (Proceedings of the British Academy 114), London, 105-130.

Zanker, Paul (2009), "Da Vespasiano a Domiziano. Immagine di sovrani e moda", in: Filippo Coarelli (ed.), *Divus Vespasianus. Il bimillennario dei Flavi*, Milan, 62-65.

Zanker, Paul (2018), "Zu einer neuen Bildnisbüste des Kaisers Domitian in Toledo (Ohio)", in: Catherine M. Draycott et al. (eds.), *Visual Histories of the Classical World: Essays in Honour of R. R. R. Smith*, Turnhout, 223-230.

Zevi, Fausto (2000), "Traiano e Ostia", in Julián González (ed.), *Trajano. Emperador de Roma*, Rome, 509-547.

Zevi, Fausto (2001), "Histoire et topographie des ports de Rome", *Pallas* 55, 267-284.

Ziegler, Ruprecht (1985), *Städtisches Prestige und kaiserliche Politik: Studien zum Festwesen in Ostkilikien im 2. und 3. Jahrhundert n. Chr.* (Kultur und Erkenntnis 2), Düsseldorf.

Zink, Stephan / Pienig, Heinrich (2009), "Haec aurea templa: The Palatine temple of Apollo and its polychromy", *JRA* 22, 109-122.

Zissos, Andrew (ed.) (2016), *A Companion to the Flavian Age of Imperial Rome*, Malden, MA/Oxford.

Zwierlein-Diehl, Erika (2007), *Antike Gemmen und ihr Nachleben*, Berlin/New York.

Zych, Iwona (2017), "The harbor of early Roman 'Imperial' Berenike: overview of excavations from 2009 to 2015", *Polish Archaeology in the Mediterranean* 26.2, 93-132.

Index

Printed by Printforce, United Kingdom